BEHIND THE MULE

W9-BJP-073

BEHIND THE MULE

RACE AND CLASS IN
AFRICAN-AMERICAN POLITICS

Michael C. Dawson

PRINCETON UNIVERSITY PRESS   PRINCETON, NEW JERSEY

Copyright © 1994 by Princeton University Press
Published by Princeton University Press, 41 William Street,
Princeton, New Jersey 08540
In the United Kingdom: Princeton University Press, Chichester, West Sussex
All Rights Reserved

Library of Congress Cataloging-in-Publication Data
Dawson, Michael C., 1951–
Behind the mule: race and class in African-American politics /
Michael C. Dawson.
p.   cm.
Includes bibliographical references and index.
ISBN 0-691-08770-9   ISBN 0-691-02543-6 (pbk.)
1. Afro-Americans—Politics and government.   I. Title.
E185.615.D39   1994
323.1'196073—dc20   93-44088

This book has been composed in Palatino

First Princeton paperback printing, 1995

Printed in the United States of America

10   9   8   7   6   5   4   3

Contents

Figures

Tables

Acknowledgments

THIS WORK is the result of a collective effort of family, colleagues, and friends. I have been fortunate in that there is a very large overlap between the three groups. The University of Michigan has proved an ideal place to engage in serious work on black politics. In particular, the Center for Afroamerican and African Studies, the Race and Politics Program of the Center for Political Studies, and the Program for Research on Black America (the latter two both part of the Institute for Social Research) have all provided material support and wonderful colleagues as well as a real home for my work. The Rockefeller Foundation, through the Program for Research and Training on Poverty and the Underclass, provided a needed postdoctoral fellowship that supported this work during the most critical stage. Many colleagues have read and critiqued parts of this book. I am grateful to the many colleagues at UM who discussed these issues with me, including Christopher Achen, Walter Allen, Robert A. Brown III, Nancy Burns, Cathy Cohen, Doug Dion, Pat Gurin, JoAnn Hall, Kim James, Todd Shaw, Lynn Sanders, Jocelyn Sargent, Ernest Wilson III, and Rafia Zafar for sharing their wisdom with me. A number of colleagues provided the exceptional aid of reading through the entire work. My sympathy and great thanks go out to Don Herzog, Jennifer Hochschild, James S. Jackson, John Jackson, Robin Kelley, Donald Kinder, Earl Lewis, and Steven Rosenstone. Many of the battles we waged not only made the work better, but have profoundly influenced how I approach scholarship. Dianne Pinderhughes and Hanes Walton, Jr., not only incisively critiqued the work, but also helped to introduce me to the complexities and importance of work in the field of black politics. Conversations with them and with many other colleagues in the National Conference of Black Political Scientists will continue to shape the direction of my work and keep me grounded in my roots. I have been extraordinarily fortunate in working *with* a group of graduate students unmatched in the country. They have been real friends, and will help shape the field of political science in the future. After I moved to the University of Chicago I received critical aid in the final manuscript preparation from two exceptional students—Pamela Cook and Taeku Lee. Ronald Brown shared the pain, frustration, and joy of scholarship and family life with me during the entire period of this work's creation. Without him, this book would not have existed. My family provided the anchor and love needed to sustain me over the past several years. I am constantly made proud of and annoyed by the fact that our children are easily my severest critics. But the most supportive and incisive critic I have is my partner in life, Aiko Furumoto. Her work in epidemiology and the example of her life are a constant reminder that our work must at least attempt to change the world. I will attempt to aid her on her first book as she has aided me on mine. Finally, this book is dedicated to three African-American elders who each taught me important life lessons: Crosby and Mary Ramey, my grandparents, who taught me the dignity of honest labor and the importance of ideas, and St. Clair Drake, my first mentor, who lived the life of scholar and activist without compromise.

Part One

BEHIND THE MULE: THE HISTORICAL ROOTS OF
AFRICAN-AMERICAN GROUP INTERESTS

> Whatever else the blues was it was a language;
> a rich, vital expressive language that stripped
> away the misconception that the black society
> in the United States was simply a poor, discour-
> aged version of the white. It was impossible not
> to hear the differences. No one could listen to
> the blues without realizing that there are two
> Americas.
>
> (Samuel Charters, quoted in Houston A.
> Baker, Jr., *Blues, Ideology, and Afro-American Lit-
> erature: A Vernacular Theory*)

> You want to know where did the blues come
> from. The blues come from behind the mule.
> Well now, you can have the blues sitting at the
> table eating. But the foundation of the blues is
> walking behind the mule way back in slavery
> time.
>
> (Bluesman Booker White, quoted in Houston
> A. Baker, Jr.,*Blues, Ideology, and Afro-American
> Literature: A Vernacular Theory*)

1

The Changing Class Structure of Black America and the Political Behavior of African Americans

> Most people are totally unaware of the darkness
> of the cave in which the Negro is forced to live.
> A few individuals can break out, but the vast
> majority remain its prisoners. Our cities have
> constructed elaborate expressways and elevated
> skyways, and white Americans speed from sub-
> urb to inner city through vast pockets of black
> deprivation without ever getting a glimpse of
> the suffering and misery in their midst. But
> while so many white Americans are unaware of
> the conditions inside the ghetto, there are very
> few ghetto dwellers who are unaware of the life
> outside. . . . Then they begin to think of their
> own conditions. They know that they are always
> given the hardest, ugliest, most menial work to
> do. . . . They realize that it is hard, raw discrimi-
> nation that shuts them out. It is not only poverty
> that torments the Negro; it is the fact of poverty
> amid plenty. It is a misery generated by the gulf
> between the affluence he sees in the mass media
> and the deprivation he experiences in his every-
> day life.
> (Martin Luther King, Jr., *Where Do We Go from
> Here: Chaos or Community?*)

Introduction: Images of Unity and Conflict

During the 1988 presidential primary season, African Americans
marched to the polls in support of Jesse Jackson. Northern and Southern, urban and rural, rich and poor, large numbers of African Americans supported Jackson's quest for the Democratic party's nomination
for president of the United States. Five years earlier, Harold Washington had been elected the first black mayor of Chicago when the city's
black community, often divided by political bickering, came together

with an unprecedented degree of political unity. And in 1990, when Jesse Helms of North Carolina conducted a racist campaign to retain his seat in the U.S. Senate, the black turnout rate for Helms's opponent, black Democrat Harvey Gantt, was 95 percent. These instances of electoral solidarity typify the political unity of African Americans in what many have come to call the New Black Politics (Preston 1987b). This New Black Politics is characterized by the transformation of protest politics into electoral politics with high levels of black political unity. This is the first image given by the evolution of African-American society and politics—an image of a profound political unity that transcends class.

But there is a second image. In Chicago, a city torn by interracial strife, middle-class blacks and whites united in a fight to keep poor blacks from attending the excellent public schools in Dearborn Park, one of Chicago's few well-integrated neighborhoods (Thomas 1989, 1990). One of the poor black parents stated, "There is a lot of politics behind this. I don't believe it is so much color as it is economics. . . . People have this fear of their children going to school with project children, but a project child wants an education like everyone else" (Thomas 1989). This type of conflict, argue scholars such as Wilson (1980), is one of the political consequences of the class divisions that are becoming more pronounced among African Americans. When members of a racial or ethnic group become affluent, they seek to preserve their "well-earned" measure of security and privilege by forming coalitions with other racial or ethnic groups whose economic interests are similar. This second image of African-American politics is one in which the growing economic polarization within black America leads naturally to increasing class conflict among African Americans.

This book examines the tension—highlighted by these two images—between racial interests and class interests as factors shaping African-American politics. The tension arises from the historical legacy of racial and economic oppression that forged racial identity of African Americans. As bluesman Booker White suggests, the key to the historical origins of African-American social identity can be found "behind the mule." It is this legacy of a social identity in which racial and economic oppression have been intertwined for generations that has been the critical component in understanding not only the cultural basis of African-American politics, as Henry (1990) has argued, but also the material roots of black politics. As blues analyst Samuel Charters suggests, only when one "stripped away the misconception that the black society in the United States was simply a poor, discouraged version of the white" could one understand African-American society (Baker 1984). Although Charters was referring to the blues, his point is equally applicable to black politics. African-American politics, including political behavior, is *different*. It has been shaped by historical forces that produced a different pattern of political behavior from the pattern found among white citizens.[1]

But as some African Americans move from behind the mule and develop a stronger class identity, does their racial identity become politically less relevant? To answer this question, I develop a framework for analyzing African Americans' racial group interests. This framework aids in predicting which social identities of African Americans are politically salient. It also helps predict the conditions under which African-American political diversity is likely to increase. I test the framework by analyzing both individual and aggregate data on African-American political behavior and public opinion. A consequence of this test is an increased understanding of the circumstances under which race or class (or the interaction between the two) becomes the dominant influence in shaping African-American political behavior and public opinion.

The Problem: Race and Class as Competing Theories of African-American Politics

This study was motivated by a set of questions that have captured the attention of scholars such as W.E.B. Du Bois, Robert Dahl, and William Wilson. The central question, simply stated, is whether race or class is more important in shaping African-American politics. This question has been central both to the study of African-American society and to the study of ethnic politics. Both traditions have investigated when social scientists should expect racial and ethnic loyalties to decline, and when that decline is accompanied by a parallel decline in racially or ethnically oriented politics.

These questions are of general interest for two reasons. First, America is becoming racially and ethnically more diverse, and the effects of that diversity are being felt politically: rapidly growing Asian and Latino populations are reshaping politics in politically important states such as Florida and California, and, in addition, the increasing racial tensions that accompany increased diversity are sometimes played out in the political arena. Examples of the salience of racial tensions in the political arena during the 1980s and early 1990s include the 1983 mayoral races in Chicago and Philadelphia (won by Harold Washington

---

[1] By extension, the degree to which the politics of Latinos and Asian-Americans deviates from standard American politics also warrants an investigation.

and W. Wilson Goode, respectively), the strong showing among white voters in David Duke's 1991 gubernatorial race in Louisiana, and the English-only referenda in several states. Jesse Helms's 1990 Senate campaign, already mentioned, was a model of how to exploit racial fears, tensions, and outright racism.

Second, racial politics presents analysts of the American party system with several puzzles. One is the lack of diversity in African-American politics. Many scholars and political activists ask, Where are the black Republicans? Another puzzle is why the study of black politics has not become more central to the study of American political parties and other major American political institutions, despite the recognized importance of racial politics. Carmines and Stimson (1989) have argued that the party system has been transformed by racial politics, whereas Huckfeldt and Kohfeld (1989) argue that class politics has been submerged by racial politics. This research responds to these puzzles by focusing attention on the presumed lack of diversity in black politics.

To sum up, the two major questions I address are these: Why have African Americans remained politically homogeneous even while becoming economically polarized? Is greater political diversity likely in the near future? To arrive at answers, I explain the relative importance of race and class in shaping black political behavior and public opinion, and I suggest the conditions under which African Americans will become politically more diverse.

In the remainder of this chapter, I briefly sketch the competing arguments that claim that race or class is the major determinant in African-American life in the late twentieth century. The themes introduced will be much more extensively developed in later chapters. Next, I present the framework for analyzing African Americans'racial group interests, that is, for using individual perceptions of African-American group interests as a tool both to predict current political behavior and to describe the conditions under which one would expect a decline in the political salience of race. This framework, too, is more extensively developed in later chapters. I conclude this chapter by describing the structure of the rest of the book.

Race

Most students of black politics generally, and of black political behavior specifically, argue that one should expect continued political homogeneity among African Americans. This position is based on the belief that the primary imperative in black politics is to advance the political interests of African Americans as a racial group (Barker 1988; Pinderhughes 1987; Walters 1988).

This belief, in turn, is based on studies by numerous observers showing that race is still a major social, economic, and political force in American society and a major shaper of African-American lives. Socially, scholars of this school argue, residential segregation is still a fact of American life and has major ramifications. Residential segregation, they argue, determines the quality of schooling available to African Americans; it means that the property of the black middle and working classes appreciates more slowly than the property of the white middle and working classes, contributing to the enormous gap in wealth between black and white Americans; and by concentrating poverty in black neighborhoods, it negatively affects the neighborhoods even of the black middle class, which is less able to escape neighborhoods with significant concentrations of poverty than it would be if residential segregation did not exist (Massey 1990). These scholars also point to the apparent increase in violent racial incidents during the 1980s in cities and suburbs and on college campuses as a social factor that affects African Americans regardless of their class (Nelson 1990).

Within the economic sphere, adherents of this view argue, the entire class structure of black America is distorted by the legacy of racism (Boston 1988). A black capitalist class does not fully exist. Further, the black middle class is economically vulnerable because of its extreme reliance on public sector and quasi–public sector employment. In addition, middle-class blacks own less wealth per family than poor whites. The median and mean levels of household wealth are less for black families that earn over $50,000 a year than for white families that earn under $10,000 a year (Oliver and Shapiro 1989).

Wealth is an often ignored but important indicator of life chances because it signifies the ability to transmit resources from one generation to the next, to produce income from resources, and to survive financial setbacks (Landry 1987; Oliver and Shapiro 1989). Thus, the lack of wealth in the black middle class means that even affluent black families often find it difficult to pass resources to their children, that a pool of capital (often necessary for the survival of small businesses) is not available, and that many black middle-class families are, in Landry's words, "one paycheck from disaster" (Landry 1987; Oliver and Shapiro 1989). Glass ceilings (unspoken barriers to the promotion of minorities and women to partnership in firms and top managerial ranks) and other forms of inequity have also harmed the financial stability of the black middle and working classes.

Politically, these same scholars argue, race remains a major force in the lives of African Americans. The lack of competition between the two parties for the black vote, in combination with the recent shift to the right in American politics, reinforces the need for African-American political unity to continue. Whether one is talking about the cutback of means-tested programs of vital importance to the black poor or about the massive attack on the affirmative action programs that benefit the more affluent African Americans, these scholars conclude that the political interests of all African Americans are still bound by race.

According to this line of reasoning, because the social, economic, and political realities of whites and blacks differ substantially *because of race*, racial interests continue to override class interests (whether individual or family). And as long as this is true—as long as the political interests of African Americans are bound by race—one should expect high levels of political unity among African Americans *regardless of economic status*.

Class

There is, however, increasing support for the competing hypothesis that race is no longer the most salient factor in African-American lives because economic polarization within the black community is accelerating. University of Chicago sociologist William Wilson has been the most forceful proponent of the thesis that class has become the most salient social determinant of African Americans' life chances. In *The Declining Significance of Race* (1980) he makes three important claims. The first (the one that has given the book so much notoriety) is that discrimination is now less important in determining a person's life chances than social status or economic class. His second claim (which several scholars and politicians have embraced) is that the civil rights movement benefited mostly middle-class, well-trained, younger African Americans. Wilson's third claim is that to some degree the civil rights movement was consciously led by black middle class mainly to benefit their own class interests.

Wilson's claims taken as a whole have profound implications for African-American politics. If it is true that in the 1960s American society changed so much that race ceased to be the overwhelming or even the major determinant of the fate of individual African Americans, one would expect African-American political behavior to reflect increasing diversity. As Dawson and Wilson (1991) have detailed, most major social science theories would predict that increased economic heterogeneity in a population would lead to increasing diversity in political behavior. Social theorist Robert Dahl, for example, in *Who Governs?*

(1961), a sophisticated presentation of ethnic political development, certainly predicted this growing political diversity.

Some empirical evidence exists to support Wilson and like-minded scholars. Economic polarization among African Americans has indeed been increasing over the past twenty years. Both the black middle class and the group of economically marginalized African Americans have grown.[2]

From 1960 to 1991, the black middle class more than doubled in size. Approximately one third of employed blacks now have middle-class occupations. (But when the unemployed and discouraged workers are added to the pool, the relative size of the black middle class shrinks to approximately 15 percent.) So on the one hand, there is a growing, if vulnerable, black middle class. Moreover, those such as Wilson would argue, despite glass ceilings, job and social segregation, residential segregation, and the like, this class has more opportunities than any group of African Americans in history. This is held to be particularly true of the new black middle class, which has grown as a result of advances in black civil rights—blacks whose economic status is based on employment in sectors not traditionally tied to the black community, such as multinational corporations, the media, predominantly white universities, and businesses that sell to predominantly white markets or to the government (Boston 1988; Landry 1987). In the future, the new black middle class may not identify as strongly with the black community, the Democratic party, or liberal causes.

On the other hand, the number of African Americans without stable employment is also growing. In the 1980s, black unemployment rates in states such as Illinois and Michigan were significantly higher than 20 percent (U.S. Department of Labor 1989). Among key age cohorts of black men—those who should be at the beginning or in the middle of their prime earning years—labor force participation rates have been decreasing (Smith and Welch 1989). The result is that African Americans—adults and children alike—are three times more likely to live below the poverty line than whites. And when we look at families as opposed to individuals, as late as 1987, 30 percent of black families, containing 45 percent of black children, were below the poverty line (U.S. Bureau of the Census 1990). Nearly 70 percent of these poor families are headed by women (Pinkney 1984). The lives of economically marginalized African Americans are dominated by the struggle for economic survival.

Many would argue that economic polarization within the black community will continue to increase throughout the 1990s and will

---

[2] Chapter 2 contains a detailed analysis of the economic status of African Americans.

bring in its wake increasing political polarization. African Americans already display an unusually high degree of class consciousness when compared with other Americans (Jackman and Jackman 1983). Such consciousness is likely to grow, particularly among less affluent African Americans; as the objective importance of race in the lives of African Americans declines interests diverge. According to the proponents of the class thesis, the dire *economic* status of large numbers of African Americans, especially in contrast to the improved economic status of large numbers of other African Americans, dictates that class will supersede race as the most politically salient factor for African Americans.

A Solution: A Group-Interests Perspective on African-American Politics

This book develops a framework for analyzing African-American political choice by testing whether race or class is the primary determinant of contemporary African-American political behavior and public opinion. This framework draws in recent work in the psychology of social groups to help explain how psychological processes are critical for the formation of social identity. Particularly the work of Turner (1987) is used to help develop a theory of African-American group interests that explains the continued political homogeneity of African Americans and describes the conditions under which African Americans will begin to display political diversity.

My framework is based on two assumptions. First, it is quite clear that, until the mid-1960s, race was the decisive factor in determining the opportunities and life chances available to virtually all African Americans, regardless of their own or their family's social and economic status. Consequently, it was much more efficient for African Americans to determine what was good for the racial group than to determine what was good for themselves individually, and more efficient for them to use the status of the group, both relative and absolute, as a proxy for individual utility. I call this phenomenon the *black utility heuristic*.[3] The black utility heuristic is the basis for my framework for analyzing micro black politics. It was more efficient to use group status

---

[3] This heuristic should in principle be applicable to other groups; the particular way it is manifest would depend on the historical context. For example, in many periods and places, a Jewish person's religious identity might well have dominated all other social identities; in the France of the 1980s, North Africans' identity and political struggles with other French were tied to the North Africans' belief in Islam. For African Americans, I shall argue, identity has been tied to subordinate economic status.

as a proxy not only because a piece of legislation or a public policy could be analyzed relatively easily for its effect on the race but also because the information sources available in the black community—the media outlets, kinship networks, community and civil rights organizations, and especially the preeminent institution in the black community, the black church—would all reinforce the political salience of racial interests and would provide information about racial group status.

Second, I assume that cognitive psychological processes are critical in shaping perceptions of racial group status. Psychological theories of attribution and self-categorization suggest that psychological processes on the individual level would reinforce the salience of racial politics for African Americans. Information that either minimized intragroup differences or exaggerated intergroup differences would be accepted more easily than information that contradicted current images of the importance of race in politics. Errors in information processing and biases in decision making would tend to favor racial explanations of the social world. The salience of one's racial identity, or of any other group identity, is a function of the cognitive accessibility of information pertinent to that identity, and the fit of that identity with social reality. This fact suggests two ways in which racial identity can become less salient for African Americans. One way is if information about the political, economic, and social world of black America becomes less accessible, either because individual blacks do not live in the black community (some members of the black middle class are in fact moving out of black communities) or because social networks in the black community are breaking down, as has happened in some of the most economically devastated inner-city neighborhoods (Marable 1983; Wilson 1980, 1987). The other way, particularly for the new black middle class, is if race becomes less salient in individuals' own lives. This is essentially the process described by Wilson and Dahl.

If neither of those developments takes place—that is, if information does not become less accessible and race does not become less personally salient—we should expect the combination of the cognitive phenomenon of accessibility and fit to slow the growth of political diversity in the African American community. And, in fact, exiting from their community is much harder for black Americans than it was for European ethnic groups earlier in the nation's history or for Asians or Latinos today (Massey and Denton 1988). In addition, to the degree to which the political and social climate is still perceived to be racially hostile, economic information is counteracted, with the result that racial group politics remains salient for African Americans. It is upon these assumptions that my framework for analyzing African-American political choice is based.

A Note on Social Structure, Culture, and Methodological Individualism

At this point I would like to clarify the approach to the study of politics, particularly African-American politics, adopted in this book. The main subject matter of this work is the testing of competing explanations of individual-level African-American politics. Consequently, the theoretical and methodological base that this work stands on can be found in theories and methodologies that focus on individual behaviors. Both psychology and economics give considerable attention to individual decision-making processes. Psychological theory describes how individuals process information and how groups influence individual cognition and behavior. Economic theories of rationality offer clues about the decision-making process in which individuals engage once identity has been determined and preferences have been formed.

I rely to a significant extent on nonreductionist theories of the social group—theories for which group psychology is more than the aggregation of interpersonal behaviors (Turner 1987). I make more use of psychological theories of the social group and Simonesque approaches to rationality than of economic approaches to rationality. In one sense, my approach is similar to Hardin's (1991), which provides a rational choice foundation for the formation of group identity. However, unlike Hardin, for whom rationality is optimal, I argue that rationality is procedural, based on assessments of what works as opposed to what is best. I also use theories of rationality (Simon 1985) to gain insight into the decision-making processes of African Americans both as individuals and as part of a politically active group within the American polity.[4]

In advanced industrial societies, however, citizens have multiple identities, as the pluralists have been pointing out for much of the second half of the twentieth century. Further, many scholars have pointed out that preferences are not exogenous—they do not fall like manna from the sky. Preferences are clearly endogenous. To determine which identity (group and individual) is salient, where preferences come from, and how norms and values are formed, one must turn to the study of society, its culture, and its institutions (Gerber and Jackson 1990; Przeworski 1985). In the black community, institutions—particu-

---

[4] "Simonesque" approaches to rationality tend to emphasize procedural rationality rather than strict maximization of utility. See Simon (1985) for a good summary of these approaches.

larly the black church—are critical in shaping culture, norms and values, policy positions, and modes of behavior (Henry 1990; Pinderhughes 1990). To study individual political behavior in a vacuum is at best to gain only an incomplete understanding of the motivation for and consequences of that behavior.

Politics itself, of course, is much more than simply the behavior of individuals or the sum of these individual actions. Institutions, groups, cultures, and organizations all affect and shape society and its politics. Consequently, to understand black politics one needs to draw on many methodologies, and one clearly needs to pay more attention to the boundaries between society and the individual, with the group as the intermediary phenomenon. No single work can hope to embrace the range of methodologies and approaches necessary to study black politics. In addition to using quantitative analysis, this work draws particularly on historical approaches to help set the context within which individual African Americans' behavior can be understood.

Overview of the Book

My basic theoretical and historical arguments are presented in Part One. Chapter 2 lays out the basic empirical evidence for the two competing arguments: that race remains the primary factor affecting the life chances of African Americans, and that class is now the major determining factor. This chapter also presents evidence about the role of government in politicizing the economic status of African Americans. Chapter 3 provides the historical and theoretical arguments for describing whether race or class becomes the primary politically salient identity for African Americans.

Part Two turns to the empirical tests of my framework for analyzing African-American micropolitics. The primary source of data is the 1984–1988 National Black Election Panel Study (NBES), a national political survey of African Americans that provides a detailed political portrait of black America. The analysis of the NBES is supplemented by analyses of other surveys as well as of aggregate time series data.

Chapter 4 presents and examines the basic building blocks of African-American group interests and then uses the—concepts to analyze African Americans' perceptions of economic status and racial influence in American society. In Chapter 5 I analyze African Americans' political partisanship. In Chapter 6 I develop a model of African-American political choice and test it by using the 1984 and 1988 national elections as exemplars. In Chapter 7 I further probe African-American presidential approval by analyzing changes in African-American presidential approval over time. I also consider how changes in the party that controls macroeconomic policy affect the races differently. Chapter 8 focuses on whether the lack of class differences in political behavior demonstrated in Chapters 5 and 6 can also be found in the realm of African Americans' policy preferences and issue positions. Chapter 9 includes a summary of my main findings and speculation on the possible future of African-American politics and the politics of race and class.

2

Race, Class, and African-American Economic Polarization

The old bee makes de honey-comb,
The young bee makes de honey,
Colored folks plant de cotton and corn,
And de white folks gits de money.
  (Song sung by African Americans from times
of slavery to the Great Depression, in Laurence
Levine, *Black Culture and Black Consciousness*)

The Structure of the African-American Political Economy: A Short Review

The central question introduced in Chapter 1 was whether race or class had a stronger influence on African-American politics. Specifically, the question was asked whether changes in the class structure of African-American society had led to a situation in which African Americans who belong to different economic strata no longer share sufficiently similar interests to ensure a high degree of homogeneity in African-American political behavior and public opinion. This chapter investigates two questions: How do the different structures of black and white economic reality differ from each other? Do different strata of blacks experience a common economic reality?

The structure of the American political economy has helped determine the shape and scope of life chances for African Americans at any given moment. Further, since the 1960s this structure has undergone extensive changes that have had profound implications for African-American life chances. Specifically, the changing structure of the American economy and the distribution of life chances of African Americans has had and continues to have a massive impact on the development of African-American class structure.

The major questions addressed in this chapter are: (1) Is there continued economic polarization between the races? To what degree have African Americans as a whole, or any group of African Americans, closed the economic gap with white Americans? (2) What evidence is there for economic polarization within the black community? If economic polarization in the black community has indeed taken place, how permanent and stable are the changes in the African-American class structure likely to be? (3) How has government policy affected African-American economic status, racial polarization among African Americans, and the size of the economic gap between blacks and whites? This chapter lays the basis for understanding the political importance of black economic status and the economic environment for African-American group interests.

African-American Political Economy in the Twentieth Century

The first great migration of African Americans to the North took place in the period immediately before World War I and marked the beginning of the urbanization and industrialization of blacks in both the North and the South. At the turn of the century, 88 percent of all black men worked in agriculture and related industries, fishing, or domestic service (Pinkney 1984). But increased demand for black labor was stimulating migration out of the rural South. Demand for labor was produced in the urban South by shipbuilding and heavy industry. In the North, labor was needed by the nascent auto industry, the steel industry, and meat-packing concerns (Baron 1971). A major transformation in the occupational structure of African Americans—the transformation that would culminate between 1940 and 1970—was beginning.

The year 1940 is a convenient benchmark year for comparing the economic status of black Americans in the periods before and after World War II. It marked the end of the Great Depression as U.S. war production began to grow for the exponentially rising needs of the Allies and the anticipated needs of the American armed forces. While the Depression was catastrophic for many Americans, and disproportionately so for many blacks, New Deal programs were often able to ensure black survival, even though they were administered in a discriminatory fashion (Weiss 1983). It was also the period of the greatest migration of blacks, who moved from the South to the industrial areas of the North and Midwest. For the first time African Americans were also drawn to the West by the new aircraft and shipbuilding industries. The black population in Los Angeles doubled from 75,000 to 150,000 during the war (Franklin 1974). Between 1940 and 1970 the net migration out of the South was 4.2 million African Americans (Farley and Allen 1987). Urbanization accompanied this exodus from the land. For most of

American history blacks had trailed whites in degree of urbanization. By 1940, blacks had achieved the same degree of urbanization that whites had reached in 1910 (Baron 1971). Blacks went from an urban area residence rate of 49 percent in 1940 to over 76 percent in 1973 (Baron 1971; Wilson 1980). By 1973, 60 percent of all blacks lived in the central cities (Wilson 1980). When disaggregated by region, the results are even more striking. By 1970, over 97 percent of African Americans living in the Northeast, the north central region, and the West lived in urban areas (Reich 1981). The South also saw a large increase in African-American urbanization. The comparable figure for the South was 67 percent (Reich 1981). The black population of some Southern cities grew extremely rapidly. In cities such as Birmingham, Montgomery, and Baton Rouge, the African-American population grew anywhere from 40 percent to 453 percent between 1940 and 1960 (Morris 1984). During these decades the profound transformation of African Americans from a largely Southern and rural population to a highly urbanized people in the space of a generation would produce an immense shock in the American political system.

The massive migration between 1940 and 1970 led to a rapid increase in the proportion of blacks in industry (and was also associated with the rapid postwar economic modernization of the South). This occupational shift helped improve the absolute and relative economic status of African Americans. Industrialization produced changes in the distribution of occupations and industries in which blacks were employed. In 1940, 470,000 black workers were employed in manufacturing. By 1970 this number had grown by almost 300 percent to 1.3 million (Reich 1981). In 1940 one third of all blacks were employed as farm laborers (Pinkney 1984). Over half of all blacks were involved in agriculture in some capacity (Baron 1971). By 1970 this figure had declined to under 3 percent (Pinkney 1984). Conversely, the number of blacks in white-collar occupations rose from 6 to 24 percent in the same period (Pinkney 1984). Still, in 1970, 81 percent of black men were concentrated in service and blue-collar industries (Reich 1981). The overall impact of these changes on incomes, earnings, employment, and the overall economic status of blacks will be explored later in this chapter.

The end of the war and two decades of American supremacy during the "Pax Americana" led to several important structural changes in the American political economy. These changes in turn had an important effect on the economic status of blacks. One of the results of the enormous economic growth in the postwar era was the creation of a new black middle class. An often overlooked feature of this increase in its size and of other changes in the black middle class is the concentration of much of the increase in the state sector. This class made great strides from the mid-1960s well into the late 1970s. During the late 1970s and the 1980s, however, the vulnerability of this class in the private and state sectors of the economy was highlighted by the detrimental impact of fiscal crises, attacks on affirmative action, and the hostility of the Reagan administration to programs aiding minorities. A negative economic feature of this period was the rapid growth of black unemployment, which had been hovering at around twice the white rate since 1954 (Wilson 1980). Furthermore, the rise in the black unemployment rate has been accompanied by a decrease in the black labor participation rate, which was 90 percent for black men in 1945 but fell to 70 percent by 1970 (Pinkney 1984). Evidence for the narrowing of the income gap between whites and blacks is mixed. These trends of the postwar period will be explored below.

The Black/White Economic Gap

Is there a convergence in black and white economic status in recent years? This question has political as well as economic consequences. A key finding in cognitive science is that intergroup differences are a prime ingredient in the forging of group identity. As will be shown in Chapter 3, the relative as well as the absolute economic status of African Americans is critical in the politicization of African-American perceptions of racial group interests. Consequently, the degree to which interracial economic differences persist or decline is a critical element in African-American political decision making.

Black and white economic status is examined along a number of dimensions. Black/white differences in income, unemployment and labor force participation, poverty, and stability of the middle class are all studied. Persistent large gaps between black and white economic fortunes are found across the range of the two races' economic strata.

Black and White Income Trends

This section begins with an analysis of postwar income trends. Income inequality (particularly *net* inequality, which includes government transfer payments—the so-called safety net) declined throughout most of the postwar period until the 1970s (Dennis 1983; Moss and Tilly 1991). As Dennis has pointed out, disagreement over the distribution of income has been perhaps the most conflictual area of American politics—one could argue that racial conflict is another candidate (Dennis 1983). Tax policy, affirmative action, transfer and entitlement pro-

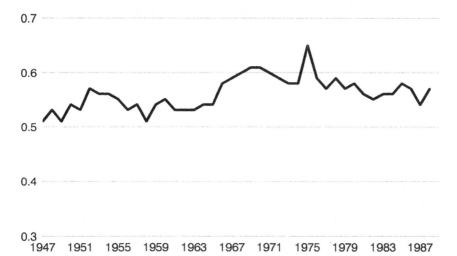

Figure 2.1. Ratio of black to white median family income, 1947–1987 (*Sources and notes*: The data for 1947–1974 come from *The Social and Economic Status of the Black Population in the U.S.: An Historical View, 1790–1978*, Current Population Reports, Special Studies, Series p-23, no. 80. The data for 1975–1987 are compiled from U.S. Bureau of the Census, *Statistical Abstract of the United States, 1990*, Table 727. The data for 1947–1954 are for black and "other"races; after 1954 the data are tabulated separately for blacks.)

grams, and agricultural subsidies all fall under the rubric of income-enhancing or income-redistributing programs.

Figure 2.1 shows the relative ratio of black to white median income from 1947 to 1987. While there was an improvement in the ratio during most of the 1960s and the first half of the 1970s, the ratio was relatively flat throughout the 1980s. As Reich (1981) details, the ratio of black to white male incomes rose until the early 1970s, when black men were making approximately 75 percent of white men's income outside the South. Comparison of this data with the data for women is most enlightening.

By 1977 black women's income had reached or exceeded parity in all regions but the South, where it remained less than 75 percent of white women's income. Because women's incomes lag male incomes, while reaching parity with white women's income, black women's income still seriously lagged that of white males. Reich concludes: "The secular national improvement ... appears to result largely from an upward trend within the South and from the migration of blacks out of the South to regions that continue to have higher absolute and relative incomes for nonwhite males" (Reich 1981).

Looking specifically at urbanization further confirms the arguments that the decline in the black/white income gap can be largely explained by migration out of the South and improvement of black incomes in the South. As will be detailed below, much of the improvement in incomes in the South is due to federal civil rights intervention (Heckman and Payner 1989). This decline in racial income inequality in the South is responsible for *two thirds* of the overall decline in income disparity between the races that has occurred since 1964. Improvement in black education has also contributed to this decline (Smith and Welch 1989).

Urban black/white income ratios have gone from 0.50 in 1930 to 0.64 in 1969. However, the income ratio has declined from 0.73 in 1949 to 0.69 in 1959 in the urban non-South (Reich 1981). This evidence is not as straightforward as it might seem. Much of the disparity in income across regions and cities might be due to structural changes in the American macroeconomy—specifically, the large declines in manufacturing employment over the past several decades, first in the cities and then in the nation as a whole.

Reich reports that the largest relative declines in employment were in Detroit, Pittsburgh, and Birmingham, all cities that have or had very large auto and steel industries. These two industries have faced intense competition from foreign companies. However, major differentials between white and black earnings persist even when the income gap is declining (Farley 1984). Reich attributes this difference to the concentration of blacks in industries they entered in the past several decades at the lowest occupational and earnings categories. Reich (1981, 53) points out: "Blacks approached equality with whites by 1970 in only two industries. . . . Preliminary investigation of the same industries . . . indicates that these inequalities had not diminished by the mid-1970s."

The very large exception to Reich's argument is the state sector. The government versus private sector ratios in 1970 were 0.76 and 0.65, respectively, for men and 0.93 and 0.74 for women (Reich 1981). As will be shown later in the chapter, much of the expansion of the black middle class was in the government sector. The relative equality of earnings and the greatly increased employment opportunities for blacks in the state sector combined to magnify the *economic* importance of the state during the 1960s and 1970s for blacks. A review of the volatility of the private sector, particularly in manufacturing and other sectors sensitive to the structural readjustments of the economy and to cyclical downturns, will further emphasize this point as well as help draw a fuller picture of black income and earnings trends in the postwar period.

Despite this, there has been a steady decline in income parity in all regions but the South since the mid-1970s. The gap between black and white incomes holds for all types of families (Jaynes and Williams 1989). Even African-American incomes for married couples still lagged white incomes by 20 percentage points. The biggest racial gap was for female-headed households. For all families, the ratio of black/white income was only 57 percent in 1986, the same as it had been in 1971 (Jaynes and Williams 1989). The decade of the 1980s brought about a powerful reversal in the convergence of incomes. In particular, the incomes of black men suffered absolute and relative declines when compared with the incomes of white men. Bound and Freeman (1990, 1) state: "Our evidence shows that the era of relative black economic advance ended in the mid-1970s. The racial earnings gap between recent male labor market entrants widened from 1976 to 1989, especially among college graduates and workers in the Midwest."[1] Black male college graduates and high-school dropouts in the Midwest fared the worst during the 1980s. Among the factors that contributed to the deterioration of African-American absolute and relative earnings during the 1980s were weakness in aggregate demand, the location of African-American workers in regions such as the Midwest that had suffered particularly heavy economic damage, the employment of African Americans in industries that were in decline, the placement of African Americans at the end of hiring and seniority queues, the movement of jobs from the central cities to the suburbs, the reduction in enforcement of fair employment laws and regulations, and a continuation of racial discrimination in employment (Bound and Freeman 1990; Holzer 1989; Johnson and Oliver 1990; Kirschenman and Neckerman 1991; Moss and Tilly 1991).[2] These factors that contributed to the erosion of black economic status during the 1980s have been perceived by many African Americans as being the result of either direct interracial economic conflict (discrimination on the part of employers), government policy (macroeconomic policies leading to reduced aggregate demand), or both (the reduction in enforcement of fair employment laws during the 1980s). Consequently, the deterioration of African-American economic

[1] One problem that Bound and Freeman report with their and other studies that use the Current Population Survey data from the census is that undercounting of some of the relevant populations is quite severe. For example, 30 percent of young black men (as opposed to 10 percent of young white men) are omitted from the survey (Bound and Freeman 1990).

[2] One of the difficulties with analysis of African-American economic status is the lack of work on the economic status, particularly the employment status, of black women. A critical area for future research is the experiences of African-American women in employment markets.

status has shaped how African Americans perceive the *political* salience of racial identity.

The earnings of blacks are also adversely affected by underemployment because blacks still work fewer hours than whites (Farley 1984). As Bluestone and Harrison (1982) point out, there is often a "ripple effect," or a community-wide adverse effect over and beyond that resulting from the direct unemployment of individual workers. When examining income and earnings trends one has to be careful to control for structural as well as cyclical changes in the American macroeconomy. Some of the decline in black-to-white income ratios is the result of the departure of manufacturing from the cities, the distressed state of manufacturing employment nationwide, the damaging effects of the relatively depressed state of industries such as steel and auto on workers in cities where these industries are major employers, and the differential reduction of black wages, due not only to concentration of black workers in lower-wage occupations but also to the fewer hours that blacks work. Deconcentration of jobs within a metropolitan area has at least as much impact on black employment as deindustrialization. The structural changes in the economy have a particularly detrimental effect on minority income, since 80 percent of minority income are due to wages and salaries as compared to 75 percent for whites (Bluestone and Harrison 1982). As Bluestone and Harrison (1982, 55) state, "The nearly immutable code of 'last hired, first fired,' combined with entrenched patterns of housing segregation, have left minorities at a real disadvantage when manufacturing plants close down, retail shops move out and economic activity spreads to the suburbs and beyond. The dream of jobs with high wages and decent fringe benefits that once lured blacks to the North has turned into a nightmare for those who now face termination in the once bustling factories of the industrial Midwest." Let us now turn from the discussion of income to the most severe economic problem facing African Americans—unemployment.

Trends in Unemployment and Labor Force Participation

Unemployment is the most dismal area of discussion in black political economy. Figure 2.2 shows trends in black and white unemployment rates between 1954 and 1990. By May of 1983, during the Reagan recession, official black unemployment rates had soared to 20.8 percent (*Black Enterprise Magazine* 1983). Black unemployment rates declined to the high teens during the Reagan recovery, but continue to be more than double white rates. By 1988, fourteen states still had black unemployment rates of greater than or equal to 15 percent (U.S. Department

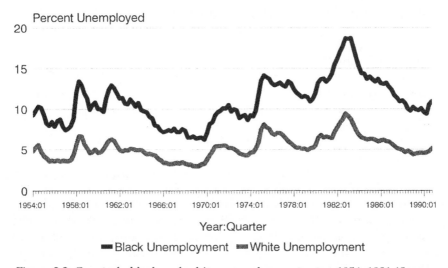

Figure 2.2. Quarterly black and white unemployment rates, 1954–1991 (*Source*: Citibase Econometric Database)

of Labor 1989). States with such high black unemployment rates are concentrated in the South and Midwest and include those with large black populations such as Illinois and Michigan. The gap between black and white unemployment, unlike that of income, shows no signs of narrowing. Farley (1984, 40) states that "there has been no racial convergence in unemployment rates. At all dates, the racial discrepancy was at least as large at the end of this period as at the beginning. In fact, a closer look at the data reveals that unemployment rates have risen more over time among nonwhites than among whites."

A combination of factors has led to the precipitous rise in African-American unemployment. Government action, spurred by black protest, opened up employment opportunities for blacks from the 1940s to the 1960s. These opportunities had narrowed owing to Jim Crow legislation and custom throughout the first forty years of the century (Farley 1984). The advent of war and massive pressure from black workers under the leadership of A. Philip Randolph led to "the greatest economic gains, in terms of both real advances and in relation to whites, since the Civil War" (Harris 1982). The pressure led to President Franklin D. Roosevelt's establishment of the Federal Employment Practices Committee (FEPC). Harris (1982) describes the effect of the establishment of the FEPC on the war industries and concludes that the structure of the labor market had been changed largely in favor of blacks. John F. Kennedy and Lyndon B. Johnson followed with a combination of executive orders and legislation in 1961 (Kennedy's executive order barring employment discrimination in federal employment) and 1964 (the 1964 Civil Rights Act) that broadly extended employment antidiscrimination law (Farley 1984).

However, structural changes in the American political economy were producing conditions that would eventually have a tragic impact on black labor force participation. Black labor force participation reached its height in the early 1950s (Farley 1984). As mentioned earlier, Pinkney reports that between 1945 and 1970 black labor force participation declined from 90 to 70 percent. By 1982 this rate had declined to below 60 percent (Pinkney 1984; Farley 1984). Farley comments that both white and black men's participation rates have declined, but that the decline for white men is almost entirely explained by the drop in participation of men in the over-55 age bracket. For blacks the decline in the participation of elderly workers accounts for only one third of the decline. Discouraged workers—workers unemployed for so long that they are no longer on the unemployment rolls—account for much of the difference between black and white rates.[3] In 1979, for example, the National Urban League estimated that the true black unemployment rate, including discouraged workers, was 23.1 percent—twice the 11.3 percent official rate (Pinkney 1984). The difference in rates has widened from five points to twelve points between 1950 and 1982. The sea change that saw the rapid decline in labor participation occurred around 1970. The rate of discouraged workers was highest for black males aged 25 to 54 (Farley 1984). This cohort would ordinarily represent the primary income-earning group.

Wilson (1980) asserts that the changes that led to the 1954 doubling of the ratio of black to white unemployment rates, the rise in the number of discouraged black workers, massive minority teenage unemployment, and the reduction in hours for workers in manufacturing (especially blacks) were structural in nature. Among the underlying reasons he cites for these changes are the shift from a goods-based economy to a service-based economy; the migration of jobs from the cities to the suburbs and from the Northeast and the Midwest first to the South and Southwest and finally offshore; and the growth of corporate power in the economy.

Several forms of economic restructuring in addition to the deindustrialization described by Wilson have accelerated black losses in employment. Johnson and Oliver (1990) argue, "Among cities with high rates of deconcentration, black male unemployment rates, idleness,

---

[3] Labor force participation rates, unlike unemployment rates, include discouraged workers.

and total black male joblessness were significantly greater than in cities in which job deconcentration was low." Holzer (1989) summarizes several studies that show that greater transit times from central cities to suburban-based jobs, deindustrialization, and deconcentration are factors that lead to greater black joblessness. Further, Holzer points out that residential segregation and the propensity for manufacturing plants to locate away from concentrations of African Americans are further barriers that make it more difficult for African-American workers to relocate to the suburbs or other regions when central-city factories and businesses move.[4]

Among the most significant structural changes were the growth of the importance of corporate industries in the economy and the subsequent development of a surplus black labor force. Several factors are at work in these industries. They emphasize technology in order to maximize profits, thus making many black workers redundant. Wilson also argues that there is now a greater demand for well-educated, technologically oriented workers, technicians, managers, and professionals and a declining demand for unskilled and semiskilled labor. Wilson claims that black workers face a ceiling in occupational and wage levels in these industries. Entry-level jobs have become scarce, putting a particularly severe strain on minority youth seeking jobs (Wilson 1980).

BLACK YOUTH UNEMPLOYMENT

The lack of entry-level jobs has particularly harmed the employment prospects of black youth. Structural changes in the economy have been exacerbated by cyclical downturns. U.S. Department of Labor statistics show that twelve months after the start of the 1981–1982 recession, black teenage unemployment (ages 16 to 19) soared over 50 percent (*Black Enterprise Magazine* 1984). The *New York Times* estimated that there were 400,000 unemployed black youth (Pinkney 1984). By May of 1985, in the midst of a strong recovery, the official black teenage unemployment rate was 39 percent, almost triple the 15 percent rate of white teenagers (Koepp 1985).

Holzer (1989), Koepp (1985), and Pinkney (1984) cite the geographical distance of available jobs from the residences of minority teenagers combined with the lack of affordable public transportation as one reason for the high black teenage unemployment rate. The research confirms that blacks tend to be employed by firms located in or near the

[4] For a more extensive discussion of the racial dimensions of plant relocation see Cole and Deskins (1988).

inner city (Leonard 1986). However, the effect of geographical distance on the likelihood that individual youths will take a given job appears more problematic (Ellwood 1986; Leonard 1986). The combined effects of the increasing distance of jobs from the inner city and of racial discrimination aimed at black youth on the part of employers have disastrous implications for the future of black youth (Culp and Dunson 1986; Freeman and Holzer 1986). The increasing propensity of some groups of firms, such as Japanese automakers, to locate plants far from minority residential concentrations suggests that black unemployment could become even higher in the future (Cole and Deskins 1988). The evidence already suggests that bouts of unemployment are not becoming shorter as black youth age (Freeman and Holzer 1986). The labor force participation rate of those 18 to 19 years old in 1979 will not reach 80 percent until they reach their mid-thirties.

Other reasons given for the high black youth unemployment rate are black youths' lack of education, "bad attitudes," inappropriate aspirations, and lack of social skills (Datcher-Loury and Loury 1986; Koepp 1985). Pinkney would disagree, claiming that discrimination in the administration of federal youth programs and in the private-sector hiring process bears more responsibility (Culp and Dunson 1986; Pinkney 1984). However, increased education does have a positive effect on teenage unemployment (Freeman and Holzer 1986).

A look at the evidence in a different light provides some additional clues about some of the structural factors underlying the high black teenage unemployment rate. Black teenage unemployment ratcheted upward during the past four recessions (*Black Enterprise Magazine* 1984). From 1970 to 1982 the starting point of black teenage unemployment at the beginning of each recession had risen approximately seventeen percentage points. After each business cycle, black teenage unemployment had a much higher baseline. This suggests that structural factors are also critical in contributing to black youth unemployment. During the period from 1970 to 1982 the American economy underwent a series of major readjustments. The series of structural changes discussed earlier changed the structure of the labor market. Hence there is no single factor responsible for teenage unemployment; rather, a plethora of factors have combined to result in this problem (Freeman and Holzer 1986).

The problem that this increasing pool of unemployed African-American youth presents for future black economic status can be seen in the labor force participation rates displayed in Table 2.1. As Smith and Welch highlight, what is remarkable about this table is not the relatively stable lack of labor force participation on the part of African-American youths, but the erosion in the labor force participation of

TABLE 2.1
Activity Status of Black Men

	1980	1970	1960	1950	1940
18 years old					
SEM (%)	79.3	79.5	78.6	82.1	78.3
UOJ (%)	20.6	20.4	21.4	17.9	21.7
24 years old					
SEM (%)	71.8	78.9	80.2	86.2	82.7
UOJ (%)	28.2	21.1	19.8	13.8	17.3
35–36 years old					
SEM (%)	79.7	86.3	82.9	86.5	85.3
UOJ (%)	20.3	13.7	17.1	13.5	14.7

Source: Adapted from Smith and Welch 1989, 549.

Note: SEM = in school, employed, or in the military; UOJ = unemployed, out of the labor force, or in jail.

older black men. This decreasing labor force participation, together with the continued slow growth of the economy, *marks an end to black income gains relative to those of whites*. Most of the historical supports for income gains—rapid growth in the economy, large black out-migration from the South, aggressive enforcement of equal opportunity laws by the federal government, and improvement in black skills through improved education—were steadily eroded in the 1970s and 1980s. Indeed, Smith and Welch (1989) find this point disturbing even though they hold a generally optimistic outlook on the future of black economic status. They concur with Wilson (1987) that the deterioration of inner-city schools has dire prospects not only for the future of the devastated black poor, but for black economic status more generally. However, Moss and Tilly (1991) argue that the suggestion of declining skills is a poor explanation for lack of black employment success because African Americans' test scores have steadily, if modestly, continued to approach those of whites. However, a trend that does have negative implications for the ability of black youth to enter the labor market is noted in the studies of Turner et al. (1991) and Kirschenman and Neckerman (1991). Turner and colleagues' study demonstrated that black youth faced discriminatory treatment from employers even when black job applicants *were matched with whites on all possible characteristics, including demeanor and dress, other than race.* The Kirschenman and Neckerman study demonstrated widespread prejudice on the part of employers against black job applicants. This study is particularly interesting because of its demonstration of the very strong and very negative stereotypes about inner-city residents held by employers. The employers in the study held the negative stereotypes of African Americans similar to those demonstrated by Bobo and Kluegel (1991) to be held generally by whites of African Americans. This is a disturbing finding because it suggests, as does the Turner study, that blacks are denied jobs *even when they act like whites*. Racist stereotypes of African Americans present a significant hurdle for blacks entering employment markets. Exacerbating this phenomenon is the decline in enforcement of equal employment laws by the state (Moss and Tilly 1991). The combination of factors leading to black joblessness in general and black youth joblessness in particular has led to accelerating economic devastation in the black inner cities of America.

BLACK POVERTY

All of the factors discussed in this section have led to a situation in which African Americans are three times more likely to live below the poverty line than whites. Nearly 70 percent of these poor families are headed by women (Pinkney 1984). Poverty afflicted 55 percent of all blacks in 1959, 30 percent in 1974, and 36 percent in 1982 (Farley 1984). Even when we look at families below the poverty line, as opposed to individuals, in 1987, 30 percent of black families were below the poverty line. Despite enormous variation in poverty rates by family type, black poverty is greater than white poverty for all family types (Jaynes and Williams 1989). Figure 2.3 shows the trends in black and white poverty.

A few comments on poverty and African Americans are appropriate at this juncture. Poverty is widespread among African Americans. Black youth as well as the elderly suffer disproportionately. Both black youth and the black elderly are three times more likely to live in poor households than whites (Farley 1984). In 1987, 45 percent of black children age 14 and under lived in poor households, as opposed to 15 percent of white children (U.S. Bureau of the Census 1990). The percentage of African-American children living below the poverty line has fluctuated between 40 and 47 percent since 1979 (U.S. Bureau of the Census 1990).

The fact that nearly half of all black children grow up in poverty, coupled with the long-term erosion in black labor participation rates, portends the establishment of a permanent class of desperately poor African Americans. This trend, if unchecked, will have enormous consequences not only for black progress, black politics, and American economic productivity, but for the stability of American society.

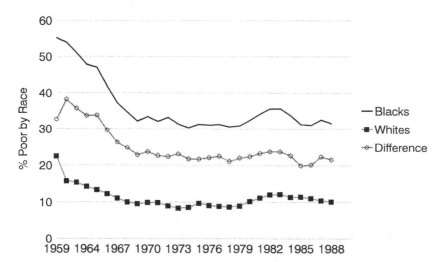

Figure 2.3. Black and white poverty rates, 1959–1988 (*Source and notes*: The data are compiled by the author from U.S. Bureau of the Census, *Statistical Abstract of the United States*. *Abstracts* from the following years were used: 1964–1966, 1968–1971, 1973–1975, 1977–1982, 1984–1986, amd 1990. Data for blacks were not available for 1959–1965 and 1967; the reported data for "nonwhites" appear here. There were reported changes in measurement in 1969, 1974, and 1987. For more details, see the notes in the cited *Abstracts*.)

The Vulnerability of the Black Middle Class

Those who argue that the economic status of African Americans is improving and converging with that of whites often point to the explosion in the size of the black middle class. As pointed out in Chapter 1, the black middle class doubled in size in the period from approximately 1960 to 1980. However, some features of this growing black middle class suggest that the black middle class is far from reaching parity with the white middle class and in fact is fairly vulnerable. First, according to 1989 Census Bureau figures, the black middle class comprises approximately 40 percent of African-American households. This is significantly less than the 70 percent of white households that have achieved middle-class status (Wilkerson 1990). African-American middle-class households are, on average, a third poorer than white middle-class households. Black middle-class status, unlike white middle-class status, is dependent on two paychecks (Wilkerson 1990). Finally, black businesses and middle-class occupations tend to be concentrated in fewer fields than their white counterparts (Jaynes and Williams 1989).

Another distinctive feature of the increase in the black middle class is the large size of the government sector. Pinkney (1984) documents the tremendous size of this sector, showing that 67 percent of all black professionals and managers (as opposed to 17 percent of this class in the general population) and 42 percent of all black administrators work for the government. (These were 1980 figures.) Part of the black job growth in the government sector was due to the enormous growth of the state itself as a result of the Great Society programs, what Dwight D. Eisenhower termed the military-industrial complex, and regulatory government (Wilson 1980). Furthermore, as of 1969 black women working for the state earned 93 percent of what white women did. They only made 74 percent of white women's earnings in the private sector. Black men earned 77 percent of white male government work-ers' earnings while earning only 65 percent of the wages of white men in the private sector (Reich 1981). Such earning differentials would tend to draw black wage earners into the government sector.

Smith and Welch (1989) argue that there has been a shift in the 1980s toward middle-class blacks leaving traditional middle-class occupa-tions and joining the nation's economic elite in the private sector. They base much of their optimism on the future economic status of African Americans who have recently entered the labor force in prime eco-nomic sectors but are just beginning to move up the occupational lad-der. However, they offer little evidence in support of this observation, and many other observers underline the economic vulnerability of the black middle class (Landry 1987; Updegrave 1989).

These figures highlight the importance of the government sector for middle-class blacks. Just as Drake and Cayton's postman was the stable pillar of the middle-class community of "Bronzeville," today's mid-level federal administrator and local agency head play the same role.[5] The important role played by the state in the growth of the black mid-dle class has several implications for the main theses of this work. One implication is the material basis for the preference that African Ameri-cans have compared to other Americans for an economically active state since the black middle class still depends to a significant degree on government employment. More than for other middle-class Ameri-cans, it is in the self-interest of many middle-class blacks to support a large activist state. The dependence of the black middle class on the

___

[5] For more on the social structure of "Bronzeville," see Drake and Cayton's (1970) clas-sic description of black Chicago in the 1930s and 1940s.

state also leads to increased vulnerability both of government workers and of the class as a whole. Fiscal crisis, leading to state cutbacks, is one source of vulnerability. During New York City's mid-1970s fiscal crisis 40 percent of all black males employed by the city were laid off, as opposed to an overall rate of 19 percent (Shefter 1977). Thus blacks, who were 11 percent of the work force, made up 13 percent of the overall decline in laid-off New York city government workers (Pinkney 1984). Hostile national administrations can be extremely harmful to black employment. One historical example occurred when numerous White House staff were fired when Woodrow Wilson became president in 1912. During his first term he issued an executive order segregating federal employment and phased out as many blacks from the civil service as possible (Franklin 1974). The same results, regardless of motive, were achieved in the first year of the Reagan administration as massive federal cutbacks led to severe layoffs of black federal workers (Anderson 1982). During the 1980s the reduction in government employment contributed significantly to the erosion of the absolute and relative gains of the black middle class (Moss and Tilly 1990). This reduction contributed to the instability of the black middle class. Middle-class status for individual African Americans and their families has been insecure over the second half of the twentieth century (Hochschild 1989). Despite the more cosmopolitan nature of the black middle class in the 1980s alluded to by Kilson (1983), in many ways it is still an economically marginal class disproportionately affected by changes in the economic and political environments. Hochschild and others summarize the potential problems of this class quite well when they suggest that those hired on the basis of affirmative action guidelines have relatively little power in their jobs and often walk a tightrope (Hochschild 1989; Pinkney 1984). Time will be needed to tell how vulnerable this "new" black middle class and potential black bourgeoisie is to the fortunes that have at times decimated its predecessors (if indeed, "ceilings" do not limit career growth). As a result of these forces, members of the black middle class are nearly twice as likely to become unemployed than members of the white middle class (Updegrave 1989).

Worse, African-American male college graduates suffered a "massive drop in relative earnings" during the 1980s (Bound and Freeman 1990). Bound and Freeman suggest that the massive movement away from parity with white college graduates in the mid-1970s can be explained by the reduction in government efforts to maintain equal opportunity and affirmative action programs, leading to occupational downgrading for black college graduates. This occurred at the very

TABLE 2.2
Percentage Shares of Aggregate Wealth Held by Each Fifth and by the Top 10,
5, and 1 Percent of Households, 1984

	Net Worth		Net Financial Assets	
	White	Black	White	Black
Lowest fifth	0	—	—	—
Second fifth	3	0	0	—
Third fifth	11	4	3	0
Fourth fifth	21	21	13	1
Top fifth	65	77	85	99
Top 10 percent	47	53	67	91
Top 5 percent	33	35	51	76
Top 1 percent	14	12	24	30

Source: Adapted from Oliver and Shapiro 1989, 16.

time that college graduates in general experienced a "widening distribution" of earnings, resulting in a massive erosion in the fortunes of one of the groups that could have provided the economic foundations for increased black political heterogeneity.

The vulnerability of the black middle class is apparent along yet another dimension—the lack of wealth this class possesses. Oliver and Shapiro use the information in Tables 2.2 and 2.3 to show that household wealth is less for black families earning over $50,000 per year than for white households earning less than $10,000 per year.[6] The net financial assets of white households with incomes of less than $10,000 per year total over $10,000. The only African Americans with positive net financial assets belong to households with incomes of more than $50,000 per year.

The disparities in wealth are due in part to the lack of return on the human and other capital that members of the black middle class possess. Black men with a bachelor's degree earn 26 percent less than their white counterparts while those with graduate training receive 15 percent less (Landry 1987; Updegrave 1989). Segregation in housing also retards the accumulation of black wealth. Real estate in black middle-class communities appreciates at a much slower rate than real estate in

[6] The same definition of wealth is found in Oliver and Shapiro (1989). They use two measures to define wealth. One measure is net worth, which is simply a household's assets minus its debts. The other is net financial assets. This measure includes only assets that can realistically be used to secure additional resources. Thus, personal vehicles and one's own home are excluded from the calculation. For more details, see their article.

TABLE 2.3
Wealth and Family Status of Householders (in dollars), 1984

	Median Net Worth			Median Net Financial Assets	
	White	Black	B/W Ratio	White	Black
Married couple	54,499	13,848	.25	7,540	0
Woman, no children	29,575	3,675	.12	4,217	0
Woman, children	3,320	0	—	0	0
Man, no children	a	a	—	a	a
Man, children	11,825	3,100	.26	1,663	0
Married couple, two workers	50,475	19,470	.39	5,600	(265)
Married couple, ages 24–35, two workers	18,617	4,000	.21	900	(450)

Source: Oliver and Shapiro 1989, 17.
a Subsample too small to analyze (1 percent or less).

white middle-class communities. Typical differences in appreciation rates over five years can range from a difference of 21 percentage points in Atlanta to 91 percentage points in Washington, D.C. (Updegrave 1989). The dollar differences in accrued equity over five years for these same cities range from approximately $40,000 in Atlanta to $50,000 in Washington, D.C. The end result is that black wealth accumulates slowly, if at all. The black middle class remains vulnerable to individual setbacks, changes in government economic policy, and swings in national and local economies.

SUMMARY

Large gaps between black and white economic status are still found in late-twentieth-century America. Evidence for the large gaps in unemployment, poverty, and even income confirm that the Kerner Commission's judgment that the United States was moving toward two societies—one black, one white—is clearly reflected in the American landscape. Further, many of the causes of the erosion of some African Americans' absolute and relative economic status can be traced directly or indirectly to state policy or the lack thereof. The management of aggregate demand which plays a major role in both the erosion of black earnings and employment, enforcement of antidiscriminatory statutes, support for affirmative action remedies, etc., are all within the purview of the national government. These are all factors that affect black income which are responsive to government policy. The devastation caused by industrial deconcentration and deindustrialization has led African Americans to support politicians such as Jesse Jackson in their demands that *public* control over private-sector decisions such as the closing of plants be significantly strengthened. All of these factors would tend to reinforce the political salience of race. Let us now examine whether black society itself is dividing into two subsocieties—one relatively stable with slowly improving economic prospects and one waging a desperate struggle for economic survival.

Economic Polarization among African Americans

Several different opinions exist regarding the *degree* of economic polarization that is present in the black community. The question most commonly addressed today is not whether there is economic polarization among American blacks but rather what degree of polarization exists and what political implications are to be drawn. The National Academy of Science's report on the status of black America summarized its views on African-American economic polarization: "One effect of the improvement in blacks' occupations and wages for those who are employed has been the development of an appreciable black middle class that exists in the presence of a large percentage of low-status blacks whose condition has persisted through periods of recession and prosperity" (Jaynes and Williams 1989, 324). In this section we will review the evidence for African-American economic polarization.

Changes in Black Class Structure and the Rise of the Black Middle Class

There has been a significant upgrading in the occupational structure of *employed* blacks for most of the post–World War II period. Between 1950 and 1970 the percentage of employed black men working in white-collar jobs rose from 8 to 19 percent. By 1980 this figure had reached 25 percent. The comparable figures for black women are 11 percent in 1950, 36 percent in 1970, and 49 percent in 1980 (Reich 1981; Kilson 1983). It should be noted that the *true* black middle and upper classes (true in the sense of being professional, managerial, and technical rather than "merely" white-collar classes) are still small—particularly as compared with whites. The term *black bourgeoisie* is somewhat of a misnomer in that the number of blacks owning even moderate-sized businesses, let alone owning or managing large corporations, is minuscule. Professionals, managers, and technicians grew from 4 percent of black male workers in 1950 to 14 percent in 1980. The comparable figure for white men in 1980 is 31 percent. The percentage of black women in this category rose from 6 percent to 17 percent. The 1980 figure for white women is 24 percent. Unlike white women, black women have reached some parity with black men in level of professionalization. Both black men and black women trail both groups of whites.

The greater parity for black women with white women than for black men with white men is typical of a variety of occupational and income measures. The increase in white-collar jobs has been accompanied by a phenomenal decrease in the number of both male and female black agricultural workers since the turn of the century. There has also been a major reduction in the number of black women working as household workers—although a significant minority of women were in this category as of 1970. The overall patterns justify both Farley's (1984) and Wilson's (1980) conclusion that there has been an upgrading of the black occupational structure since the end of World War II. Wilson cites the major factors in this upgrading as migration, increased unionization of blacks, government fair employment laws (at both local and national levels), and the prolonged postwar economic expansion.

Several unique features characterize this newest rise in the fortunes of the black middle class. According to Kilson (1981), one of these features is that, on a large scale, African Americans are now able to transfer both wealth and poverty intergenerationally. The result has been the creation of two economic realities for African Americans, one with immense potential and another leading to generations of dead-end prospects (Kilson 1981). This has led to a "pulling away" of the African-American class structure at both ends as the top becomes a mainstream bourgeoisie and the bottom is condemned to "ever-widening poverty." Loury (1983) agrees, as mentioned above, that class stratification has occurred and that the benefits have been spread unevenly, creating a schism in the black community. Wilson is the source of much of this analysis. In fine detail, he describes the structural sources of the plight of the black poor (Wilson 1980, 1987). He argues further that, although the black middle class still suffers from discrimination, their greater economic power allows for more options in avoiding what he terms the new arenas of racial strife than are available to their poorer cousins (Wilson 1980). The contradictory forces working on the black middle class have led to what Kilson (1983) has referred to as the "insider/outsider" syndrome. He documents that over 80 percent of this class still feel racial obligations. On the other hand, Pinkney (1984) reports that the black poor tend to feel at least somewhat alienated from their more fortunate brethren. Blacks in the middle class, according to Kilson, have begun the process of "status deracialization." He explains: "This occupational shift reflects a fundamental fact: upper-strata blacks are employed increasingly not in ghetto but in national job markets—in national (white) banks, insurance companies, retail firms, industries, universities, and government agencies. The last employ heads of 30 percent of white-collar black families, compared to 16 percent for whites. Such occupational dispersion of white-collar blacks affects their class identity; it alters the historical mode of racial or ethnic interaction. It allows, above all, new milieus to shape class awareness and identity" (Kilson 1983, 86–87). It is argued that the degree to which this process has developed along the lines outlined by Kilson will determine whether black politics becomes increasingly marked by class divisions.

Economic Polarization and African Americans' Incomes

The potential for class divisions due to the rise of the black middle class become clearer when one examines African-American income inequality. Farley (1984), in an analysis of 1980 census data, finds generally mixed evidence regarding black economic polarization. All employed black workers benefited from the economic trends of the past two decades. Amount of education in particular appears to be an area where there is convergence in the black community. Farley also argues that distribution of income to the richest fifth has remained steady during the postwar era.

However, census data clearly show that in 1982 and 1983 the amount of black income distributed to the richest 5 percent and Gini measures of income inequality among blacks reached levels not seen since World War II. The trend is clearer for black families, as opposed to individuals, suggesting that the polarization is affecting entire families of blacks.[7] From 1961 to 1968 income distribution among African Americans became more equal. From 1968 to 1983, income inequality among black families increased, with the 1983 figure representing the greatest income inequality since 1962.

Farley (1984) is correct in observing that the income distribution among the highest fifth of African Americans remains relatively stable. Although he argues that income distribution has remained steady over

---

[7] The Index of Income Concentration, the Gini statistic, measures the degree of income inequality in a given population. The statistic declines toward zero as income becomes equally distributed among a population.

the years, he believes that polarization among African Americans has increased in other areas. He believes that the trend toward lower labor force participation, the rise in the number of discouraged workers, and the high black unemployment rate, resulting in one out of four blacks being out of work, have contributed to this polarization.

Income inequality is more pronounced when black men are considered separately. The share of the highest-earning 20 percent of black men increased from 50 to 60 percent between 1959 and 1984 while the share of the lowest-earning 40 percent declined from 8 to 5 percent over the same period (Jaynes and Williams 1989). Level of education constitutes a clear dividing line for younger African-American males. Black men aged 25 to 34 with some college education narrowed the black/white income gap to the point where they were earning 80 to 85 percent of white incomes in early 1980s. This group constituted one third of this age cohort, while high-school dropouts represented another quarter (Jaynes and Williams 1989). This class-based polarization is also evident when one examines families. The proportion of families earning less than $10,000 per year grew from 27 to 30 percent between 1970 and 1986, a period during which the black middle class, particularly the upper end of it, was also growing (Jaynes and Williams 1989).[8] A major contributing factor to the devastation at the distressed end of the economic spectrum was the massive losses in manufacturing jobs, particularly in the Midwest, in the black community. This meant both that established blue-collar workers moved to worse-paying jobs (which paid worse than jobs obtained by similarly displaced white males) *and* that relatively unskilled young job entrants had fewer possibilities for securing jobs with stable incomes (Bound and Freeman 1990; Moss and Tilly 1991).

Freeman, in *Black Elite: The New Market for Highly Educated Black Americans* (1976), predicted that the income picture for the black middle class would continue to improve owing to affirmative action and the opening of new employment markets for highly educated African Americans. This trend was expected to be (and the preliminary data seemed to support this) of primary benefit to young cohorts entering the labor market with advanced degrees during the period from 1965 to 1980. Although Freeman *was* generally optimistic, he was concerned that "the serious danger of future discrimination in promotion decisions cannot be denied. Two-thirds of the placement directors in the Black Elite survey expressed concern that at least some black graduates being offered good jobs in 1970 could face dead-end careers 10 years

---

[8] Income and wealth inequality is also increasing for whites, but both types of inequality are increasing more rapidly among blacks (Jaynes and Williams 1989).

hence" (Freeman 1976, 36–37). But his optimism showed through as he concluded, "Even granting these possibilities, however, the achievement of equal starting salaries in the late 1960s was a major advance over the experience of previous generations and past decades."

Freeman's book, like Wilson's, was controversial, and for the same reason. They both attempted to depict the declining significance of race in determining economic outcomes of individual Americans. Freeman was much more optimistic, partly because his book was much narrower, focusing only on the most advantaged African Americans—the highly educated. However, Bound and Freeman (1990) convincingly document how by the 1990s this young cohort of well-trained African Americans lost massive ground to their white counterparts.

Darrity and Myers (1980) attempted to test Freeman's hypotheses. Using census income data, they formulated a model of income determination. Their model shows that different equations for blacks and whites are necessary to estimate income. This suggests that different processes underlie the generation of income for black and white men.[9] In terms of income generation, they found that the migration factor was critical, as did Reich, in the rise in black incomes. They found that for the cohort aged 24 to 33 in 1968, relative inequality had increased in the period from 1968 to 1978. When combined with the effect of the interaction between age and education (the interaction Freeman posits), they found that there is some "relative improvement" for blacks. While they found the evidence "mixed," there does seem to be limited evidence for at least a short-range reduction in inequality for young, highly educated cohorts, if not for blacks as a whole during that time period. The National Academy of Science study found a similar convergence in incomes between young highly educated blacks and whites. They found that black families with a college-educated head of household under the age of 35 earned 93 percent of the incomes of their white counterparts (Jaynes and Williams 1989). Nevertheless, only one half of 1 percent of black households fall into this category.

These findings provide limited evidence in support of Wilson's thesis of the declining significance of race. Class is becoming more important than race in determining life chances. The strength of this conclu-

---

[9] These authors also found that the structural models for blacks and whites were statistically different (Darrity and Myers 1980). As the results from the models of black political behavior reported in Chapters 4 through 6 also show, Darrity and Myers demonstrate that it is often necessary to use different structural equations to model social processes for blacks and for whites. The problem of how to model the political and economic behavior of blacks and whites is a vexing one. See also Dawson, Brown, and Cohen (1990).

sion is still open to question. However, these hypotheses do provide the political scientist with ample reasons to test whether class is becoming a salient variable in the formation of black political attitudes. If well-off blacks are becoming more like whites economically, are they becoming more like whites politically? This critical question will be addressed in the next two chapters.

The Economic Impact of Federal Intervention and African-American Economic Status

The evidence presented to this point suggests that large gaps in economic status persist between blacks and whites. Further, there is solid evidence that economic polarization is increasing among African Americans. There is both a growing black middle class and a growing group of African Americans who are economically devastated. The question remains, however, to what degree has African-American economic status been politicized? To what degree do African Americans see their individual and group economic interests tied to their individual and group political interests? This question will be addressed through a variety of approaches. The next chapter provides historical evidence in support of the argument that a historical link was forged between African-American economic status (both absolute and relative vis-à-vis whites) and the perception of African-American racial interests. At this juncture, I will explore the degree to which current African-American economic status is a result of government intervention in the economy and enforcement of civil rights legislation.

Government Policy and African-American Economic Status

Whether interventionist government policies have aided blacks is a hotly debated question, particularly among economists. Many of the justifications for the dismantling of the New Deal and Great Society programs by the Reagan administration are found in the claims that these programs have not helped and may have hurt minority workers (Mead 1986; Murray 1984). Two leaders of the movement to dismantle these programs are black conservative economists Walter Williams and Thomas Sowell. Sowell (1975) attacks the principle of "discriminatory" (affirmative action) hiring policies of the government. He cites the high number of blacks in the U.S. Postal Service as one example of government discriminatory policy. This example shows some of the problems with his analysis. As mentioned above, black wages in the public sector are much nearer to parity with white wages than black wages in the private sector. Given even moderate mobility and diffusion of information among black workers, neoclassical economics would predict a large influx of black workers into the postal service (and, indeed, into all government agencies with relatively high wages and equal opportunity employment policies). Concentrations of blacks in the state sector can be explained not by the discriminatory policies of the government but by the relative lack of discriminatory policies in the state sector, as opposed to the private sector, and correspondingly higher wages.

Walter Williams has addressed the proposition that the state has an exceedingly harmful economic impact on African Americans. His initial argument is that prejudice, and specifically discrimination against African Americans, need not be economically harmful. To support this claim he cites the examples of many other groups (e.g., Japanese Americans in the United States and Chinese in Southeast Asia) that face prejudice and social and political discrimination but have achieved economic success (Williams 1982). However, these comparisons are spurious. Williams admits that these populations constitute less than 3 percent of the population. Their small size makes it impossible (as in the case of Japanese Americans) to discriminate through strict segregation; Japanese-American high schools are unknown outside of Hawaii, where Japanese Americans dominated political life for several decades. In contrast, "Blacks made up nearly 40 percent of the southern population in the years following the Civil War; they were central to the economy as cheap laborers; and they were highly visible in virtually every region of the South. They proved to be particularly worrisome. . . . It was this concern that motivated the most threatened of white Southerners to attempt to eliminate black competition after the collapse of Reconstruction. And they did it well. The Jim Crow system of segregation was virtually unchallenged until the 1950s" (Wilson 1980, 137).

Wilson had described how the same process was reproduced in the urban ghettos in the period following World War II. The visibility and relative economic importance of African Americans, as well as their potential concentrated political power, have always made African Americans a threat to those who benefited from black powerlessness. It is these differences that makes Williams's interethnic comparisons suspect.[10] Williams mainly examines state regulatory functions, not oc-

---

[10] In addition to ignoring the ramifications of population size, Williams also rejects all of the econometric evidence detailing discriminatory wage gaps: he states that one cannot accept any of the evidence from these studies unless one is absolutely confident that all variables have been considered that could possibly affect racial income ratios

cupational, employment, or transfer payments. His primary objective is not so much to analyze policy objectively but to support freedom of markets and call for the end of all state intervention in the economy (Williams 1982).

Early evidence for the economic impact of the state on African Americans was provided by William Landes's analysis of the effect of state fair employment laws on change in relative wages between blacks and whites (Landes 1968). Using primarily cross-sectional data (most of this data was from 1959, but he also uses 1949 cross-sections as a control) and controlling for region, degree of unionization, and other variables, Landes (1968, 544) found that "relative wages were higher by about 5 percent and discrimination lower by between 11 and 15 percent in states with fair employment laws compared with states without these in 1959." While Landes felt that the above-mentioned effects were probably understated, he found a tendency toward a rise in "unemployment differentials" in the states that had fair employment measures.[11]

Much has been accomplished in this area since the mid-1970s. Although studies during the 1970s seemed to suggest that federal laws did not have much of an effect on black earnings and had a negative effect on black employment, more recent work suggests that there is a clear positive economic effect associated with affirmative action legislation and executive orders (Butler and Heckman 1977; Leonard 1984b). Leonard looks at demand effects such as Executive Order 11246, which calls for contract compliance, and Title VII of the 1964 Civil Rights Act, which set up the Equal Employment Opportunity Commission (EEOC). His conclusion is that affirmative action goals, while less rigid than quotas, help improve black employment in covered industries (Leonard 1984b).

Freeman (1976) observed that improvement in black employment at the federal level was due to state activities, while at the state and local

---

(Williams 1982). On one hand, he does not examine evidence from studies such as Reich's that do control for many other factors while testing for discrimination. On the other hand, he does not hold his own analysis to the same standard.

[11] Economist George Stigler correctly pointed out that Landes's model suffered from a serious statistical flaw: employment legislation, which appeared on the right-hand side of the equation, was not a predetermined variable but was also endogenous to the system (Heckman 1976). Stigler, in his own work, found that there were no benefits to blacks from fair employment legislation (Heckman 1976). But Stigler's work, too, contained flaws. His measure of beneficiaries was actually a measure for tastes in discrimination. He used an incorrect statistical estimator to estimate the model (Heckman 1976). Correcting for these problems, Heckman found that Landes's original findings were largely correct (Heckman 1976).

levels it was due mainly to increased black political activity. He concludes: "The principal forces [for improved black public employment] appear to have been the growth of black voting power, which resulted from the 1965 Voting Rights Act, selected antidiscriminatory voting laws and activities, and the growing concentration of blacks in the North" (Freeman 1976, 174). This critical observation about the economic importance to blacks of both political activity (both electoral and the type of protest that led to the 1965 Voting Rights Act) and state activity flies directly in the face of the work of those who deny the economic importance of either politics or government.

The importance of government intervention for all classes of African Americans is further demonstrated by Heckman and colleagues. They show that the improvement in black wages between 1964 and 1973 was due largely to the increased availability of manufacturing jobs in the South, from which African-American workers had been barred for racist reasons (Heckman and Payner 1989; Donohue and Heckman 1989). In a study of the largest industry in South Carolina, the textile industry, Heckman and colleagues have found that the combination of federal civil rights and affirmative action practices directly led to the elimination of Jim Crow laws in employment and the entry of black labor into crafts and operative-category jobs (Heckman and Payner 1989). Their work emphasizes two aspects of the federal effort. First, the federal effort was concentrated, for historical and political reasons, in the South. It was in the South of the mid-1960s where, with the full cooperation of state governments, the most egregious civil rights violations occurred. Moreover, the South was responsible for two thirds of the national improvement in wages between 1960 and 1970 (Donohue and Heckman 1989). While the intervention of the federal government does not account for the total improvement of black wages over this period (tight labor markets and improvement in black educational levels also contributed), it is responsible for a significant portion of the improvement in black wages in the South at a time when black wages were stagnant in all other regions of the country (Donohue and Heckman 1989; Heckman and Payner 1989). The evidence for the withdrawal of state support for antidiscriminatory policies has already been introduced. Bound and Freeman (1990, 25n.19) declare: "The number of employment discrimination suits in federal district courts stabilized in the 1980s at about 9,000 per year after having risen rapidly . . . ; the number of class action discrimination suits fell; and most employment discrimination cases involved termination rather than hiring. . . . From 1979 to 1985 the Equal Employment Opportunity Commission . . . reduced its staff by 20 percent while holding real expenditures constant; and the Office of Federal Contract Compliance, which administers affirmative action, reduced its employment by 10 percent and its real budget by 20 percent." The "weak" American state has always had a great amount of influence over African Americans' economic outcomes—if for no other reason than that the state response or lack of response to the continued discrimination suffered by African Americans in labor markets has often had far-ranging effects. This simple fact highlights the importance of African-American relative and absolute economic status both in the shaping of black racial identity and in African Americans' political decision making.

Conclusion

The evidence clearly indicates continued economic polarization between the races and growing economic polarization among blacks. Two different economic realities exist for blacks and whites. The black community is literally divided into the haves and have-nots, those who have steady jobs and those who do not. The government has had multiple effects on black economic status. Black incomes have moved toward parity with white incomes, owing in part to enforcement of equal protection and affirmative action regulations. The black middle class is still heavily dependent on government employment.

The vulnerability of the black middle class may affect its politics to a large degree. As Kilson (1983) has pointed out, it is not clear where this class stands on class-based issues (i.e., tax policy), race-linked issues (policies aimed at discriminatory actions), and issues that are both class- and race-linked (job policies). The relationship between class and public opinion will be examined in Chapter 8. Some representatives of the new cosmopolitan black middle class urge abandonment of old alliances and policies, claiming that they are unrealistic in a profoundly conservative era (Loury 1983). This entails abandoning much of the agenda of the civil rights community. Some of these representatives, such as Loury, recognize the persistence of racism in the *social* arena, as well as the economic arena, and call for continued attention to race-linked policies (Loury 1983). However, they still argue that, on balance, civil rights policies are not desirable in this era. In refutation of the view that the black middle class no longer suffers from discrimination and that civil rights and affirmative action policies are no longer needed to protect nearly all African Americans, Pinkney (1984) presents a long list of discriminatory situations faced by today's black middle class.

The politics of this class are important not only because of its growing size but also because this class is able to influence opinion in the black community. On the one hand, if this elite develops as other ethnic elites have developed in the past, one would expect to see increased political heterogeneity as members of the race act in their own separate interests (Dahl 1961; Dawson and Wilson 1991). On the other hand, it is quite possible, given the history of political unity in the black community, that if this class began moving toward the mainstream of American politics, it could carry the whole distribution of black public opinion to the right. How much polarization there is within the black community depends not only on the politics and situation of the black middle class but also on the effect of government programs on blacks as a whole.

This last point cannot be overemphasized. African-American economic advances occurred in large part owing to an expanding economy and what the National Academy of Science called "the vigorous enforcement of equal opportunity laws and employment programs" (Jaynes and Williams 1989, 324). Since the end of World War II, the economic status of African Americans has been powerfully linked to the economic policies of the federal government.

The degree to which economic polarization among African Americans and the rise in status of the black middle class affect the formation of black politics will be explored in depth in Part Two. How the economic status of African Americans has been historically tied to the political group interests of the black community is the subject of the next chapter.

3

The Politicization of African-American Racial Group Interests

> Negroes have illuminated imperfections in the
> democratic structure that were formerly only
> dimly perceived, and have forced a concerned
> re-examination of the true meaning of American
> democracy. As a consequence of the vigorous
> Negro protest, the whole nation has for a decade
> probed more searchingly the essential nature of
> democracy, both economic and political. . . . The
> twice forgotten man in America has always been
> the Negro.
> (Martin Luther King, Jr., *Where Do We Go from*
> *Here: Chaos or Community?*)

IN THE LAST chapter we saw that in the economic sphere, African Americans, although not yet as well-off as whites, are becoming increasingly polarized among themselves. The black middle class, though very vulnerable, is growing, as is the sector of the black community that is economically devastated. Yet systematic manifestations of these class divisions in the political arena have been difficult to find. The puzzle for researchers and political observers is why, given the growing economic cleavage among black Americans, political unity among blacks appears to remain fairly strong. After all, as Dawson and Wilson (1991) have documented, virtually all social science theories of race and class, except black nationalism, predict that black political diversity will follow black economic diversity.

In this chapter I develop a framework that allows us to analyze the elements of African-American political choice and their interrelationships—thus allowing us to understand the puzzling persistence of African-American political unity. My framework requires that we relate African Americans' political beliefs and actions as *individuals* to their perceptions of racial *group* interests. The relationship between a black person's sense of his or her own interests and the same person's sense of the interests of the racial group is the key to the apparent political homogeneity of African Americans. It is also key to understanding how perceptions of racial group interests shape black public opinion and political behavior. If we understand that relationship, we will understand what conditions will have to be fulfilled before African-American political diversity increases. My framework shows that African Americans' perceptions of the interests of the racial group explain to what degree and under what circumstances the economic divisions within the African-American community will become politically salient.

In modern societies, individuals may indeed have multiple social and political identities (as pluralists argue), but not all of those identities are equally salient; some assume greater importance than others, for historical reasons. The two identities of primary historical importance for African Americans are race and class. Since at least the late nineteenth century, scholars and activists have been debating which is more important in determining the social status and life chances of African Americans.[1] Thus, race and class have been the prime candidates for shaping black identity. This is not to deny the importance of gender and religion. In fact, survey research shows the continued importance of racial identity for black women (Robinson 1987; Brown, Allen, and Dawson 1990). Indeed, Robinson finds that gender and race consciousness reinforce each other. Religion has also been shown to be an important force in shaping African-American group identity (Allen, Dawson, and Brown 1989). However, Higginbotham (1992) has correctly argued that the "overdeterminancy of race . . . particularly in the United States" has led many researchers and activists to ignore how class and gender divisions within races shape reality differently and ignores nonracial forms of oppression. But an example cited by Higginbotham clearly demonstrates how, *historically*, black racial identity has overwhelmed other salient identities such as class. When Chicago congressman Arthur Mitchell attempted to ride in a first-class

---

[1] In the late nineteenth century, socialists in labor organizations argued that black progressive leaders such as Frederick Douglass's son should stop pushing the socialist movement to adopt an antilynching agenda. The younger Douglass was accused of using secondary issues to divert the socialist movement—a charge that white leftists would often level at black activists during the heyday of the Communist party and during the period of the New Left. More complex debates occurred within the African-American movement. During the early part of the twentieth century, the African Blood Brotherhood debated with Marcus Garvey, and during the 1960s and 1970s the Black Panthers and the League of Revolutionary Black Workers, among others, debated the relative importance of class with black nationalist forces such as the Congress of African Peoples and the US organization.

rail car in Arkansas in the 1930s, he experienced the following rebuff: "'When I offered my ticket, the train conductor took my ticket and tore off a piece of it, but told me at that time that I couldn't ride in that car. We had quite a little controversy about it, and when he said I couldn't ride there I thought it might do some good for me to tell him who I was. I said . . . : "I am Mr. Mitchell, serving in the Congress of the United States." He said it didn't make a damn bit of difference who I was, that as long as I was a nigger I couldn't ride in that car'" (Higginbotham 1992, 261). Similar claims about the "real" status of middle-class African Americans can be found in the speeches of Malcolm X during the 1960s and in some rap artists' musical lyrics during the 1990s. However, many have convincingly argued that the economic polarization within the black community described in Chapter 2 reflects important differences in the realities of middle-class and disadvantaged African Americans (Hochschild 1989).

In this chapter I extend the discussion of the importance of group interests in two respects. On the one hand I draw upon social and cognitive psychology, which emphasizes group identity, group interdependence, and group subordination (Brown 1986; Conover 1988; Tajfel 1981; Turner 1987). On the other hand, I combine a commitment to methodological individualism—which, in this context, means seeing the decision-making processes of the individual as the foundation for group behavior—with an approach that views individuals in relation to their place in the social structure and in relation to the political environment. In other words, I take individual preferences to be endogenous and structured, at least partly, by one's placement in the social structure (Przeworski 1985). For African Americans, this means that one's individual preferences are partly shaped by one's ties to the black community, one's perception of group interests, which, in turn, is partly shaped by one's place in the African-American class structure as well as by one's race in a society structured by a racial hierarchy.[2] Thus, for African Americans group interests are forged both by tensions of class and status within the African-American community and by the racial climate in the wider society.

In this chapter, then, I provide the foundation for the study of the relative salience of racial and economic group interests as compared with other identities and interests, but I emphasize economic interests

---

[2] For a discussion of how race structures American society along with class, see Greenstone and Peterson (1973). For a look at some implications of racial cleavages for American politics, see Carmines and Stimson (1989). Finally, for a discussion of the interaction between race and class in American politics, see Huckfeldt and Kohfeld (1989).

as a foil for racial group interests. First I derive the theoretical basis for understanding the importance of African Americans' perceptions of their group interests in shaping blacks politics. Then I present a model of how perceptions of African-American racial group interests structure microlevel black politics.

The Politicization of Black Racial Group Interests

The racial group interests of African Americans have both a social component and an economic component. The social component, which Lewis (1991) calls "the home sphere," includes the relationship between African Americans and both society and state; thus, the social component includes politics. The economic component of black racial group interests includes those aspects of African-American life that involve African Americans' economic subjugation. As Lewis (1991) points out, these two components are closely related: the political, social, and economic environments of African Americans, in contrast to those of most other Americans, are very intermingled. Both components were forged during the historical experiences that linked a general subjugation of black life with economic domination of blacks by whites.[3] The experience of slavery, reinforced by the post–Civil War destruction of Reconstruction, ensured that both the general social component and the economic component of African-American group interests would be tied to black politics.

The critical era for the politicization of African-American group interests was the period from the beginning of Reconstruction through the beginning of World War I. During Reconstruction, African Americans entered the political system for the first time as they began to participate in Southern politics. But by the end of this period, during Redemption, African Americans had learned that when they were deprived of political rights, they quickly lost economic and social rights

---

[3] It is *not* argued here that all whites benefited equally from black economic subjugation either during the slavery period or in the era that followed. Neither am I arguing that black economic subjugation was in the *long-term interests* of lower- and working-class whites. I am not attempting to determine whether the lower wages that poor whites received owing to the overall suppression of wages (Reich 1981) were greater than income flows received owing to decreased labor market competition (Wilson 1980). What I am arging is that, owing to the formal and informal exclusion of blacks from labor markets, discriminatory wages, and the weak property rights of blacks as compared with whites, at any given time blacks not only were in a worse position economically than whites but also were economically subjugated by whites. That both races were aware of their relative positions is revealed by numerous accounts.

as well. It was during these five decades, Zafar (1989) and others claim, that blacks became a nation within a nation.[4] It was during these five decades that the great majority of African Americans gained and then lost the right to vote, were forcibly segregated, and were reduced to an economic condition that was, for most, remarkably grim. In the latter part of this period, lynchings became a major tool to maintain African-American subservience. Between 1889 and 1940, four thousand African Americans were lynched, the great majority between 1890 and 1920. By 1905, Williamson (1984) argues, lynchings and Jim Crow legislation together had made African Americans nearly "powerless" in the South. But it was also between the beginning of Reconstruction and 1914 that the seeds of resistance were sown, first in the South during Reconstruction, and later, in the early twentieth century, in the North. For several decades the fruit from these seeds flowered mainly in the North, but in the mid- and late twentieth century black politics and black protest emerged in both the North and the South.

By the beginning of the First World War, the brutal pattern of social segregation and economic subjugation and political disenfranchisement that Morris (1984) calls the "tripartite system of domination" had been solidified in the South, despite ongoing African-American resistance that took the form first of flight and then of radical movements. Neither the desperate exodus of African Americans from the South to Kansas in the late 1870s and to Oklahoma at the turn of the century nor the first great migration to the North in the years preceding World War I nor the radical movements of the first three decades of the twentieth century seriously broke the system of domination under which the great majority of African Americans in the South lived (Kelley 1990; Lewis 1991; Painter 1976, 1987). In fact, this system of political, social, and economic domination of blacks by whites was also extended into the black urban ghettos in the early twentieth century, sometimes resulting in explosive violence. From 1898 to 1919, bloody race riots raged in Wilmington (Delaware), New Orleans, New York City, Tulsa, Springfield (Illinois), Chicago, Charleston, Atlanta, Akron, Washington, D.C., and elsewhere (Franklin 1974; Painter 1987). These riots usually took the form of white mobs attacking black individuals, with

---

[4] Zafar summarizes the view held by scholars across a number of disciplines. Although her focus is the origins of a separate African-American voice in literature during the period following the end of Reconstruction, those writing on black politics, music, and culture hold a similar view. She argues that blacks created a nation within a nation owing to the disappointments of Reconstruction (Zafar 1989). As Higginbotham explains, the concept of a black nation is an old tradition among black nationalists (and a newer one among black radicals). Martin Delaney described African Americans as a "nation within a nation" as early as the 1850s (Higginbotham 1992).

casualties occasionally reaching into the hundreds (in Tulsa, for example). In cities such as Chicago (1919), the black community vigorously defended itself.[5]

During the next period, from 1910 to the beginning of World War II, African-American political and social action gradually shifted from the South to the North. Still, the bloody cycle of day-to-day oppression, racial violence, and black resistance continued unabated from the days of Reconstruction throughout the 1930s. The African-American women's club movement, the antilynching movement of the early decades of the twentieth century, the Garvey movement, the urban radical movements of the 1930s, and the trade union organizing of A. Phillip Randolph all had urban and predominantly Northern roots. Further, it was during this period that African Americans made their first tentative moves into the electoral arena in the growing Northern ghettos. Except for periodic outbreaks such as in Alabama in the 1930s, Southern organizing remained steady, but was quieter and more clandestine—particularly in the rural areas (Kelley 1990; Lewis 1991).

As they also experimented with different forms of political behavior, ranging from participation in a white political machine (Chicago) to formation of a left-labor coalition (Harlem), African Americans, acting on their group interests, tended to display high degrees of political unity. In the economic arena, the decades-long fight by A. Phillip Randolph's black workers' movement for economic justice culminated in a proposed march on Washington in 1941, on the eve of America's entrance into World War II. This threat forced FDR to issue the first executive order in support of equal opportunity in employment—specifically, employment in defense-related industries. Throughout the war, African Americans waged a "Double V" campaign, aiming for victory against fascism abroad and racism at home (Franklin 1974). In addition, during this period urban race riots flared, the most serious one occurring in Detroit in 1943 (Franklin 1974). Then in 1945, with the formation of the United Nations in San Francisco, African Americans tried to focus the world's attention on the pattern of human rights violations of African Americans.

The seventy-five-year legacy of continual organizing made available trained, experienced cadres with a strong sense of historical mission. The conclusion of yet two more wars to preserve democracy (World War II and the Korean War) provided the momentum needed for the civil rights movement to begin. The first incident was the Baton Rouge bus boycott of 1953. That example ignited other bus boycotts, such as

[5] These attacks were the subject of some of the literature by Harlem Renaissance figures such as Claude McKay.

the one in Montgomery, Alabama, which sparked the civil rights movement across the nation.

Although the long legacy of black resistance did not, until the 1950s, break the basic pattern of white supremacy, the histories of black activists such as the Alabama sharecroppers of the 1930s and Ivory Perry of the St. Louis civil rights movement make it clear that the collective memory of the African-American community continued to transmit from generation to generation a sense that race was the defining interest in individuals' lives and that the well-being of blacks individually and as a group could be secured only by continued political and social agitation. Yet it is often forgotten that political organizing had been occurring for decades before the civil rights movement. Equally forgotten is the fact that such organizing resulted from African Americans' perceptions of their subordinate economic status throughout the United States. Thus, economic subjugation was as important as political and social oppression in politicizing African Americans' racial interests.

The Intertwining of Economic and Social Group Interests

The economic history of African Americans illustrates how their economic status has become integral to their perceptions of racial group interests. Several studies have documented the special significance of economic evaluations as a component of African-American group interests (Conover 1984). The interrelationship between African-American group interests and absolute and relative economic status has roots in the late nineteenth and early twentieth centuries. During that period, black economic subjugation became pervasive. Blacks were allowed only limited property rights, and individual and group economic progress was blocked. The pattern of economic subjugation that became fixed during Reconstruction seared into the memories of African Americans the importance of their economic status relative to whites. It also seared into their memories the political basis on which economic subjugation rested.

Letters written by blacks are filled with testimonials on the use of force to deprive entrepreneurial, successful African Americans of their property, and often their lives as well. Richard Wright ([1937] 1966) describes the murder of his uncle by whites for economic reasons in *Black Boy*. Nate Shaw's 1974 autobiography details his continual struggle to foil the attempts of Alabama whites to steal his property, with the end result of his confinement to prison for a long period. Ida B. Wells, one of the leading protesters against lynching in the early part of the twentieth century, was motivated in good part by the lynching of three black men for having successfully launched a black "People's Grocery" in Memphis (Giddings 1984). One of the three, Thomas Moss, the city's first black federal employee, had stated, "There is no justice here." Wells herself wrote, "Lynching was merely an excuse to get rid of Negroes who were acquiring wealth and property and thus keep the race terrorized and 'keep the nigger down'"(Giddings 1984, 28).

White economic supremacy was maintained by the use of violence, law, the local government apparatus, the credit system, and psychological oppression. In particular, violence was a potent means of enforcing labor discipline so that blacks could not benefit from their own labor in the South as that region evolved during Reconstruction and Redemption (Higgs 1977).

As Jaynes (1986) points out, however, violence was not as powerful a means of coercion as was the exercise of local state power, particularly through laws and the judiciary. Anti-enticement laws were used to control the mobility of labor, and vagrancy laws ensured that black workers not under contract to white planters would face criminal sanctions and become part of a government-supplied labor supply for planters (Jaynes 1986; Ransom and Sutch 1977). Sundown laws—which forbade the selling of cotton between sundown and sunup, the only period of time when black tenant farmers could leave the land on which they were tenants—made it exceedingly difficult for black farmers to sell their own crops (Jaynes 1986). Lien laws gave the planter-renters sole control over the crop until all advances, fees, and the like were paid. (But because the planters controlled the gins and the stores, these bills were often never paid [Jaynes 1986].) The judiciary ensured that blacks would not be enticed away from their employers and established that independent blacks could be legally used as bonded labor through the penal system.

The state served to reinforce and enforce the merchants' and landlords' structure of economic coercion and exploitation of credit arrangements imposed on African-American sharecroppers. Store merchants were an especially vicious segment of the Southern political economy, and black farmers who were cheated by the planters on whose farms they were tenants had little recourse—the state system of "justice" was part of the system of tyranny (Higgs 1977). By manipulating the credit system, merchants were able to expropriate over 10 percent of black farmers' income (Ransom and Sutch 1977). Jaynes labels the system "debt slavery."

By the interaction between the racist system of state power and unfree markets, racism governed rural Southern political economy. Although the black labor market might have been in some respects competitive (Higgs 1977), it was by no means a free market (Jaynes 1986). Property rights were severely curtailed owing to government actions and terrorism (Higgs 1977; Jaynes 1986). To ensure that blacks "knew their place," economic exploitation was occasionally combined with psychological oppression. The resulting violence reinforced the mechanisms designed to keep African Americans in a subordinate position. Ransom and Sutch (1977, 98) report the following advice from a planter about how to bargain with sharecroppers: "A little plain talk too, to Sambo in the right way as soon as the bargain is made, as to the course of conduct by which the employer expects to be governed, and what he expects of him, is also productive of good. . . . We expect all orders to be promptly and cheerfully obeyed; that if we tell him to peel the bark off of a long, tall, sleek, slim pine sapling, grate it with tallow and climb it feet foremast, we will expect him to make a faithful effort to accomplish the undertaking, and that if he fails after a faithful trial, we will be satisfied."

Ransom and Sutch (1977) claim that although the success of such "bargaining" was limited, the racism of landlords and merchants prevented black farmers from taking advantage not only of labor markets but also of credit markets, opportunities for self-education, and improved land management techniques. Worse, there was extreme hostility to African Americans' owning land. Whites who sold land to blacks faced severe sanctions, and blacks who owned land faced the worst forms of violence. When laws such as those in Mississippi that actually forbade black landownership were overturned, norms about, and sanctions against, black landownership were sufficient to raise the costs to both seller and buyer (Ransom and Sutch 1977). Secret organizations of white farmers practiced "whitecapping." This practice involved the use of warnings, burnings, shootings, and beatings to "encourage" black farmers to work on the large plantations. This practice backfired somewhat, as many African Americans left these areas entirely (Higgs 1977). The collective refusal to allow blacks to own land helped ensure a state of debt, peonage, and political powerlessness for nearly a century more. In the long run, white planters' collective action against black farmers was decisive: "In sum, the white man who wished to indulge successfully his taste for discrimination was well advised to join together with his fellows of like persuasion. Only as a group would they possess the power to resist competitive forces. Where individual employers or workers attempted to extract discriminatory premiums in the market place, their efforts generally met with failure. A unified group, especially if it possessed some legally enforceable sanctions against recalcitrant members, stood a much better chance to gain from discrimination. And finally, that strongest and most forceful group of all, the occupants of public office, met with little or no resistance in discriminating against blacks" (Higgs 1977, 133).

It was not only Southern black workers who were facing economic attacks based on race. Urban blacks in the North during the late nineteenth and early twentieth centuries found their economic status controlled by white private associations and government. Unions often made the exclusion of blacks from the work force a condition for labor peace (Baron 1971; Higgs 1977; Jaynes 1986). Waves of European immigration made it easier for the unions to displace African-American laborers from their traditional occupations in the street-paving, bricklaying, and restaurant trades. As the new immigrants became involved in the union movement, Baron (1971) reported, "at least" fifty strikes developed between 1881 and 1900 to protest the employment of black workers. Black labor was severely constrained and kept subordinate to white labor by the collective action primarily of white employers (in both the North and the South), but also by poor and working-class whites, who saw blacks as potential rivals in the labor market. African Americans remained largely outside of the family of labor until the CIO organizing drives of the 1930s. This pattern of African-American economic subordination would remain in place, in the North as in the South, in urban as in rural areas, until the dawn of the civil rights movement (Lewis 1991; Morris 1984; Wilson 1980).

This historical pattern has two major implications for this study. One, which I consider in greater detail later, is that African Americans' lack of equal participation in labor and other markets and their nearly nonexistent property rights help explain the statist orientation of African Americans as compared with other groups in American society.[6] But it is a limited statism, because local and state government units, particularly in the South but also in the North, were often allied with racist and terroristic forces, and the federal government was an inconsistent guardian of black rights. During some periods the federal government was relatively remote compared to the extremely powerful and hostile local and state authorities. But during other periods, notably Reconstruction, the New Deal, and the Great Society, the federal government proved to be the only ally (even if a poor one) of African Americans. It should not be too surprising, then, that the federal government, rather than local and state governments or the market system, has been the authority African Americans have turned to in time of need.

---

[6] See Hamilton (1982) and Dawson (1986) for more evidence on African Americans' attitudes toward the state. This issue is also discussed in somewhat more detail in Chapter 7.

Second, and of immediate importance in the present context, is that the perceived economic domination of blacks by whites became intertwined with a sense of political domination as well. Indeed, Ransom and Sutch (1977) argue that when the economic system that had managed to keep African Americans subordinate in the late nineteenth and early twentieth centuries began to decline, the planters and their allies in local government turned to political domination as the main vehicle for maintaining black subjugation, instituting Jim Crow laws and stripping African Americans in the South of all citizenship rights, including the right to vote and to participate in political life. What formal rights African Americans held during the period from 1877 to 1890 were even more severely curtailed, and in many states virtually eliminated. The law now mandated white supremacy and black exclusion.

Ransom and Sutch are on the right track but do not take a broad enough view. Behind the establishment of Jim Crow laws lay two other developments. First, planters perceived a breakdown in the ability of the economic and legal systems based on "King Cotton" not only to keep blacks subordinate but also to keep them economically and geo-graphically immobile—literally, on the farm. Jim Crow laws made it easier to keep the black labor force immobile. Second, as a result of the populist movement in the late nineteenth century, there was a hint of alliances between poor black and white farmers in the South. Jim Crow laws were also a response to this development. By declaring that any white person was superior to any black person, Jim Crow laws tried to stifle this potential challenge to the planters' political power. These two developments—greater black labor mobility and incipient alliances between poor black and white farmers—motivated Southern economic and political elites to make full use of the political and governmental system to reinforce economic control of one race by another. Thus, from the period of slavery through the late twentieth century, a critical interest of African Americans as a group, and of African Americans' evaluations of their economic status as a group relative to the economic status of whites, was the reinforcement of the close connection between economic status and political status. As a result, in all spheres of African-American politics, economic evaluations have been accentuated.

African Americans have become the most politically liberal group in American society on most issues, particularly economic and racial issues. This liberalism is not surprising given the oppression African Americans have suffered in all spheres of life throughout American history (Brady and Sniderman 1985; Dawson 1986; Kinder et al. 1989; Nie, Verba, and Petrocik 1979). This political liberalism exhibited by African Americans has served to further isolate this group politically.

Racial Hierarchy and the Link between African Americans' Individual and Group Interests

In African Americans' historical experience, life chances have been linked to the ascriptive feature of race in all spheres of life. Stone (1989, x) describes well the pervasiveness of black oppression for much of American history.

> Blacks were excluded from many jobs, sometimes given less pay for the same work . . . , confined in business and professional life to serving other blacks, allowed no position of authority over whites, demeaned in forms of personal address, not allowed to try on clothes and shoes in "white" stores or drink from "white" drinking fountains, excluded from restaurants, hotels and other public accommodations, sent to the back of the bus or separate rail cars in public transportation, residentially segregated (even to the point that street names changed as the racial character of the residents shifted), denied participation in the Democratic party (the state's dominant party), and subjected to personal abuse and brutal treatment by police officers, especially for any sign of behavior that departed from complete submissiveness.

This description of Atlanta in the post–World War II era is applicable to the South during most periods of American history. Lewis (1991) describes the struggle of African Americans in Norfolk to achieve advancement in both the "home" sphere (which Lewis describes as the nexus between African-American community and household life) and the economic sphere. He argues that great advances were made through the civil rights movement in achieving political and social rights, but that commensurate advancement was not attained in the economic realm. This is true for most working-class and poor African Americans. The black middle class has somewhat expanded in the years since the achievements of the civil rights movement. It is not clear, however, that enough advances have been achieved by more affluent African Americans to undermine the political salience of their racial identity.

Economic and social discrimination still plagues African Americans. In the economic sphere, blacks continue to face employment discrimination. For example, the state government sued four New York City employment agencies in 1989 for discriminating against blacks both by refusing to refer blacks for certain jobs and by not sending them to certain firms, such as Morgan Stanley and other investment houses and the cosmetics firm Estée Lauder (Kirschenman and Neckerman 1991). Further, as described in Chapter 2, large black/white gaps in income and wealth continue to exist. In the social sphere, blacks continue to fight police brutality cases in small cities such as Ann Arbor, Michigan, as well as in megalopolises such as Chicago. From Massachusetts to Michigan to Mississippi, African-American college students have struggled against racist harassment. In the 1980s middle-class blacks complained of being excluded from certain Boston stores and nightclubs. What must be determined is whether this current level of racial discrimination and harassment in the economic and social spheres is sufficient to keep race the most politically salient identity for African Americans.

The political importance of group interests is a result of at least two historical aspects of American racism. First, until at least the late 1960s, individual African Americans' life chances were overdetermined by the ascriptive feature of race. Because being black did much to determine one's place in the world, determining what political and social policies would provide the most utility for each individual African American by calculating the benefits for the group was more cost-effective than the calculation of individual utility. Hardin (1991) also argues that in societies ravaged by racial or ethnic conflict, individual success may be strongly linked to group success. It is much easier for an individual African American to determine if a given government policy is good or bad for the racial group—an evaluation often provided by black political and economic elites—than to determine the ramifications of a given policy for oneself as an individual. Attempting to limit the amount of information required is an integral aspect of the decision-making process (Elster 1989). Citizens' ability to focus cognitive resources on the issues that are most salient to their own life makes it easier to make informed decisions without having to gather a lot of general information across several issue domains (Iyengar 1990). Cues from important racial organizations and their leaders further aid the process of becoming sufficiently informed on policy issues, parties, and candidates without having to spend an inordinate amount of time gathering information (McKelvey and Ordeshook 1986). Thus, as long as African Americans continue to believe that their lives are to a large degree determined by what happens to the group as a whole, I would expect African Americans' perceptions of racial group interests to be an important component of the way individual blacks go about evaluating policies, parties, and candidates. I call this phenomenon the *black utility heuristic*.

The black utility heuristic is based on the procedural view of rationality (which is somewhat akin to Downs's [1957] views on economizing the decision-making process when less than perfect information is available). This heuristic suggests that as long as race remains dominant in determining the lives of individual blacks, it is "rational" for African Americans to follow group cues in interpreting and acting in the political world. This tendency of African Americans to follow racial cues has been reinforced historically by institutions developed during the forced separation of blacks from whites during the post-Reconstruction period. These institutions, particularly the black church, tended to transmit the lessons of how to respond to the shifts in race relations, economic climate, and political environment across generations.

Group mobilization and black institutions provide another mechanism for reinforcing group identity and group behavior (McAdam 1982). During key periods, the institutions that were formed in the South and often reproduced in urban areas across the country provided a network for politically mobilizing African Americans (Morris 1984). These mobilization networks, besides being responsible in the post–World War II period for the civil rights movement and, more recently, for large voter mobilization campaigns for local black candidates in cities such as Chicago and for Jesse Jackson around the country, are also responsible for helping to perpetuate the perception that racial group interests take precedence over class interests for many blacks (Kleppner 1985; Morris 1984; Pinderhughes 1987). Both Kleppner's (1985) and Alkalimat and Gills's (1984) studies of Harold Washington's first successful campaign for mayor of Chicago vividly illustrate how the perception of a single racial group interest overcame long-standing ideological and class divisions within the black community and how the campaign itself helped reinforce African-American group consciousness. As was demonstrated by the 1983 Chicago campaign specifically and the history of black politics generally, African-American group consciousness helps form a political worldview at odds with the "American ethos" on a number of key points, ranging from evaluations of the local police force to the advisability of expanded government intervention in the economy (Pinderhughes 1987). Further, political elites can strategically utilize appeals to group interests and group consciousness to further their own organizational goals (Peterson 1979). In fact, a strength of politically unified collectivities, according to Hardin (1991), is that power is produced for the group because the group's unity gives a leader "capacity to act." All of these various social and political factors serve to reinforce individual perceptions of group interest.

This view of black decision making would suggest, on the one hand, that black political behavior and attitudes are relatively sensitive to short-term changes in the political, racial, and economic environments and, on the other hand, that black social attitudes and behavior will take longer to reflect shifts in the structure of American racial relationships or in beliefs about which party or candidate will better advance black interests. An excellent example of the process by which black elites and institutions can quickly inform and mobilize the black community at times of great perceived risk (during the Reagan administration) or opportunity (Harold Washington's 1983 mayoral campaign) was the rapidity and near-unanimity with which black religious, civil rights, and other leaders responded to the Reagan administration's perceived hostility to blacks and sought to mobilize the community congregations and constituencies to the "danger" that the administration, its policies, or both posed for the black community. On the other hand, owing to black social networks that reinforce group decision making and homogeneity of behavior and attitudes, shifts in the structure of American racial relationships or beliefs about which party or candidate better advances black interests take longer to be reflected in black social attitudes and behavior. George Bush's initially high approval ratings among African Americans were a result of a combination of an initial willingness on his part to at least meet with recognized black elites and relief over the ending of the Reagan era. However, his ratings steadily declined after the upswing that followed the Panama invasion as the veto of a civil rights restoration bill (over the protests of many black Republicans) and similar acts signaled a fairly traditional Republican presidency, at least in terms of racial issues.

Black institutions and social networks also serve to limit the reduction of black political homogeneity. Political heterogeneity, such as that caused by the creation of a new black elite, takes longer to take hold because such changes are presumably mediated, at least at first, by familial and other ties between the new elite and less affluent African Americans. If one belongs to a family in which some members are in trouble economically, or if one lives in a racially segregated community, one may be more likely to support liberal economic and racial policies despite middle-class status. As ties with the black community and community institutions became progressively weaker, one would expect to see a decline in group consciousness in this stratum.

A second, but related, historical factor leading to the development of the black utility heuristic is the forced segregation of the races following the end of Reconstruction, in the period from 1890 to the beginning of World War I. This segregation, as we have seen, was enforced by lynchings and backed by the full power of the state, exerted through the implementation of Jim Crow legislation, electoral disenfranchisement of blacks, and the protection of white racial terrorists. During this period lynchings occurred at a rate of one every four days (Williamson 1984). Lynchable offenses included succeeding economically, poisoning a mule, "writing an insulting note to a white girl," and acting white (Giddings 1984; Jaynes 1986; Williamson 1984).[7] Jim Crow laws, electoral disenfranchisement, and "scientific" and "historical" justifications for white racism were all integral elements of the structure of white supremacy and forced segregation.

This segregation caused the development of indigenous black institutions, including political organizations, fraternal organizations, businesses, and—by far the most important *politically*—the black church (Du Bois 1961; Morris 1984). Hechter (1986) argues that "differential association" is a major determining factor in the formation of individual preferences and identifies the family and other community institutions as critical in this process. In fact, segregation encouraged the formation of a separate culture (Baker 1984; Gates 1984), separate values (Rokeach 1976, 1979; West 1982), and a separate political philosophy (McClosky and Zaller 1984; Pinderhughes 1987; Verba and Orren 1985). In the realm of values, egalitarianism and communalism played the same important role in black life that individualism did in the dominant society (Rokeach 1976, 1979; West 1982). The forced separation of the races in the South and the development of independent black institutions served to reinforce the overwhelming salience of group status and interests for individual African Americans. Further, the creation of two societies, separate and unequal, provided African Americans with a benchmark against which to evaluate their own group interests: the well-being of white Americans. As immigrant group after immigrant

---

[7] The reason Southern whites universally gave for lynchings was to protect white women from rapacious black men. Some modern commentators, such as Williamson, tend to agree that the perception of black men as beasts and white women as objects to be protected was integral to the lynching culture of the South (Williamson 1984). However, contemporaneous black observers and their modern interpreters tend to analyze lynchings in the context of racial power relations. Indeed, the wave of riots that swept the South at the turn of the century, including the infamous Atlanta riot of 1906, was associated with successful efforts to disenfranchise African Americans. To ensure black disenfranchisement, a gubernatorial candidate in Georgia promoted the symbol of the black "beast"—an effort that led directly to the lynchings of 26 Atlanta black men [Williamson 1984]). It is true, however, that further serious study of Southern lynchings from the standpoint of both racism and sexism is needed. Demonstrating the continued explosive interaction of racism and sexism are the use of the symbol of Willie Horton by the 1988 Bush presidential campaign, the racial hysteria that swept Boston after an unidentified black man was accused of killing a pregnant white woman (who in fact turned out to have been murdered by her husband), the racial overtones of the media's coverage of the vicious rape of a white woman in Central Park, the killing of a Detroit-area Asian American, Vincent Chin, by white men, and the "justification" of a racial letter-bombing campaign as necessary for the protection of white women, all in the late 1980s.

group came to these shores and prospered, from the late nineteenth century to the early decades of the twentieth, African Americans saw their own position as a group remain relatively unchanged. The consequences of all these inequities for African Americans' perceptions of group interests will be considered in the next section.

Group Theory and the Black Utility Heuristic

I argued in the introduction to this chapter that African-American group interests have two components: one social, the other economic. The social component has reinforced the racial identity of African Americans because it has strengthened the perceived link between one's own fate and the fate of the race. The greater the perceived link between one's own fate and that of the race, the more politically salient becomes racial identity. The economic component of African-American group interests has led individuals to evaluate the status (particularly the economic status) of African Americans as a group vis-à-vis whites as a group. Turner and colleagues (1987) argue that "meta-contrasts," the ongoing comparison between in-group and out-group members, is an intrinsic feature of group psychology. The oppressive economic history of African Americans makes the contrast between black and white economic status particularly important. I believe that these two aspects of African-American group interests, the social and the economic, are critical in African-American political decision making and constitute the foundation of the black utility heuristic.

The black utility heuristic is a mechanism enabling one to specify the conditions under which African-American group interests become stronger or weaker relative to individual interests. It simply states that as long as African-Americans' life chances are powerfully shaped by race, it is efficient for individual African Americans to use their perceptions of the interests of African Americans as a group as a proxy for their own interests. The black utility heuristic is based on a conception of rationality drawn from Herbert Simon. Simon's (1985) view of bounded procedural rationality is more similar to the social psychologists' view of rationality than to that of the economists.[8] Simon sees human cognition as procedurally rational, given the limited computational and informational resources available to individuals. Rationality is measured not by how well humans achieve rational ends by maximizing one's own utility but by how rational the process of decision

[8] For an extended discussion of the differences between psychological and economic approaches to utility and cognition see Simon (1985).

making is. In the historically risky environment within which African Americans have lived, procedural rationality would tend to reinforce the salience of racial identity. Constant conflict between blacks and the dominant groups in society and the institutionalization of mechanisms within the African-American community for dealing with the shifts and vagaries of black life help provide researchers with a framework for understanding black behavioral responses to social stratification within the African-American community and shifts in the environment of race relations. According to this view of rationality, the episodic intensification of racial hostility would lead African Americans to continue basing their political choices and behaviors (at least partly) on a calculation of racial group interests, even if over a short period of time race has seemed to be less of a factor in determining one's life chances (Brown 1986; Kleppner 1985; Pinderhughes 1987).

Underlying this view is the notion that "group membership is a powerful basis for the development of self-identity and perceptions of individual interest" (Bobo 1983). Individual political and social attitudes are formed partly as a response to individual perceptions of the status of the group.[9] An individual's attitudes toward other groups are formed by perceptions of the threat that the other groups pose for the individual's own group, even though the individual may not feel personally threatened. For example, Coleman (1986) finds that blacks are much more pessimistic about the prospects of blacks as a group than about their own individual prospects.

The asymmetry often found between dominant and subordinate groups illustrates a critical point about group differences and group interests. Social psychologists such as Tajfel and Brown seem to suggest that social identity or ethnocentrism has the same form across groups (Brown 1986; Tajfel 1981), but one should not expect group consciousness to have the same content, the same strength, or even the same structure across groups. As discussed earlier, for African Americans racial group interests have a powerful economic component because of the structure and historical development of the economic subjugation of blacks in the post–Civil War South and the intertwining of economic and political subordination for African Americans. For no other group in American society are political and economic status in-

---

[9] Hardin, in his work on self-interest, also describes a state where "for historical personal reasons of the particularity of our experience, our interests are causally associated with our group's interest." He takes more of a game-theoretic approach—he uses coordination games to produce the basis for group identity—to reach a very similar description of the interrelationship between self-interest and perceptions or group interest (Hardin 1991).

tertwined to such a degree. Consequently, we should expect economic status, both relative and absolute, to be integral to the political decision-making process of African Americans. We should also expect the ways in which group interests influence individual decision making to differ among African Americans, as well as between African Americans and other groups in American society.

We should also expect the nature of racial identity *within* the black community to change over time. Just as African-American racial identity was forged as a response to racial oppression, as conditions and institutions within the black community change, so should the nature of racial identity. The process of change and the growth of political heterogeneity, if any, would be accelerated to the degree that black social networks and institutions were eroded or that black elites with strong ties to the black community were gradually outnumbered by individual blacks (particularly newer members of the black middle class, with weaker ties to the black community) who had joined white middle- and upper-class networks and institutions. In this framework, a critical variable in the development of black political heterogeneity would be the racial climate for individual blacks and the strength of autonomous black institutions.

Of course, not all individuals possess the same degree of group consciousness or substitute group utility for individual utility. Yet the seeming homogeneity of African-American social behavior and beliefs is due to three powerful forces. First, racial group measures of well-being have been substituted for individual measures of well-being as a satisficing, efficient, procedurally rational method of obtaining individual utility (Simon 1985). As long as this heuristic holds, individual differences will be submerged. Further, Turner (1987) argues that a critical aspect of social identity is the minimization of intragroup differences and differences between the individual and the group. Thus the stronger the political salience of African-American racial identity, the more homogeneous will be African-American political behavior and beliefs. Second, the constraint of the American political ideological space by comparative standards masks much variation among African Americans regarding ideas about the best strategies for pursuing common goals. The class differences that do exist emerge not in traditional measures of partisanship and political choice but in questions that concern the political direction and organization of the black community. Finally, individual differences among African Americans can also be explained by different conditions of socialization (e.g., between age cohorts or between those who grew up in urban as opposed to rural environments) and by the severity and salience of individual experiences with discrimination.

The Black Racial Interests Model

The basic model used in the book for the relationship of self-interest to individual perceptions of racial interests is shown in equations 1 though 3:

$$mbp = f(pgi, ises, mpp) \tag{1}$$

$$pgi = f(binst, binf, belitop, ises) \tag{2}$$

$$mpp = f(pgi, ises) \tag{3}$$

where
  mbp is microlevel black politics
  pgi is respondent's perception of racial group interests
  ises is respondent's socioeconomic status
  mpp is mainstream political phenomenon such as party identification
  binst is membership in black community institutions that promote collective identity
  binf is exposure to black information sources
  belitop is the influence of black elite opinion on the respondent

The first equation simply states that individual black political behavior and public opinion are a function of racial group interests, individual socioeconomic status, and the traditional political variables such as party identification used in microanalysis. The second equation states that perceptions of racial group interests are a function of integration into black organizations such as the black church, exposure to black information networks, degree of reliance on messages from black elites, and—once again—socioeconomic class. The third equation posits that for African Americans, traditional political attributes such as party identification are themselves structured by perceptions of racial interests and socioeconomic status. Standard demographic characteristics as well as factors normally included in models of American political behavior such as perceptions of the national economy were also included in the modeling as alternative explanations to the group interests framework.

$$U_{it} = f(pgi, ises, U_{t-1}) \tag{4}$$

where
  U_{it} is the utility flowing to an individual from a given policy, candidate, or political party
  U_{t-1} is the past utility flowing to an individual from the same policy, candidate, or political party

Equation 4 states that the perception of the current utility flowing to individual African Americans from a policy, candidate, or political party is a function of perceptions of racial group interests, individual economic status, and the utility that flowed to the individual in the past from a given policy, candidate, or political party. Past information about the probable utility of a given policy, candidate, party, or piece of legislation is transmitted through the formal and informal networks of the black community and used to predict current racial group utility. The assessments of each of the components are influenced by the cost of information. If information is costless, then the full impact of socio-economic status and perceptions of racial group interests is incorporated into the perceptions of current utility. The more costly the information is, the "noisier" the perceptions of utility will be. If information on race is easier to incorporate into calculations of political utility, it will have greater weight than nonracial information based on one's status.

In Chapter 1 I argued that information on group utility has been less costly to acquire than information on individual utility. To the degree that this is the case, perceptions of individual utility depend increasingly on perceptions of racial interests. But let us consider the opposite case. As perceptions of racial group interests become less able to predict individual utility, perceptions of racial group interests are less likely to be considered. As this becomes the case for more African Americans, political diversity within the black community will increase. This is essentially a restatement of the phenomenon of the declining political salience of ethnic identity described by Dahl in *Who Governs?* (1961).

The decline of the salience of racial group interests does not automatically result from a change in socioeconomic status, which would make class more salient. First, one's perception of the benefit flows may be wrong. There may also be systematic "error" component. For example, because the rate of social mobility varies across strata, the prominence of class and race cues could depend on the stratum to which one belongs. Further, the transmission of information about "what's good for the race" through numerous information sources, including critical black institutions (for example, the church), black leaders with an interest in providing information about the "state of the race," and formal and informal social networks (such as kinship networks or other networks with "loose ties"), would tend to reinforce the importance of racial interests.[10] Information about the impact on the group may also

---

[10] To avoid confusion, I am using the term "loose ties" where sociologists talk about "weak ties." I use the term "weak ties" to describe the weakening relationship between some elements of the new black middle class and the black community as a whole. This is different from the sociologists' use of "weak ties" to describe relationships in informa-

be more cognitively accessible than information about the impact on the individual (Iyengar 1990).

Second, the term U_{t-1} provides a counter to the importance of information about current benefits. It brings history into the calculus by incorporating evaluations of past perceptions of racial group interests. The inclusion of this term is contrary to the normal wisdom of rational-choice theory, which generally incorporates forecasts of the future but not retrospective components (Elster 1989). I argue not only that use of the perceived past utility of group interests as a proxy for that of individual interests is the starting point for the calculation of utility, but also that past values continue to have an effect on current utility calculations. These values are updated as new information becomes available. My use of the updating mechanism of group utility is similar to the use by some scholars of combined prospective and retrospective evaluations of party affiliation and voting (Achen 1989; Fiorina 1981).

There are several ways bias can be introduced into the utility calculus. To the extent that either racial or class cues contain significant noise, we would expect more reliance on heuristics (Kahneman and Tversky 1982). To the extent that formal and informal institutions are strong in a given black community or that individual African Americans have strong ties to these networks, we would expect racial cues to dominate class cues, because the role of institutions in reinforcing the importance of racial group interests would lead to greater cognitive availability of psychological constructs that support a group utility calculus. This, in turn, follows from the availability heuristic, which suggests that the construction and retrieval of more prominent and available memories and other cognitive structures will bias the decision-making process toward utilization of group conflict (Taylor 1982). Thus, if black institutions are emphasizing a racially oriented analysis of candidates, policies, and social progress, perceptions of the group utility calculus are likely to be more favorable than those of the individual calculus. The type of racial belief system found by Allen, Dawson, and Brown (1989) would also bias decision making toward group calculus (Taylor 1982). Moreover, relatively slow changes in African-American class relations leading toward greater economic heterogeneity are less likely to decrease the relative salience of the group than sharp, prominent, and violent racial confrontations. Finally, information that counters long-standing beliefs will be discounted, while infor-

---

tion networks. See Granovetter (1973) on the importance of weak ties in propagating information.

mation that reinforces such beliefs will be overemphasized (Kahneman and Tversky 1982).

Poor individuals living in relatively disorganized communities would probably have lower group efficacy than other African Americans, because the group beliefs would not be reinforced by community institutions and networks. Further, the despair caused by their surroundings would be overemphasized in the utility heuristic of such people. Conversely, affluent African Americans with weak ties to the black community are likely to have biased calculations in favor of the individual calculus. Again, the availability heuristic suggests the reason for this. The information obtained by these African Americans would be drawn largely from their white colleagues. While such information might include mixed signals about their own worth and achievements, it would also convey the individualistic norms and values prominent among white citizens (Feldman 1983). These norms would tend to bias the African Americans' calculations toward the individual calculus.

Let us again consider the U_{t-1} term. This term represents the transmission of historical information across generations and acts as a brake on the influence exerted by new information. As has been stated, historical information is transmitted through black institutions, kinship networks, and other social networks. The "memory" of the African-American community resides in its formal and informal institutions.

The importance of U_{t-1} explains how quickly individual class status begins to dominate racial group interests. Consider two middle-class individuals, one with strong ties to family and other black community institutions, the other *with the same household or individual utility function* but with very weak ties to the black community. The individual with strong ties to family and community will be slower to deemphasize racial group interests than the individual with weak ties because of the greater impact of information from the black community for that person. This phenomenon may explain why much of the black middle class has been slow to change its political orientation and may point toward the segment of the black middle class in which change would first occur.

The transmission of history has another implication for the relationship between changes in African-American social structure and black politics. If, as Marable (1983) and Wilson (1987) argue, family structure and indigenous institutions in poor black communities are breaking down, then information obtained from black institutions will approach zero, and the black poor will base their political evaluations and choices only on current information. If the only source of information is the community around them, their group political efficacy and perhaps their individual political efficacy could decline. The less costly a particular source of information becomes compared with other sources, the more likely it is that one's view of the world will become consistent with that source.

Conclusion

In this chapter I have demonstrated the historical importance of the economic and social components of the black utility heuristic, then showed how the black utility heuristic can help us understand the relative importance of race and class in shaping black political behavior. We should be clear what is at stake. If among African Americans the black utility heuristic is used widely and more or less uniformly across social classes and if perceptions of group interests prove to be more politically salient than perceptions of individual interests, then Wilson and other social theorists are wrong in believing that class has displaced race as the most politically salient factor in the lives of African Americans. If, on the other hand, the relationship between African Americans' racial identity and their position in the black social structure follows the lines described in this chapter, we will be in a better position to specify the conditions under which perceptions of racial group interests will remain critical in shaping African-American politics.

Part Two

AFRICAN-AMERICAN POLITICAL BEHAVIOR
AND PUBLIC OPINION

> The Negro must . . . work passionately for
> group identity. This does not mean group isola-
> tion or group exclusivity. It means the kind of
> group consciousness that Negroes need in
> order to participate more meaningfully at all
> levels of the life of our nation.
>   (Martin Luther King, Jr., *Where Do We Go
> from Here: Chaos or Community?*)

4

Models of African-American Racial and Economic Group Interests

> When sticks and stones and beasts form the sole
> environment of a people, their attitude is largely
> one of determined opposition to and conquest of
> natural forces. But when to earth and brute is
> added an environment of men and ideas, then
> the attitude of the imprisoned group may take
> three main forms—a feeling of revolt and re-
> venge; an attempt to adjust all thought and ac-
> tion to the will of the greater group; or finally, a
> determined effort at self-realization and self-de-
> velopment despite environing opinion.
> (W.E.B. Du Bois, *The Souls of Black Folk*)

Introduction

Political and economic concerns have been at the forefront of African-American activism throughout American history. While either economic or political concerns may be more prominent during any given period in African-American history, politics and economics have been constant arenas for black struggle. Several scholars have documented the historical interplay between African Americans' efforts to achieve both racial and economic justice. Lewis (1991) documents the dynamics of this interplay in Norfolk, Virginia. Marable's work (1983, 1985) uses an approach that integrates black political and economic struggles at the most fundamental level.[1] Hamilton and Hamilton (1986) document the keen early interest of twentieth-century black advocacy organizations in economic progress. As Hamilton and Hamilton—and other scholars—show, whether emphasis should be placed on political or economic struggle has long been a matter of dispute among activists and intellectuals. The fierce Booker T. Washington–W.E.B. Du Bois debate was partly over the relative importance of economic and political

---

[1] Marable's political economy approach to black politics is based partly on the political economy approach of Poulantzas (see Poulantzas 1974).

strategies for black advancement. However, most African Americans, and Du Bois himself later in his career, have believed that advancement on both fronts is necessary and that the two types of progress are intertwined. The New Deal policies of Franklin D. Roosevelt confirmed the importance of the link between politics and economics for African Americans (Weiss 1983). As numerous scholars have shown for the white electorate, evaluations of the status of the American economy itself structure African-American individual-level as well as aggregate-level political choices and evaluations (Beck 1987; Hibbs 1987; Kinder, Adams, and Gronke 1989). Not surprisingly, however, *how* economic evaluations structure political decision making for blacks differs from how it does for whites. These interest-based evaluations of the economy powerfully structure African Americans' political behavior. Economic group interests directly and indirectly influence such basic political phenomena as African-American party identification, candidate evaluations, and voting behavior.

Measures of Class and the African-American Class Structure

Wilson, in *The Declining Significance of Race* (1980), calls class a "slippery concept." For African Americans the concept of class is even more problematic than usual because of the severe distortion of the African-American class structure due to the historical legacy of racism and exploitation. Several students of the American class structure have noted the extreme attenuation of the African-American class structure as compared with that of whites. Wright and colleagues (1982), working from a neo-Marxist framework, state that the black middle class is much smaller and the black working class is much larger than those of whites. According to Wright, for example, the black working class comprises 64 percent of the black population while the white working class comprises only 44 percent of the white population. Black managers are only 7 percent of the black population while white managers are 14 percent of the white population. Small-business owners (the Marxist petty bourgeoisie) and capitalists/employers combined only make up 3 percent of the black population as compared to 25 percent of whites. Boston (1988) finds similar divergence in his work on black social classes. He also argues that a black capitalist class with any social influence within the black community does not exist. He finds that the black middle class, when adjusted for the high rate of black unemployment, comprises 11 percent of the black population as opposed to an unemployment-adjusted white percentage of 27 percent.

This distortion of the African-American class structure is apparent whether one looks at various occupational structures, as Landry (1987), Boston (1988), and Wright and colleagues (1982) do, or looks at income and employment patterns, as do many of the economists surveyed in Chapter 3. Wilson (1980) and Boston (1988) have similar definitions of class; a class of African Americans is a group of African Americans who have similar life chances. Wilson (1980, ix) defines class as "any group of people who have more or less similar goods, services, or skills to offer for income in a given economic order and do therefore receive similar remuneration in the marketplace." This is the definition adopted here.

Several reasons—some theoretical, others pragmatic—support the adoption of Wilson's admittedly broad definition. First, it is flexible enough to accommodate both changes in the structure of the American political economy and changes in the African-American political economy. For many observers of African-American society, the stunning change in the African-American class structure that has occurred in the second half of the twentieth century is the creation of a new black middle class at the same time that many African-American workers became economically marginalized (Boston 1988; Kilson 1983; Landry 1987; Wilson 1980, 1987). This definition allows for the possibility that as the structure of the economy changes, new segments within classes (Boston's terminology) may develop, or over time new classes may develop. Certainly, new structural opportunities have led to a situation in which a new segment has developed consisting of people whose income is less dependent on the black community and more dependent on traditionally white enterprises, both in the government and in the private sector (Boston 1988; Kilson 1983; Landry 1987; Wilson 1980). For Wilson, higher class means, among other things, greater life chances and higher income. Although Landry rejects a notion of class based on income or education, he argues that education is an enabling factor for higher class position while income is a reward for higher class position. Indeed, Boston argues that the new black middle class, in particular, is distinguished both by its members' possession of "scarce skills" and by their resulting relatively high salaries.

Boston and Wilson explicitly argue that different classes within the African-American population have different political interests. Of course, Wilson argues that race is declining in importance as a factor for determining African-American life chances and that class is an increasingly important factor. Boston, who directly challenges Wilson, still argues that within each class there are strata of African Americans who share similar class-based interests and political beliefs, even though for virtually all classes of African Americans, class positions have been influenced by racism. Consequently, he argues that if there is a social basis for the media pronouncements of a new black conservatism that were frequent during the Reagan administration, it is to be found in the new black middle class (Boston 1988). This is because the financial well-being of the new black middle class is separate from that of the African-American community as a whole. Wilson (1987) would add that this class has also physically separated itself from the black community in a new suburban exodus from the inner city.

However, as Boston and others have pointed out, this class is so small as to be almost undetectable using social surveys. Research strategies such as participant observation or analysis of the social organizations of this new, up-and-coming black economic elite may be more fruitful in understanding the political beliefs of all classes of African Americans. Surveys, however, do provide tools with which to test the basic *political* proposition that as African Americans' station in life has improved in the late twentieth century, their political beliefs have become increasingly divergent from those of less affluent blacks. Most of the arguments advanced by scholars such as Boston and Wilson restate fairly directly the somewhat simplistic phrase "being determines consciousness." In other words, as *objective status* improves, African Americans become more conservative.

Jackman and Jackman (1983), however, argue that while individuals' perceptions of social class are highly correlated with income, education, and occupation, cultural beliefs are also important in all Americans' perceptions of class; for African Americans, they further contend that cultural beliefs are more important than objective criteria. They do argue that simple white collar–blue collar schemes of class, which ignore, for example, the routinized work of those such as secretaries, are inadequate for understanding even objective perceptions of class.[2] When exploring the "class consciousness" of African Americans, Jackman and Jackman found that working-class and middle-class blacks, unlike whites, exhibit higher degrees of racial identity than class identity. Those who are in a subordinate position seem to feel that they share a common fate, according to the Jackmans. Thus, racial identity cuts across class lines. However, because I am concerned in this book to test Wilson's and others' thesis that *objective changes in the African-American class structure should lead to political divergence*, the objective measures of economic status are the ones that will be utilized here.

---

[2] Thus, they argue, secretarial work is misclassified as white collar both because of the way the work has changed with the coming of large office pools, and because of the relatively low prestige ranking of secretarial, clerical, and related occupations that employ a significant percentage of women.

I also considered measures of occupation, income, and education. As previously mentioned, the new black middle class possess unprecedented educational opportunities and subsequent remuneration that allegedly follows their investment in "human capital." I also considered occupation, but the lack of variation among African Americans in their occupational attainment captured in social surveys limits the utility of occupation as a measure of class in this analysis. On the other hand, even those such as Landry who strongly prefer occupational measures state that one's education and income are closely related to one's class position. Further, the type of complex analysis of occupation and job content preferred by those influenced by the Marxist tradition such as Wright and colleagues (1982) is unsuitable for this analysis for two reasons. First, as Wright himself reports, the small number of African Americans falling into the petty bourgeois and employer categories makes any systematic analysis of how African-American political behavior and public opinion vary with class extremely difficult. Second, political surveys of African Americans do not contain the instrumentation necessary to probe the complex class positions suggested by Wright. Third, the concept of occupation itself becomes fuzzy when one examines a population such as African Americans in which a significant portion is either temporarily out of the labor force or has never been in the labor force.

More fundamentally, the concept of occupation imperfectly captures the shifts in the African-American class structure. Consider two black lawyers. One is a recent graduate from an elite law school who is working at a major corporation or law firm. She is earning an excellent salary that is at least somewhat on par with those of her white classmates. The other is an older lawyer who was not allowed to go to an elite law school and has a practice based in the black community. This lawyer's income hardly matches the salary of the other lawyer, but both share the same occupation. In this case, income better captures the disparities between class segments than does occupation. Income and education are the primary class measures used in this study.

Components of Group Interests: Measures and Data

The central assumption of the black utility heuristic is that the more one believes one's own life chances are linked to those of blacks as a group, the more one will consider racial group interests in evaluating alternative political choices. This evaluation includes choosing between different public policies and evaluating candidates and parties, as well as engaging in other forms of political action. Such consideration of racial group interests contrasts with the use of other criteria for evaluating self-interest, particularly individual economic status. It has been argued that economic domination has been (and, many would argue, continues to be) an important aspect of African-American *political* reality over the past three centuries. Hence, a belief about the economic subordination of blacks is a component of racial group interests.

This theory is based to a significant degree on the self-categorization and social identity theories of Turner and colleagues (1987). Individuals form their concepts of self at least in part by judging their similarities with and differences from others. This social identity theory allows for multiple self-concepts, prompted by different contexts, but the key to understanding the self-categorization process for African Americans is the fact that *the social category "black" in American society cuts across multiple boundaries*. African Americans and whites pray, play, and get paid differently.

Crucial to the formation of social identity is the active process of comparing in-group and out-group members. The more differences that are perceived between the in-group and the out-group on the salient social dimensions, the stronger the group identity of in-group members. A salient contrast between blacks and whites is the difference between black and white economic status. As a consequence of the process of comparison, black economic status shapes evaluations of the national economy. In the political domain, black evaluation of the political parties is based on African Americans' perceptions of how well the political parties serve black interests.

This approach is different from that of scholars who analyze social identity from the standpoint of group consciousness. While the concept of linked fate is similar to Conover's concept of interdependence and very close to Gurin's and colleagues' concept of common fate, it differs in that it explicitly links perceptions of self-interest to perceptions of racial group interests (Conover 1984, 1988; Gurin, Hatchett, and Jackson 1989). Gurin's concept of group consciousness incorporates discontent with illegitimate social inequities, social comparisons, social identity, and collective action (Gurin, Hatchett, and Jackson 1989). Conover's definition also incorporates social identification, causal attributions concerning in-groups' and out-groups' status, and cognitive structures that incorporate affect as well as the other psychological attributes.[3] While these definitions of group consciousness provide a use-

---

[3] Conover's attempt to incorporate affect as an integral theoretical and pragmatic aspect of the analysis of group consciousness is an important contribution. The NBES, like most social surveys, does not incorporate many of the measures that make this possible. More work is needed on the role of affect in African-American social identification.

ful measure of available psychological resources, the heuristic introduced here is intended to suggest a simpler mechanism by which the proposition that African-American political solidarity breaks down as economic polarization increases can be directly tested. Conover (1984) suggests that one's perceptions of group interests can become "personally relevant," but not "synonymous" with self-interest. My claim is somewhat different: the historical experiences of African Americans have resulted in a situation in which group interests have served as a useful proxy for self-interest.

Measures of African-American Racial Interests

Two components of group interests are critical to the political process for African Americans. For group interests to affect the political process, a significant number of African Americans must believe that what happens to the group as a whole affects their own lives. A construct of *linked fate* is needed to measure the degree to which African Americans believe that their own self-interests are linked to the interests of the race. Second, evaluations of relative group status, particularly economic status, are essential for understanding African-American perceptions of racial group interests.

The National Black Election Panel Study (NBES) of 1984–1988 demonstrates both the basic underpinnings of black group interests and the role they played in shaping African-American political behavior and political beliefs in 1984 and 1988. The study consisted of a national telephone survey in which 1,150 interviews were conducted with members of the adult African-American population. The NBES is one of the most extensive political surveys of the African-American population that has been conducted. A full description of the NBES and the other surveys used in this study may be found in Appendix 1.

The 1988 NBES survey provides both economic and general measures of absolute and relative group status. These measures allow us to compare the different hypotheses according to which the most important determinants of political choice are based on class, individual utility, evaluations of what is good for society, or racial group utility, respectively. Further, measures are provided that allow us to test the relative salience of both current and retrospective evaluations.

The concept of linked fate was measured in both 1984 and 1988. Survey participants were asked, "Do you think that what happens generally to the black people in this country will have something to do with what happens in your life?" Figure 4.1 shows the distribution of responses to this question. In 1984, 63 percent of the NBES sample re-

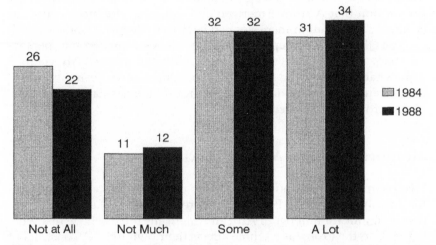

Figure 4.1. Perceptions of linked fate, 1984 and 1988: "Do you think that what happens generally to the black people in this country will have something to do with what happens in your life?" Category values represent percentage of respondents responding in that category. (*Source*: 1984–1988 National Black Election Panel Study)

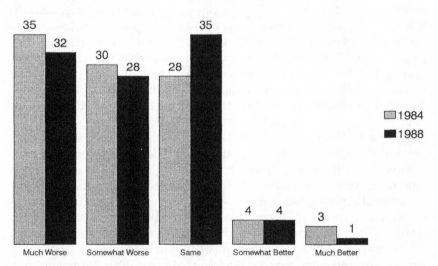

Figure 4.2. Perceptions of economic subordination, 1984 and 1988: "On the whole, would you say that the economic position of blacks is better, about the same, or worse than that of whites?" Category values represent percentage of respondents responding in that category. (*Source*: 1984–1988 National Black Election Panel Study)

TABLE 4.1

Gamma Correlations between Group Interest Variables and Selected Socio-economic Indicators

Variable	Linked Fate		Blacks Worse Off Than Whites	
	1984	1988	1984	1988
Family income	.09	.03	.16	.23
Education	.13	.10	.15	.31
n[a]	886/1064	309/315	882/1056	308/444

Source: 1984–1988 National Black Election Panel Study.

[a] First "n" is for correlation between group interest variable and income, the second for group interest variable and education.

sponded affirmatively, and in 1988, the figure was 64 percent. Perceptions of economic subordination of blacks were also measured. The question was asked, "On the whole, would you say that the economic position of blacks is better, about the same, or worse than that of whites?" As shown in Figure 4.2, 65 percent of African Americans in both years of the sampling responded that blacks are in a worse economic position than whites.

Do perceptions of either linked fate or economic subordination vary with one's class position? To answer this question I look first at the bivariate relationships between perceptions of linked fate and education, family income, and occupational class. These relationships are summarized in Table 4.1. As this table demonstrates, linked fate varies very slightly with socioeconomic variables. Variables associated with linked fate in 1984 were not associated with linked fate in 1988. Multivariate analysis will help determine what factors help predict perceptions of linked fate.

A parallel analysis was conducted for perceptions of economic subordination. The relationships between perceptions of economic subordination and the socioeconomic variables are also presented in Table 4.1. There appears to be very little covariation between the socioeconomic measures and the measure of perceptions of economic subordination. Furthermore, occupation seems to add little information to that provided by education and income. Clearly, there is a relationship between socioeconomic status and perceptions of economic subordination. Multivariate analysis will pin down the exact nature of this relationship. This preliminary analysis suggests that those with more education and status are more likely than their less affluent cousins to believe that blacks as a group are in a poor economic state absolutely and relatively.

A Model of Black Utility and Linked Fate

It appears, then, that while perceptions of group interests are important to a large majority of African Americans, there is a relationship between perceptions of African-American group interests and various socioeconomic factors. However, the bivariate analyses are unable to provide much information about the causes of this relationship. A multivariate causal model of group interests can provide more information.

It is reasonable to expect to find a relationship between perceptions of linked fate and of black economic subordination. If one believes that blacks as a group are in a subordinate position, one's belief in the linked fates of individual African Americans should be strengthened. Furthermore, if one perceives the fates of individual blacks as linked to that of the group, it is at least in part because one perceives blacks as a subordinate and exploited group in American society. One's beliefs about whether blacks are in a subordinate economic position and whether one's fate is linked to that of the racial group should be mutually reinforcing. This thesis was tested by modeling the relationship between perceptions of linked fate and black economic subordination as a reciprocal relation.

Class is another major contender for influencing perceptions of African-American group interests. If increased affluence is weakening links between individual African Americans and the race as a whole, income and education should be negatively correlated with the group interests variables. According to this logic, those with higher incomes should feel weaker attachments to the race and perceive better economic status for blacks vis-à-vis whites. To further develop the model, let us consider the causes for each construct.

First, consider linked fate. We have already proposed a positive correlation between perceptions of linked fate and of black economic subordination. The belief that one's fate is linked to that of the racial group should be relatively stable. There is some variability in perceptions of linked fate reported by NBES survey respondents between 1984 and 1988. Approximately 10 percent of those who reported perceptions of linked fate in 1984 had moved into the no-linkage column four years later. Even more important, in Chapter 3 it was argued that historical information on the importance of group interests in determining individuals' political and social choices is incorporated into current calculations of the salience of group interests. Therefore, the availability of panel data itself as historical information should be taken into account as a possible influence on the 1988 value for linked fate.

Further, it was argued in Chapter 3 that the black church was one of the institutions that helped to reinforce the political importance of the perception of group interests for individual African Americans. It is the political role of the black church that is salient for the reinforcing of group consciousness and group interests. Therefore, the measure of whether one hears political messages at church is included in the equation with the expectation that linked fate would be positively reinforced by the degree to which one heard political messages at church.

Allen and Kuo (1990) have found that exposure to mainstream media is negatively correlated with feelings of racial identity. Here I would also expect a negative relationship between exposure to mainstream media and the importance of group interests to the survey respondent. In my study, I control for a number of sociodemographic variables, which are used to test various hypotheses about whether the perception of linked fate is associated with one's socioeconomic status. A description of the control variables that I use throughout this study and the rationale for their selection can be found in Appendix 1.

The model for perceptions of black economic subordination is simpler. Again, linked fate is included in the equation. Similarly, whether one believes blacks are economically subordinate to whites, while partially a product of current conditions, should also be influenced by beliefs about the historical economic position of African Americans vis-à-vis whites. In addition, it is reasonable to expect that one's own economic status would affect one's perception of economic differences between blacks and whites. This is consistent with the findings of Kinder, Adams, and Gronke (1989). The effect of information on perceptions of black economic subordination is also measured. The same set of control variables is used as in the linked fate model. The full results of the analysis are reported in Table 4.2 in Appendix 1.

Fifty-seven percent of the variance in the dependent variable was explained by the model of the interrelationship between perceptions of black economic subordination and linked fate. Examination of the linked-fate equation reveals that, as predicted, past values of linked fate strongly predicted current values. Perceptions of black economic subordination also were strongly predictive of perceptions of linked fate.

The class variables did not affect perceptions of linked fate. This suggests that, as of yet, class-based distinctions in perceptions of linked fate are not discernible. There was an indirect link between level of education and perceptions of linked fate through beliefs about black economic subordination. However, the *more* education one had, the more likely one was to believe that blacks were economically subordinate to whites, and consequently, the more likely one was to believe that one's fate was linked to that of the race. *Education thus had the opposite effect from the one predicted by those who believed that increased opportunities for blacks should lead to a weakening of perceived attachment to the race.*

Political messages received in church weakly reinforced perceptions of linked fate. Being an urban resident and being exposed to main-stream media served to weaken the link between individual African Americans and the group as a whole. Commentators as disparate as Marable and Wilson have suggested that the increasing social disor-ganization of the inner cities has led to a breakdown of community (Wilson 1987) and a lessening of group consciousness (Marable 1983). The urban residence finding was consistent with their hypotheses. The finding that exposure to mainstream media served to weaken percep-tions of linked fate is consistent with findings by Allen and Kuo (1990) that mainstream media can act as a conservative force.

Turning to the results of the equation for black economic subor-dination, we find a confirmation of most of the predictions. Deteriorat-ing household finances and past beliefs about the economic position of blacks both contributed to a perception of black economic subordi-nation. A particularly strong predictor of a belief in black economic subordination is a strong belief in linked fate. The strongest predictor was one's past views on the relative economic status of blacks and whites. In addition, the higher one's educational level and age, the stronger one's belief in the economic subordination of blacks. The effect of urbanicity on perceptions of black economic subordination was op-posite to its effect on linked fate. The problems of the urban black com-munity, then, seem to reinforce perceptions of group subordination at the same time that they weaken the belief in a link between one's self and the race that many argue is necessary for overcoming those problems.

Although socioeconomic status, as indirectly indicated by education, was found to be a strong predictor of the belief that blacks are econom-ically disadvantaged as compared to whites, which itself is a predictor of linked fate, little evidence exists that class has a direct relationship to perceptions of linked fate. However, class-based differences become apparent when one examines the similar but more specific question, "Do you think that the movement for black rights has affected you personally?" It is one thing to believe that one's fate is linked to that of all African Americans. It is quite another to claim that African Ameri-cans have benefited equally from black social progress. Increasingly, scholars such as Wilson (1980) have asserted that the civil rights movement has benefited mainly better-trained and more affluent African Americans. Class differences are more likely to affect responses to this more specific question of whether the black movement has affected one's own life than the broader question of linked fate.

Of course, if one does not believe that one's fate is linked to that of the race, then political and social movements based on race are not likely to be seen as having aided one's own advancement. On the other hand, if those such as Wilson are correct, less affluent African Americans did not benefit as much from the civil rights movement and consequently are less likely to believe that the movement affected their own lives. An analysis was undertaken of the effect of perceptions of group interests and socioeconomic class on responses to this more specific question. The results are displayed in Table 4.3, in Appendix 1.

Belief in linked fate, higher eductional level, and higher household income increased the probability of believing that the civil rights movement had affected one's own life. Linked fate had the second greatest impact on one's views on the efficacy of the black rights movement. Those who believed that one's own fate was strongly connected to that of the race were 42 percent more likely to believe that the black rights movement had affected one's own life.[4] As with linked fate, the more exposure one had to mainstream media, the less likely one was to believe that the black movement had affected oneself. On the other hand, being a member of a black organization increased one's probability of thinking that such a linkage exists by 13 percent. This is not merely a case of institutional reinforcement of community norms. Many black organizations, ranging from black churches to the civil rights organizations themselves, have been key participants in the black rights movement.

Both higher education and higher income increased the probability of seeing the movement as having affected one's life. Respondents having postgraduate training were approximately 20 percent more likely than respondents having completed high school to answer the question affirmatively, and those having completed the twelfth grade were 20 percent more likely than those with only an eighth-grade education. Those with a family income of $50,000 per year were 10 percent more likely to answer affirmatively than those earning $10,000 per year. Unlike the question of linked fate, in which a large majority of African

---

[4] While in the text the assumption is made that linked fate predicts how one views the black movement, there was a possibility that a reciprocal relationship with linked fate existed. Such a relationship was found not to exist. Linked fate predicts the black movement effect variable, not the other way around.

Americans across socioeconomic classes perceived a common destiny, class status affected how one viewed the efficacy of the monumental struggle for black rights. We can conclude that the fruits of the movement were not shared equally.[5]

Consequences of Perceptions of Group Interests

Perceptions of racial group interests shape a variety of other perceptions critical to African-American politics. Perceptions of linked fate and perceptions of black economic subordination are the political building blocks for analyzing perceptions of racial group interests. But perceptions of racial group interests also play a more general role in shaping African Americans' political, economic, and social judgments. Perceptions of which political party best serves African Americans, and absolute and relative black economic status, are both examples of consequences of perceptions of racial group interests that are politically relevant. Group interests and class divisions affect perceptions of the economy and of the social influence of racial groups, which in turn shape many important political outcomes. Thus, before we attempt to understand how perceptions of racial group interests and class shape political outcomes, we need to understand how they shape some of the social and economic antecedents of black political choice.

Group Interests and Evaluations of Group and National Economic Performance

It has been demonstrated that for the general population, evaluations of personal and group economic performance underlie evaluations of national economic performance (Kinder et al. 1989). Evaluations of personal and national economic health have in turn been demonstrated to be important predictors of political choice (Kinder and Kiewiet 1981; Markus 1988; Tufte 1978). The present analysis is based on the strong hypotheses that (1) perceptions of black group economic status will be important in African Americans' political decision-making calculus

[5] Another hypothesis is that what one sees is an age effect. The argument is that it is the members of the post–civil rights generation who do not see a relationship between their own lives and the struggle for black rights. This hypothesis was tested explicitly, and age is not a predictor of the perception of linkage between one's own life and the various movements for racial justice. Further, when one divides the age variable into cohort ranges, there is still no effect.

and (2) the economic component of group interests will be a strong predictor of the evaluation of black economic status.

In 1984, assessing the preceding year, 34 percent of African Americans believed that their household finances had worsened, as opposed to 45 percent who thought that they had improved. However, 37 percent thought that black group economic status had become worse and 50 percent thought that the economic health of the nation had declined. The pattern is virtually identical in 1988. In 1988, more African Americans perceived that the national economy had worsened over the preceding year than perceived either a worsening of black group economic status or a worsening of household finances. However, in this year only national economic status was perceived to have declined by an absolute majority of blacks. Thirty percent of the sample thought that their household finances had declined, 38 percent thought that racial group economic status had declined, and 52 percent of the sample believed that national economic status had declined. Forty-four percent of the sample believed that their own finances had improved. Household finances was the only one of the three variables for which the modal choice, the choice made by the greatest number of respondents, was that economic status had not declined.

A simple two-equation model of the interrelationship between perceptions of group interests and evaluations of racial group and national economic health was developed to further probe the relationship between various perceptions of economic well-being and perceptions of group interests. Perceptions of black economic subordination were predicted to contribute to the perception that black economic status has deteriorated. Deterioration in household finances was predicted to have the same effect. Negative evaluations of changes in black economic status were predicted to correlate with negative perceptions of the state of the national economy. The two measures of perceptions of racial group interest, evaluations of household economic health, and the standard control variables, are included as predictors of whether black economic status has changed.

Perception of black economic subordination is the strongest predictor in the equation that models perception of change in black economic status.[6] Beliefs about household finances also play a strong role in predicting beliefs about group economic performance. As goes the household, so goes the group. Higher age and higher family income contribute moderately to the likelihood of having a more negative view of black economic performance. By far the strongest predictor of evaluations of national economic performance is evaluations of racial group

---

[6] Table 4.4 in Appendix 1 displays the results of the estimation of this model.

economic performance. As goes the group, so goes the nation. Household economic performance is a weak predictor of perceptions of national economic performance. Black men had a somewhat more optimistic view of the nation's economic health than black women—a not unexpected finding, given the large number of women heading households afflicted with poverty (Wilson 1987).

Economic distress has always been a fundamental component of African-American reality (Dawson, Cohen, and Brown 1990; Farley and Allen 1987; Reich 1981; Wilson 1980, 1987). As recently as 1984 a large majority of African Americans identified unemployment as the biggest problem facing the country. Consequently, economic evaluations are likely to play an important role in the formation of African-American political choices and patterns of partisanship. This section has shown that African-American economic evaluations are built on perceptions of group interest and household economic conditions. An important aspect of the findings on evaluations of the national economy is the relative lack of class divisions influencing perceptions of economic status. Despite the signs of increased economic polarization among African Americans documented in Chapter 2, African Americans have similar evaluations of economic status. The next section probes the interaction between perceptions of group interests and perceptions of racial group influence.

Perceptions of Relative Influence and Racial Group Interests

Whether one believes that blacks and whites, respectively, have too much, too little, or the right amount of influence should be determined by one's perceptions of linked fate and of black economic subordination. In turn, perceptions of relative group influence help predict one's political orientation. Just as group interests structure perceptions of absolute and relative economic well-being, they also structure perceptions of relative racial group social influence, which in turn shape African Americans' political evaluations.

In 1984 and 1988 there was little disagreement among African Americans as to whether blacks had sufficient influence. The question was asked, "Do blacks as a group have too much influence, about the right amount of influence, or too little influence?" In 1984, 81 percent of African Americans believed that blacks had too little influence. By 1988 this percentage had risen to 87 percent. In 1988, only 12 percent said blacks had about the right amount of influence, and less than 1 percent responded that blacks had too much influence.

When the same question was asked about white influence, there was more variation, although the overall pattern remained the same. In 1984, 62 percent of the sample responded that whites had too much influence, 31 percent said they had about the right amount of influence, and only 5 percent stated that whites had too little influence. In 1988, 61 percent felt that whites had too much influence.

The model of the interrelationship between group interests and beliefs about racial group influence is based on the belief that there is a reciprocal relationship between beliefs about current levels of black and white group influence. Those who think that whites have too much influence are likely to believe that blacks have too little influence. In addition, both components of group interests (economic and political) should predict one's view on racial group influence. These variables are the main components of the model of social influence.[7]

In 1984, all variables except those relating to age contributed to the perception that whites have too much influence. Those who believed that blacks had too little influence, believed that their fate was linked to that of the race, were more affluent, and believed that blacks were economically worse off than whites were more likely to believe that whites had too much influence. Once again, the class variables have the opposite effects from those one would be led to expect by those who argue that higher socioeconomic class correlates with a higher degree of conservatism. *Class status and perceptions of group interests reinforce each other.* In 1988, the pattern was somewhat different, with class and perceptions of group interests having weaker effects. In 1988, those who felt that blacks had too little influence as well as younger African Americans were the ones who believed that whites had too much influence. In both years, stronger perceptions of linked fate and of black economic subordination correlated with stronger perceptions that whites have too much influence.

Conclusion

This chapter, by developing models of racial group interests, has laid the foundation for the analyses to be conducted in the coming chapters. These models show that socioeconomic status only weakly influences

---

[7] Only the equation for white group interest is presented, for several reasons. First, the skewness in the data makes modeling black group influence difficult. Second, although the reciprocal relationship between the two variables would suggest that this is an ideal case to which to apply a simultaneous equation model, such an equation is difficult to identify. Finally, opinions on white group influence are much better predictors of other dependent variables than opinions on black group influence. The final results are presented in Table 4.5 in Appendix 1.

perceptions of linked fate. The economic and political components of group interest have a major role in shaping perceptions of both economic well-being and relative group influence. These models provide a set of tools that will be useful in modeling African-American political choice and public opinion. They confirm that, throughout the 1980s, individual beliefs and perceptions constituted a firm basis for relatively unified group political behavior.

Appendix 1

Data and Models for Chapter 4

A. Data

The 1984–1988 National Black Election Panel Study

The National Black Election Panel Study (NBES) sample is composed of adults of voting age. The 1984 NBES consists of 1,150 pre-election telephone interviews and 872 reinterviews conducted after the 1984 national election. The response rate in 1984 was 58 percent. The sample was selected by random digit dialing and stratification so that communities with high-density, medium-density, and low-density concentrations of African Americans were represented adequately. This design provided a weighted sample of the African-American population in 1984. The 1988 survey consisted of pre- and post-election reinterviews of 473 respondents in the 1984 post-election interview. The investigators on the 1984 panel were James S. Jackson, Patricia Gurin, and Shirley J. Hatchett. James S. Jackson was also the principal investigator on the 1988 panel. For an excellent and in-depth discussion of sample design, coverage, and other methodological issues, see Gurin, Hatchett, and Jackson (1989).

1989 Detroit Area Study

The 1989 Detroit Area Study consisted of 916 face-to-face interviews of a multistage random sample of the Detroit tri-county area of Wayne, Oakland, and Macomb counties during the spring and summer of 1989. The principal investigator in this study was Steven J. Rosenstone. The tri-county component of the sample consisted of 466 respondents and was complemented by an oversample of 450 respondents within the city of Detroit. This oversample ensured that there would be enough African Americans and Detroit residents in the sample to allow analysis of Detroit residents alone and analysis of black respondents. The response rate for the study was 70.2 percent. More information on this sample and survey can be found in the report "Separate and Unequal" (Detroit Area Study 1989).

B. Economic Evaluation, Economic Status, and Control Variables

All variables used in the multivariate analysis have been recoded to a 0–1 scale. Except where noted, the wording of the question and coding of variables are identical in both sample years. Other variables will be discussed as they are introduced in later chapters.

Household Finances

"Would you say that you (and your family living with you) are better off or worse off financially than you were a year ago?" Five-category variable, 0 = much worse, 1 = much better.

Black Economic Status

"Would you say that over the past year the economic position of blacks has gotten better, stayed about the same, or gotten worse?" Five-category variable, 0 = much worse, 1 = much better.

National Economic Status

"Would you say that over the past year the nation's economy has gotten better, stayed about the same, or gotten worse?" Five-category variable, 0 = much worse, 1 = much better.

Family Income

Unfortunately, this question was asked differently in 1984 and 1988. In 1984 a battery of questions about income range resulted in an eleven-category summary variable ranging from "under $9,999" to "$40,000 or more." In 1988 respondents were directly asked their family income, with those who initially did not give a response probed with a battery of questions about income range. Both 1984 and 1988 variables were recoded to fall into the 0–1 range.

Education

Number of years of school completed, with the top category representing "17+" years.

Black Organization

"Are you a member of any organization working to improve the status of black Americans?" 0 = no, 1 = yes.

Age

Age in years.

Gender

0 = female, 1 = male.

Southern Residence

0 = non-South, 1 = South.

Urbanicity

0 = non-urban resident, 1 = urban resident.

News Exposure

This question was asked only in 1988. "How many days in the past week did you read a daily newspaper?" 0 = no days, 1 = 7 days.

C. Results

The relationship between perceptions of linked fate and perceptions of economic subordination in 1988 was estimated as reciprocal. Lagged dependent variables were also included in each equation and had to be treated as endogenous. Consequently, the estimates were derived using the three-stage least squares estimator supplied with the Shazam Econometrics computer program (White, Haun, Horsman, and Wong 1988). The results from the estimation of the structural equations of interest are presented in Table 4.2 and described in the main text.

The results of the analysis of whether one believed that the black movement had affected one's own life are presented in Table 4.3. I tried to provide analysis of both 1984 and 1988 variables except where there were theoretical reasons to include the 1984 variable as a predictor of the 1988 variable. In this case, the 1984 and 1988 versions of the variable are different, and the 1988 version gave the respondent more choices. The coefficients have been corrected for selection bias using Achen's (1986) method. The details of the correction process are given in Appendix 1.

The analyses of the relationship between perceptions of black and national economic health presented in Table 4.4 also used 3SLS estimation to correct for correlated errors.

Estimates of the evaluations of white influence were obtained by ordinary least squares in 1984, but by the Achen two-stage correction in 1988. The basis for this correction is described below.

TABLE 4.2

Relationship between Perceptions of Linked Fate and Black Economic Subordination, 1988

	Dependent Variable: Coefficient (SE)	
Variable	Linked Fate	Belief That Blacks Are Better Off Than Whites
Linked Fate[a]		
1988	b	−.26
		(.14)
1984	.42	b
	(.23)	
Belief that blacks are economically better off than whites[a]		
(yes) 1988	−.62	b
	(.26)	
(yes) 1984	b	.40
		(.14)
Education	c	−.16
		(.08)
Family income	c	c
Urbanicity	−.14	−.08
	(.05)	(.03)
How many days a week read newspaper?	−.13	c
	(.06)	
Exposure to politics at church	.05	c
	(.04)	
Age	c	−.24
		(.08)
Did your household finances get better?	c	.18
		(.05)
Constant	.65	.48
	(.21)	(.13)
n = 242		
R^2	.15	.23
System R^2	.57	

Source: 1984–1988 National Black Election Panel Study. Estimates were obtained using the Systems Procedure of the Shazam econometric program. The estimates are 3SLS estimates.

[a] Variable treated as endogenous.

[b] Not included in equation.

[c] Found not to have an impact on dependent variable and excluded from final model on that basis.

TABLE 4.3
Determinants of Whether One Believes That the Black Movement
Affected One's Life, 1988

Independent Variable	Dependent Variable (Belief That the Black Rights Movement Affected One's Life): Coefficient (SE)
Linked fate	.42
	(.07)
Family income	.26
	(.14)
Education	.54
	(.20)
Membership in Black Organization	.15
	(.05)
News exposure	−.20
	(.08)
Constant	−.11
	(.16)
n = 211	
Adjusted R^2	.28

Source: 1984–1988 National Black Election Panel Study. Estimates were obtained using the Achen (1986) correction for selection bias described in Appendix 1.

D. Correction for Selection Bias

The 1988 study was conducted on a smaller scale than the 1984 study owing to resource limitations. As a result, the 1988 wave of the panel suffers from selection bias: the resulting censored sample is not a random draw from the original sample. As Achen and others have noted, selection bias is an inherent problem with panel studies. Achen (1986), Heckman (see Maddala 1984), and others have proposed various ways of correcting both continuous and binary dependent variable regressions for censored samples. Some of the proposed corrections are two-stage estimators; others utilize estimation of the maximum likelihood function for censored samples. In both cases the process involves the specification of an equation that predicts the likelihood that an observation will enter the censored sample. In this case a "selection" equation was determined whereby the probability of a person's being in the 1988 sample was found to be a function of one's age, income, and whether one lived in the South. Higher age and income as well as

TABLE 4.4

Relationship between Evaluations of African-American Group Economic Performance and National Economic Performance, 1988

	Dependent Variable: Coefficient (SE)	
Variable	Black Economic Status	National Economic Status
Belief that blacks are economically better off than whites	.44 (.06)	[a]
Age	−.12 (.08)	[a]
Family income	−.11 (.06)	[a]
Improvement in household finances	.22 (.05)	.09 (.06)
Belief that black conditions improved	[b]	.38 (.12)
Gender	[a]	.04 (.03)
Constant	.27 (.05)	.14 (.04)
n = 298		
R^2	.31	.17
System R^2	.32	

Source: 1984–1988 National Black Election Panel Study. Estimates were obtained using the Systems Procedure of the Shazam econometric program. The estimates are 3SLS estimates.

[a] Found not to have an impact on dependent variable and excluded from final model on that basis.

[b] Not included in equation.

Southern residence predicted a somewhat higher probability of being in the 1988 sample. Further, a respondent's being suspicious of the survey or not understanding the wording of a question decreased the likelihood of that person's being in the 1988 sample. Finally, the larger the number of phones one possessed, the greater the likelihood of entering the 1988 sample. Achen's (1986) method of correcting for selection bias was used to correct the 1988 coefficients. Table 4.5 demonstrates the effect of selection bias by comparing data for both corrected and uncorrected coefficients.

TABLE 4.5

Determinants of Whether One Believes That Whites Have Too Much Influence, 1984 and 1988

Variable	Dependent Variable (Belief That Whites Have Too Much Influence): Coefficient (SE)		
	1984	1988	1988[a]
Linked fate	.06	.03	.03
	(.02)	(.03)	(.03)
Belief that blacks are economi-	−.10	−.07	−.07
cally better off than whites	(.03)	(.06)	(.06)
Family income	.03	.06	.02
	(.02)	(.06)	(.06)
Education	.23	.07	.02
	(.05)	(.09)	(.09)
Belief that blacks have too	−.12	−.20	−.19
much influence	(.03)	(.05)	(.05)
Age	.03	−.21	−.30
	(.05)	(.08)	(.08)
Constant	.68	.91	1.00
	(.05)	(.09)	(.10)
	n = 894	n = 280	n = 280
Adjusted R^2	.10	.10	.11

Source: 1984–1988 National Black Election Panel Study. Estimates were obtained using the OLS Procedure of the Shazam econometric program. The estimates for 1984 are ordinary least squares estimates.

[a] The 1988 estimates were derived using the Achen (1986) correction. See Appendix 1 for an explanation of the corrections for selection bias.

5

African-American Partisanship and the American Party System

Democracy will not come
Today, this year
   Not ever
Through compromise and fear.
I tire so of hearing people say,
Let things take their course.
Tomorrow is another day.
I do not need my freedom when I'm dead.
I cannot live on tomorrow's bread.

. . . .

   Freedom
   Is a strong seed
   Planted
   In a great need.
   I live here, too.
   I want freedom
   Just as you.
(Langston Hughes, "Democracy")

Introduction: Partisanship and African-American Group Interests

The great majority of African Americans were legally excluded from participation in American politics from the founding of the republic to the middle of the twentieth century. Reconstruction was the only period of American history prior to the victories of the civil rights movement during which political participation by African Americans was widespread. However, African Americans throughout the history of the nation have relentlessly struggled to participate in American politics. African Americans often tried to force the main political parties of their time to recognize the interests of the black community. Independent black political organizations such as the antebellum Negro Convention Movement often led the struggle for black political rights. These efforts almost always included attempts to form coalitions with white Americans who either were sympathetic to black interests or, as was more often the case, saw some potential gain for themselves in alliances with African Americans. From Reconstruction to the present, African-American political activity, particularly efforts to build coalitions, has focused on the American political party system. Historically, African Americans have tried to work within whichever major party seemed most likely to advance black interests. They have also tried to force the major parties to incorporate black interests, built independent black political formations when neither party was meeting black interests, and worked with third-party formations when they dealt with black interests.

African Americans' laborious efforts to enter and influence the American party system have been based on the recognition that, at all levels of government, the party system is critical to shaping public policy on racial and economic policy. The great battle over slavery was first fought through titanic conflicts between the parties. The first major political party supported by African Americans, the Republican party, was created as a result of the parties' conflict over slavery. Reconstruction was both a battle between parties and a battle over which forces would control the soul of the Republican party. The 1876 compromise between the Republican and Democratic parties helped to solidify the exclusion of African Americans and their interests from American politics for the next three quarters of a century. The conflict over economic policy between the Republican and Democratic parties during the Great Depression had profound economic consequences for African Americans. By the early 1960s, the battle over racial and economic policy would shape the American party system with racial policy, and according to Carmines and Stimson (1989), had become the major dividing line in American politics. In the 1980s, Ronald Reagan led the Republican party to a series of victories that reversed long-standing economic and racial policies. The great majority of African Americans believe Reagan's policy reversals represented a severe blow to African-American racial interests.

These political battles have been of immense importance to the interests of African Americans and help to explain African Americans' great expenditure of effort on attempts to influence the party system. Despite the relatively weak nature of American political parties, the party system is the best pressure point from which to influence public policy for groups whose resources consist mainly of concentrated numbers of people. Parties, at least in theory, aggregate the preferences of the coalition partners who make up their core. As part of party coalitions, groups that are numerical minorities can get their needs addressed in return for supporting other coalition members' concerns. Historically,

African Americans have possessed few resources such as money, access to media, and elite contacts that could be used to influence government through other channels. Despite the political system's historical lack of responsiveness to African-American interests and needs, the political parties have seemed to many African Americans to be the most responsive American political institution.

In this chapter I argue that African-American support for political parties, ranging from the Communist party of the United States (and parties to its left) to the Republican party, has been based on African Americans' perceptions of the relative costs and benefits of alliances with the organized political forces of American society. Historically, African Americans' loyalty to political parties and general orientation toward the political system have been based on the ability of a party to actively further black interests. Political parties' action or inaction on behalf of African-American interests with regard to issues such as lynching, federal appointments, and the general state of American race relations has motivated African Americans to try to influence the political parties' racial policies. In 1864 the National Equal Rights League explained the importance of politics for African Americans: "In a republican country where general suffrage is the rule, personal liberty, the right to testify in courts of law, the right to hold, buy, and sell property, and all other rights become mere privileges held at the option of others where we are excepted from general liberty" (Walton 1972, 44). The continued perception of the importance of group interests to African Americans structures their evaluations of the political parties just as it structures their evaluations of group and national economic conditions.

Racial Group Interests and the History of Black Support for the Political Parties

African Americans and the Major Parties since the Civil War

The strong link between support by African Americans for a given political party and African-American group interests was firmly established in the early Reconstruction period, much to the dismay of both the ex-slaves' former masters and the many Northern philanthropic liberals who came to the South to participate in the "great task" of trying to teach African Americans how to be good citizens. What in particular troubled many Northern observers was the strength of individuals' sense of responsibility to each other and to the community as a whole, the active participation of women in determining both the political positions of the community and its elected representatives, and the former slaves' insistence on full participation in democratic decision making in the representative assemblies (Brown 1989). During this period, black women took the lead in enforcing community norms regarding which party to support, given black interests. Mrs. Violet Keeling reported to Congress: "As for my part, if I hear of a colored man voting the Democratic ticket, I stay as far from him as I can; I don't have nothing in the world to do with him. . . . I think that if the race of colored people that has got no friends nohow, and if they don't hang together they won't have one while one party is going one way and another the other. I don't wish to see a colored man sell himself when he can do without. . . . I think if a colored man votes the Democratic ticket he has always sold himself" (Brown 1989, 29). Brown (1989, 30) highlights the severity of group sanctions for those who violated African-American political norms:

> The whole issue of the ostracism of black Democrats reveals very clearly the assumptions regarding suffrage which were operative throughout Africanamerican communities. Black Democrats were subject to the severest exclusion: disciplined within or quite often expelled from their churches; kicked out of mutual benefit societies; not allowed to work alongside others in the fields nor accepted in leadership positions at work or in the community. Ministers were dismissed from their churches or had their licenses to preach revoked; teachers who voted Democratic would find themselves without any pupils. Democrats' children were not allowed in schools. And perhaps the severest sanction of all, black Democrats found themselves unaided at the time of death of a family member.

Brown also notes that many African Americans considered it a crime to vote against the interests of the black community. Furthermore, the communal approach to politics adopted by African Americans in the period from Reconstruction to Redemption violated several of the tenets of liberal democracy. Political responsibility to the African-American community was considered a higher good than the individual's right to act on his or her own preferences if those preferences were considered potentially harmful to the black community. The communalism of African-American public life shared its roots with the communalism of African-American religious thought. One of the critical differences between black and white Protestantism is the African-American belief in "self-realization of individuality within community" (West 1982). In opposition to the American liberal tradition, African Americans have adopted the worldview that individual freedom can be realized only within the context of collective freedom, that individual salvation can occur only within the framework of collective salvation.

The worldview that African Americans developed during Reconstruction was part of the overall process of building, for the first time, an autonomous black community. An ironic feature of this process was that African Americans of this era firmly believed that their social and religious autonomy would be best guaranteed by massive mobilization for political inclusion (Foner 1988). Backed by the black church and other indigenous institutions that were blossoming at the time, African Americans massively joined and participated in all aspects of the Southern Republican party (Foner 1988). While fighting to be included in the two-party system specifically and American politics more generally, African Americans set forth their own demands, participated on their own terms, and formed their own organizations (Brown 1989; Du Bois 1935; Foner 1988). Beginning in 1865, land redistribution was a major demand of freed black people—a demand that would be echoed a century later by peasants throughout the Third World. Along with land, major political demands included access to public education, creation of public health systems, a government-guaranteed safety net, and full political and economic rights. Newly created black organizations worked to advance this agenda. The churches increasingly became major political organizations in their own right. There was a high level of political debate within the black community itself, not so much over whether to support Democrats or Republicans as over how radical a Republican agenda should be supported. Class divisions within the black community manifested themselves in debates on issues such as the need for massive land distribution (Foner 1988).

The organizational forum for achieving black political demands was the Republican party. Blacks participated in the Republican party through the Union Leagues. Reconstruction saw the African-American yearning for political self-determination put into practice through a myriad of political activities.

The Union Leagues and their members often had to be protected by an armed wing—usually the state-sponsored Negro Militias that sprang up in states such as South Carolina and Arkansas (Foner 1988; Singletary 1957; Williamson 1965). The birth of mainstream black politics coincided with the birth of the black community. It also coincided with the birth of the Ku Klux Klan and an unprecedented wave of violence aimed at the freedmen and their allies as racist terrorism was unleashed throughout the South. African Americans believed that political power was necessary to safeguard their social and religious autonomy as well as any chance they might have of economic freedom.

The fears of African Americans proved to be well founded. As Reconstruction was smashed in state after state, blacks were disarmed, lost all political rights, and were subjugated economically. Widespread and horrific lynchings of entire families were reported as early as the late 1860s. By the late 1880s state and local paramilitary units such as the white state militias coordinated campaigns of antiblack terrorism with planters and vigilantes to enforce labor discipline. During this period, one hundred black striking sugar cane workers were killed in Louisiana, while in Arkansas over a dozen black labor leaders were murdered and lynched. In both cases state and local authorities were collaborating with the white mobs and vigilantes (Foner 1988). As state and local governments in the South became more and more reactionary and hostile to African Americans, blacks turned more and more to the national government for redress (Foner 1988). This pattern of bypassing local and state governments to seek help from the federal government has persisted to the present day.

The African-American political worldview forged during Reconstruction, which emphasized the importance of collective interests, has continued to shape African Americans' orientation toward the political parties to the present day. As Jones (1987, 26) argues, "the central concern in black political thinking has been how to end black oppression in the United States. Political support has been given and withheld from political formations based almost exclusively upon the extent to which their actions were perceived as advancing or compromising black liberation." The association of the Republican party with Abraham Lincoln, Congressional Reconstruction, and, to a lesser degree, the symbolic racial progressivism of the early Theodore Roosevelt administration helped consolidate African-American support for the Republican party in the period following the Civil War.

Disaffection with the Republican party grew rapidly beginning with the Theodore Roosevelt administration, although relations with the Democratic party were even worse (Walton 1972). Roosevelt called for African Americans to accept white supremacy, supported efforts to replace the integrated "black and tan" Southern wing of the party with an all-white branch, reduced the amount of black patronage, and brutally attacked black troops who defended themselves in Brownsville, Texas, without a hearing (Sitkoff 1978; Walton 1972). William Howard Taft continued Roosevelt's policies, further pushing blacks out of the Republican party and calling for them to abandon politics because they did not have "the mental status of manhood" (Sitkoff 1978).

As Walton (1972) describes, such blatant hostility toward blacks led to defections to the Democratic party. It was no longer clear to many African Americans which party best served racial group interests.

Some African Americans were initially attracted to Woodrow Wilson's candidacy for the presidency in 1912. The antiblack policies of the Roosevelt and Taft administrations led to a transfer of some votes to Wilson (Walton 1972). Wilson pledged that if he was elected, blacks could count on "justice done to the colored people in every matter; and not mere grudging justice, but justice executed with liberality and cordial good feeling" (Franklin 1974, 334). Wilson turned out to have a strange—but, to African Americans, familiar—concept of justice. He eliminated all blacks from the White House staff. Violent race riots, the violent occupation of Haiti, and the release of *Birth of a Nation*— the seminal film whose glorification of the Klan was exceeded only by its degradation of African Americans—all marked the Wilson presidency (Franklin 1974; Sitkoff 1978; Walton 1972). Wilson's tenure also featured a large number of discriminatory bills introduced in Congress. Through executive orders Wilson systematically removed African Americans from the civil service and resegregated cafeterias and rest rooms for those who managed to hold on to their jobs (Franklin 1974).

Both major political parties continued to disassociate themselves from African Americans in the period following World War I. Warren Harding, Calvin Coolidge, and Herbert Hoover all attempted to attract white Southern voters while distancing the Republican party from African Americans and their interests. In 1928 this attempt culminated in Hoover's public endorsement of a lily-white Republican party (Walton 1972). Hoover appointed very few blacks to office, abolished the Negro division of the Republican party, and nominated for the Supreme Court a Southern judge known for his support of the disenfranchisement of African Americans (Sitkoff 1978). This final abandonment of black Republicans by the Hoover administration–led Republican party, combined with the economic policies of the New Deal, set the stage for a black influx into the Democratic party during the 1930s (Weiss 1983).

The advent of the Great Depression brought "the specter of starvation" to African Americans throughout the country (Sitkoff 1978). Not only did African Americans suffer, as did all poor Americans, they suffered special racial injustices owing to their economic and political subordination. Blacks were fired and replaced with white workers throughout the nation (Lewis 1991; Sitkoff 1978). The election of 1932 did not appear to offer much choice. The Hoover administration's policies prompted the NAACP and others to mount a campaign against Republican supporters of Hoover's racist Supreme Court nominee John J. Parker. Black NAACP leaders such as Walter White claimed that this punishing strategy worked—in their view, black defections from the Republican party were responsible for defeats of several Republican gubernatorial and Senate candidates in states from New Jersey to Kansas (Sitkoff 1978). On the other hand, the Democratic campaign offered little hope of a better deal. The majority of Franklin D. Roosevelt's key advisors, with the notable exception of Eleanor Roosevelt, advised appeasement of the Southern branch of the party and actively tried to insulate the campaign and the early presidency from black leaders. The result was that most black elites continued to give at least lukewarm support to the Republicans. Hoover had won most of the black vote, although his popularity slipped in poor black neighborhoods (Sitkoff 1978; Weiss 1983).

The first years of the New Deal were very rough on African Americans. Because of their lack of political power, blacks received much less than their fair share of government-provided relief and jobs from locally administered programs (Sitkoff 1978). Some of the nonracial policies of the early Roosevelt administration had particularly severe consequences for African Americans. The National Recovery Act's guidelines for setting wages were detrimental to many black businessmen, who insisted that they needed to pay lower wages to stay competitive (Lewis 1991; Sitkoff 1978). By 1934 the combination of African-American local political machines in cities such as Chicago, Kansas City, and New York and the beginning of a flow of relief funds and programs to the black poor had set the stage for a transfer of support to Democratic congressional candidates (Sitkoff 1978). Northern Democratic political machines had started incorporating African Americans on a subordinate basis relatively early. Entrepreneurial black politicians such as Oscar D. Depriest and Arthur M. Mitchell of Chicago were able to translate individual benefits into group benefits to a small degree. As they saw their constituents begin to switch parties, more and more Northern politicians such as William L. Dawson of Chicago also began to change their party affiliation (Sitkoff 1978; Weiss 1983). The result was the first African American–supported Democratic victory in the congressional elections of 1934.

The creation of the Works Project Administration (WPA) in 1935 greatly aided the many African Americans in desperate economic straits. Not only did it provide jobs, but nondiscriminatory clauses were written into Roosevelt's enabling executive order (Sitkoff 1978). Several New Deal programs helped the black poor, and a few, such as the artistic branches of the WPA, helped the black middle class. The importance of the New Deal programs for black interests is reflected in the following passage from Lewis's (1991, 152) description of the impact of the New Deal on black Norfolk: "Blacks were the primary beneficiaries of the Federal Emergency Relief Administration and its successor, the WPA. They gained jobs at Civilian Conservation Corps camps and got a city beach through funding from the Civil Works Administration, a city hospital courtesy of Public Works Administration monies, and a sixty-thousand dollar appropriation from the WPA to improve Booker T. Washington High School's physical plant. In addition, the 1835 passage of the Wagner Act encouraged the CIO to organize blacks in several previously unorganized industries. In short, many gains realized during the 1930s came from federal sponsorship."

The Democratic party actively campaigned for the black vote in 1936, mobilizing African-American New Deal program recipients to campaign in the black community. As a result of this active campaigning, years of neglect and increasing abuse from the Republican party, and the important relief programs of the New Deal, Franklin D. Roosevelt captured 76 percent of the African-American vote in 1936 (Sitkoff 1978). The only area in which Roosevelt did not capture a large majority of the black vote was Chicago, where Democratic and Republican machines competed fiercely for black support (Sitkoff 1978; Weiss 1983). Class divisions were evident in black voting patterns, as shown in Table 5.1. Lewis (1991) describes Norfolk's black middle-class opposition to the provision of the National Recovery Act that mandated equal wages for both races. As mentioned previously, this policy hurt black businessmen paying lower wages and also led to the replacement of some black workers with white workers. Nevertheless, the economic benefits to blacks from the relief and jobs programs, the active courting of the black electorate, even in the South, through the agriculture programs, symbolic acts such as government consultation with black leaders, and the inclusion of black interests on the national agenda helped to bring about a massive transferal of blacks' loyalty from the Republican to the Democratic party (Lewis 1991; Sitkoff 1978; Weiss 1983).

The Truman administration continued to develop policies designed to attract African-American support. Both Truman's desegregation of the armed forces and his support for a civil rights commission and party plank sparked open revolt by the party's Southern branch (Carmines and Stimson 1989; Rosenstone, Behr, and Lazarus 1984). The defection of the Dixiecrats in 1948 convinced national Democratic party leaders such as the 1952 and 1956 standard-bearer, Adlai Stevenson, to once again acquiesce to the Southern bloc's wishes.

One would expect a fair degree of volatility in a situation in which neither party was clearly identified with black interests. The Truman administration's stillborn attempts to establish a pro–civil rights plank for the Democratic party platform were finally foiled by unsuccessful presidential candidate Adlai Stevenson, who established weak civil rights positions for the party in both 1952 and 1956 (Piven 1974). In 1954 the Supreme Court handed down its landmark decision on the

TABLE 5.1
Democratic Vote in Black Districts by Class, 1932 and 1936 (in percentages)

City	1932		1936	
	Lower-Middle-Class Districts	Lower-Class Districts	Lower-Middle-Class Districts	Lower-Class Districts
Chicago	17.5	21.3	41.0	49.3
Cleveland	17.6	18.3	55.9	65.3
Detroit	25.5	39.0	62.5	71.8
New York	50.3	54.4	NA	NA

Source: Weiss 1983, 217.
Note: NA = not available.

Brown v. The Board of Education of Topeka, Kansas case, with an amicus curiae brief filed by the State Department on behalf of the plaintiffs (the blacks). In 1957 federal troops were sent in to protect black children in Little Rock, Arkansas (Van Woodward 1966). Both of these earthshaking events happened during the watch of a Republican administration. Despite Dwight Eisenhower's general reluctance to rock the boat on civil rights matters ranging from desegregation of the military to the *Brown* decision, the Eisenhower administration could be interpreted as progressive on racial matters when compared to the Democratic party, particularly its Southern wing (Van Woodward 1966). By 1956 both congressional and state-level Democrats in the South had united to defeat the integration of schools mandated by *Brown*. Democratic state and local officials in the South launched massive attacks on desegregation and the NAACP (Morris 1984; Van Woodward 1966). At the same time, Eisenhower responded to the 1956 refusal of the Democratic governor of Alabama and the University of Alabama's board of trustees to implement the Supreme Court's order to admit Autherine Lucy to the university by declaring his support for the principle of nonintervention in state affairs. In March of the same year, the great majority (101 of 128) of the members of Congress from the eleven Southern states signed a "Declaration of Constitutional Principles," which condemned the Supreme Court's *Brown* decision. During the same year, both parties adopted very weak civil rights planks (Van Woodward 1966). Republican ambivalence and Southern Democratic hostility to the incipient civil rights movement led to a significant erosion of black Democratic support and increased volatility in the black vote. Between 1952 and 1956 the Democratic share of the national African-American vote declined from 79 percent to 61 percent.

This change in direction of the Democratic party, combined with dissatisfaction with Eisenhower's cool response to *Brown v. The Board of*

Education of Topeka, Kansas, increased blacks' doubts about both parties. Black support for the Democratic party declined in the late 1950s. However, the electoral calculus was such that in 1960 the Democratic party desperately needed the votes of black urban residents if they were to win such key states as Illinois (Piven 1974). In this year, both parties actively competed for the African-American vote. John F. Kennedy's supportive call to Coretta Scott King during the campaign helped the Democratic party win back some black votes. Nevertheless, the Kennedy administration moved very slowly on civil rights, despite the massive civil rights movement that had been raging across the South since the early 1950s. Indeed, the black Democratic vote would not solidify until 1964, when it became clear to the nation that the Democrats would support black interests and civil rights more than the Republican party (Carmines and Stimson 1989; Piven 1974; Walton 1972). The passage of the 1964 Civil Rights Act and the 1965 Voting Rights Act helped identify the Democratic party with African-American interests at the very time that the Barry Goldwater campaign was convincing white and black Americans that the Republicans were now the party of racial conservatism (Carmines and Stimson 1989; Rosenstone, Behr, and Lazarus 1984). The Nixon administration and its Southern strategy, combined with the defection of large numbers of supporters of racist Alabama governor George Wallace to the Republican party (at least during the national election) helped seal the racial cleavage within the American party system. Figure 5.1 highlights how blacks' and whites' party identification is shaped by these events.

African Americans, Third Parties, and Independent Political Activity

As both Jones (1987) and Walton (1972) point out, the movement of African Americans into and out of the Republican party was never blind or random but was based on a realistic assessment of which party would best further black political and economic interests. African Americans' orientation toward third parties has also been governed by these parties' utility for black group interests. Generally, third-party formation and activity is a result of local, regional, or national failures in the political system (Rosenstone, Behr, and Lazarus 1984; Walton 1988). Blacks have tended to be loyal to the two major parties (Henderson 1987; Rosenstone, Behr, and Lazarus 1984; Walton 1988). However, specific circumstances have led to active African-American support of third parties (Frye 1980; Naison 1983; Walton 1988). When the two major parties reject African Americans' political goal of inclusion, African Americans seek other political allies. This was the situation in the

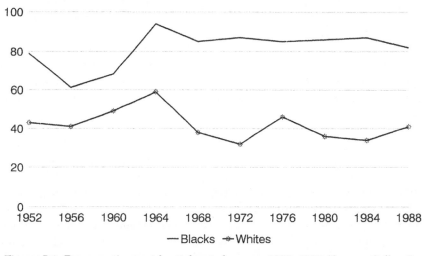

Figure 5.1. Democratic presidential vote by race, 1952–1988 (*Source: Gallup Report*, November, 1988, Report No. 27B, pp. 6–7)

1930s, when the African-American community became receptive to the organizing campaigns of the Communist party.

During the Great Depression, a time of extreme hardship for African Americans, the Communist party's willingness to fight for economic relief and redistribution of wealth while protesting the legal lynching of the Scottsboro Boys gained this third party strong support from black intellectuals, electoral support in Harlem, and national respectability in the black community (Naison 1983). Local studies of communist work in black communities such as Norfolk emphasize that black support for the Communist party was based on their willingness to fight for bread-and-butter issues as well as to conduct antiracist campaigns. Their work in the unemployment councils in opposing tenant evictions contrasted with the lack of effort by local governments to prevent black economic collapse (Lewis 1991). This base in the black community was squandered away, however, by a policy of enthusiastic assimilationism and, more critically, by the American Communist party's insistence on blindly following Stalin down every path no matter how noisome.

In the post–World War II period African Americans, particularly in the South, have themselves developed third-party alternatives to the two major parties (Frye 1980; Walton 1988). Until 1966 the official slogan of the Alabama Democratic party was "White Supremacy for the Right." Walton (1988) details how pressure from an extremely successful black third party, the National Democratic Party of Alabama, forced the main party to change its ways somewhat while providing a base from which successful county-level black political power could develop. In the North, blacks ran as independents outside of the two-party structure in order to make political gains. From the late 1960s through the early 1980s, African Americans in Chicago organized outside the confines of the Democratic political machine. This drive culminated in the election of Harold Washington as mayor of Chicago in 1983 (Kleppner 1985; Pinderhughes 1987; Preston 1987a).

The pattern of African-American support for both major and third parties reflects the importance of racial group interests in the political process. As Walton (1972) demonstrates, the slippage of African-American support for the Republicans in 1912 and the Democrats in the late 1950s can be traced to those parties' becoming more hostile toward black interests. The consolidation of black support for the Democrats in the 1934–1936 period and in 1964 occurred *after* the new regimes had implemented policies that benefited black economic and political interests. At the local, state, and national levels, African Americans' perceptions of racial group interests have dictated their choice of political party.

Contemporary African-American Orientation toward the Political Parties

Historically, large-scale shifts in African-American support for political parties have been tied to perceptions of which party best advanced black interests. The shift in support during the New Deal seemed to encompass a class component.[1] Let us now turn to the question of whether African-American support for the political parties follows historical patterns. The National Black Election Study (NBES) posed two questions intended to directly ascertain African Americans' perceptions of the two major parties' support for black interests: "How hard do you think the Democratic/Republican party *really* works on issues black people care about? Do you think they work *very hard, fairly hard, not too hard, or not hard at all* on issues black people care about?"

Figures 5.2 and 5.3 show that a large majority of African Americans in 1984 and 1988 (74 and 72 percent, respectively) believed that the Democratic party works very or fairly hard on black issues. Analysis of the panel respondents showed a great deal of stability in these perceptions: 79 percent of African Americans who thought that the Democratic party worked very or fairly hard on black issues in 1984 also

---

[1] There is also strong evidence of class differences in the strength of support for the Communist party during the 1930s (Kelley 1990; Lewis 1991; Naison 1983).

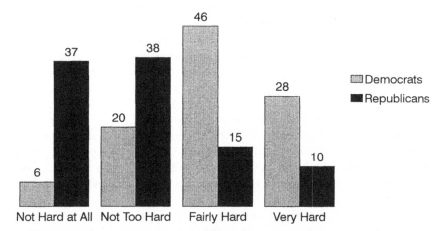

Figure 5.2. Perceptions of whether Democrats and Republicans work hard on black issues, 1984 (*Source*: 1984–1988 National Black Election Panel Study)

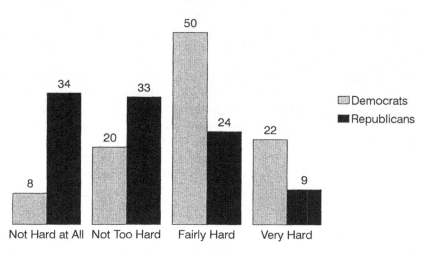

Figure 5.3. Perceptions of whether Democrats and Republicans work hard on black issues, 1988 (*Source*: 1984–1988 National Black Election Panel Study)

thought so in 1988. Less than 1 percent of the sample in both years believed that the Democratic party did not work hard at all on black issues.

As shown in Figures 5.2 and 5.3, many African Americans are convinced that the Republican party is not actively concerned with black interests. Only 25 percent of the sample in 1984 and 33 percent in 1988 believed that the Republican party worked very or fairly hard on issues important to black people. (All subsequent percentages were calculated separately by the author and therefore do not appear in Figures 5.2 and 5.3.) A full 20 percent of the sample in both 1984 and 1988 believed that the Republican party did not work hard at all on black concerns. During both sample years, a substantial majority, 61 percent of the sample, believed that the Republicans work not very hard or not hard at all on black issues. On the other hand, during both years only 13 percent of the sample believed that the Republicans work at least fairly hard on black interests.

The degree of perceived difference between the two parties can be analyzed at the individual level. Figure 5.4 shows that at the individual level a substantial percentage of African Americans—27 percent in 1984 and 45 percent in 1988—did not observe any difference in the level of effort exerted by the two parties on issues deemed important by African Americans.[2] Slightly less than 10 percent of the sample believed that Republicans work harder on black issues than Democrats. In 1988, there is a shift toward the middle of the distribution. The less positive evaluations of the Democratic party in this year are consistent with the decrease in black support for the Democratic presidential candidate in 1988 portrayed in Figure 5.1, constituting the weakest African-American support for the Democratic presidential candidate since 1960. Nevertheless, most respondents felt that the Democrats were more concerned with black issues than the Republicans.

The substantial edge the Democrats held in 1984 and 1988 among African Americans on this question is a reflection of the Democratic lead in African Americans' party identification. Figure 5.5 shows that in both 1984 and 1988 the Democrats led by more than 10:1.

According to the black utility heuristic, if one of the parties becomes identified with the interests of African Americans, that identification will grow stronger, through multiple channels. These channels include

[2] This question was constructed by subtracting an individual's score on the question of how hard they thought that the Republicans worked on issues of importance from their score on the same question as it pertained to Democrats. This yielded a measure ranging from –3 to 3, with a positive score favoring the Democrats, a negative score favoring the Republicans, and 0 denoting no perceived difference between the parties. This score was then recoded from –1 to 1.

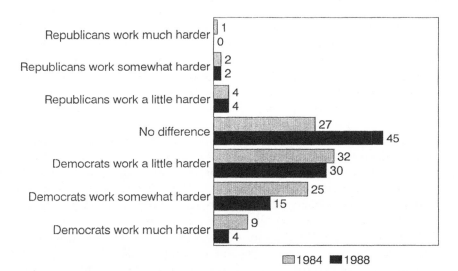

Figure 5.4. Perceptions of which party works harder on black issues, 1984 and 1988 (*Source*: 1984–1988 National Black Election Panel Study)

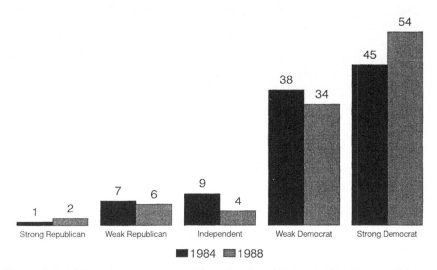

Figure 5.5. African-American party identification, 1984 and 1988 (*Source*: 1984–1988 National Black Election Panel Study)

black information networks, norms such as those operating in black communities during Reconstruction, and entrepreneurial politicians seeking to retain black voters as key constituents in their electoral coalitions. This last mechanism resulted in the defection of many black Republican politicians to the Democratic party during the New Deal. Powerful careers such as that of the late congressional committee chair William L. Dawson were built on the calculation of the appropriate time to switch (Weiss 1983). All of these factors, pointing up a clear advantage of one party over the others for the black community, should lead to stability in African-American partisanship. If a party is viewed as hostile to African Americans, identification with that party should decline. Except for those totally isolated from black social networks and norm-enforcing institutions, perception of a party as hostile to African Americans should result in defection to the other major party or abandonment of specific party affiliations. When African Americans perceive that neither major party is serving African-American group interests, their orientation toward the party system, and consequently the black vote, can become extremely volatile.

How stable was African-American party identification in the 1980s? Virtually all of the black Democrats in 1984 (94 percent) were still Democrats in 1988. Of those who considered themselves strong Democrats in 1984 (53.5 percent of the total population in 1984), 80 percent remained strong Democrats in 1988. As expected, the perception that Democrats work hard on black group interests has led to loyalty to the Democratic party. African-American party allegiance is extremely stable when compared to that of whites. Only 80 to 85 percent of the white respondents stayed in the same party when measured in only two year periods (Fiorina 1981). On the other hand, there is great volatility among those who initially identified themselves as independents and Republicans. Slightly over 50 percent of the initially Republican identifiers were still Republicans four years later. The largest group of Republican defectors had become Democrats. Seventy-four percent of the independents had become Democrats.

Causes of African-American Orientation toward the Major Political Parties

African Americans' allegiance to the two major political parties depends on their perceptions of each party's responsiveness to the needs and interests of the black community. Thus, African Americans' relationship to the two parties is likely to be influenced by general evaluations of the economy as well as perceptions of black economic and political interests.

Is African-American party identification a running tally of individual experiences with the two parties, a stable orientation toward politics learned early in life, or a result of deliberate evaluations of which party has historically been best for African Americans? The theoretical approach to party identification taken here combines the conception of party identification as a running tally of experiences with the two parties with the group interest framework outlined in Chapter 3. I view party identification as being gained initially through early political socialization in the family but then updated by one's own political experiences (Achen 1989; Fiorina 1981). To the degree that the initial socialization is congruent with prevailing norms in the black community, party identification can strengthen over a lifetime. On the other hand, evaluations of which party best addresses black political interests are sensitive to the behavior of major party candidates as well as changes in party policies, the racial and economic environment, and individual fortunes. This phenomenon is consistent with the greater volatility evident in Figures 5.2 and 5.3 when compared with the stability of party identification shown in Figure 5.5. The following variables influence African-American partisanship.

INDIVIDUAL PERCEPTIONS OF RACIAL GROUP INTERESTS

Belief in the importance of black interests translates into preference for the Democratic party. Both the historical and the survey evidence show that African Americans as well as the general public view the Democratic party as being more likely than the Republican party to support African Americans' political and economic agenda. Numerous studies have shown that poor economic conditions are a major factor in determining black support for presidents and their parties. Thus, to the degree that African Americans perceive either absolute or relative disadvantage in the economic status of blacks, they tend to hold the Republican party responsible.

INDIVIDUAL SOCIOECONOMIC STATUS

Social and economic interests are the central force in structuring the political behavior of African Americans. Many have argued that increased economic polarization should lead to increased political heterogeneity (Dahl 1961; Kilson 1983; Marable 1983; Wilson 1980). If economic polarization among blacks leads to divergence in the interests of different economic classes of African Americans, then eventually African-American partisanship should be determined at least in part by individual socioeconomic status. If the Gallup Poll estimate that 18 percent of African Americans voted for George Bush in 1988 is correct, this represents the highest black Republican vote since 1960. Indeed, both Republican operatives and some pollsters have argued vigorously that the reported 22 percent Republican African-American vote in the 1990 congressional races reflected increased conservatism on the part of the African-American middle class (Dionne and Morin 1990).[3] If greater affluence is indeed associated with a more conservative outlook, then higher socioeconomic status should also be associated with the perception that Republicans work harder on black issues, since conservative policies would be considered more efficacious in addressing problems of poverty and race than liberal social spending.

EVALUATIONS OF THE ECONOMY

Since Republicans controlled the White House at the time the study data were gathered, negative evaluations of the economy should be associated with a partisan advantage for the Democrats. Evaluations of both household and national economic status are considered to affect perceptions of which party works harder on issues of importance to African Americans, therefore indirectly influencing party identification.

LIBERALISM

Long-term party identification should be at least loosely associated with one's view of oneself as either a liberal or a conservative. Similarly, perceptions of which party works harder on black issues should be formed in part by whether one believes that liberal or conservative policies are more effective. The more liberal one is, the stronger should be the orientation toward the Democratic party on both measures.

LOCAL BLACK ECONOMIC CONDITIONS

Local black economic conditions, both absolute and relative, should also affect both aspects of African-American partisanship. The broad contours of local economic conditions change relatively slowly. For example, Michigan's black economy has been in a state of depression since the early 1970s. Such long-lasting economic hardship should affect both the formation of long-term party identification and shorter-

---

[3] It is more likely, given supporting evidence on what occurred in the Senate and gubernatorial races and the technical problems that plagued VRS, that the magnitude of the Republican vote is a result of a statistical artifact. However, the wide acceptance of the "fact" of a large increase in black support for the Republican party displays wide acceptance of the belief that middle-class African Americans will eventually display different and more conservative political behavior than their less affluent kin.

term evaluations of the parties' importance to black advancement. Following the arguments of Chapters 2 and 3, both absolute and relative local black economic status are considered. Throughout the 1980s, African Americans identified unemployment as the country's main economic—indeed, the main domestic—problem. The level of black unemployment, the difference in a state's black and white unemployment rates, and the yearly changes in both variables are considered to be measures of local black economic conditions. The perceived Republican control over the national economy during the study period would lead African Americans to hold the Republican party responsible for local black economic conditions. Thus, the higher the black unemployment rate or the larger the gap between black and white unemployment, the stronger the support for the Democratic party.

APPROVAL OF REAGAN'S PRESIDENTIAL PERFORMANCE

The Reagan presidency was considered by many to be hostile to African-American group interests (Barker 1989; Walters 1989). This perception is reflected in the very low approval ratings Reagan received from blacks (Dawson, Brown, and Cohen 1990). Approval or disapproval of Reagan's performance should be directly related to African-American party identification.

CONTROL VARIABLES

These variables are all interrelated.[4] Several additional variables, such as age, gender, and region, were included in the analysis to control for demographic characteristics. Both the control variables and the variables of major substantive focus are defined in Appendix 2.

Results

The proposed model was tested using regression analysis. This analysis provides estimates of the strength of the interrelationships among the variables.[5]

It is evident that socioeconomic status is only weakly associated with

---

[4] The relationships between Reagan approval, party identification, and perceptions of which party works harder on black issues are reciprocal. Estimation of such a model necessitates approaches other than ordinary least squares. Several versions of simultaneous equations models were tested. The results are described more fully in Appendix 2. The equation for Reagan approval is reported in Chapter 6, where African-American presidential approval is discussed in some detail.

[5] Tables reporting the details of the estimation can be found in Appendix 2.

African-American evaluations of the two parties. In both study years, socioeconomic status was a factor influencing perceptions of which party was seen as being more favorable toward African Americans. But the effect was opposite to that predicted. In 1984, the most affluent African Americans were 7 percent more likely than the least affluent to believe that Democrats work harder on black issues. In 1988, they were 18 percent more likely. Socioeconomic status had no relationship to long-term African-American party identification. In one sense this is not too surprising. There was little variation to explain in African American party identification, and the Democrats held a substantial lead in African Americans' perceptions of the parties' responsiveness to black issues. The substantial Democratic party lead portrayed in Figures 5.1 to 5.5 suggests near unanimity among African Americans across classes. What *is* important to note is that where socioeconomic status did predict either aspect of African-American partisanship it was with the *opposite sign* predicted by class theories of black political behavior. More affluent African Americans were more likely to support the Democratic party. Specifically, those with greater incomes are slightly more likely than other African Americans to have believed that the Democratic party works harder than the Republican party on issues of concern to African Americans.

Perceptions of African-American racial and economic group interests and their consequences, on the other hand, played an important role in both 1984 and 1988 in predicting both African-American party identification and perceptions of which party best advances black interests. Comparisons of the economic status of blacks versus whites, evaluations of black economic conditions, and general evaluations of the economy all influenced black evaluations of the parties. The comparison of black versus white economic status played a direct role in evaluation of the parties as well as an indirect role through perceptions of racial and national economic status. Perceptions of linked fate played an indirect role in shaping evaluations of the two parties.

Local black economic conditions also helped to predict party identification in both 1984 and 1988. In 1988, a year when ideology played less of a role than it did in 1984, those who believed that the economy had deteriorated were 30 percent more likely to identify with the Democrats than those who believed that the economy had improved. The predictive power of the various economic variables reinforces the historical evidence of the critical association of perceptions of racial group interests not only with perceptions of absolute and relative racial economic status but also with evaluations of individual and national economic health. Even perceptions of national economic health were based on evaluations of racial group interests. A key to African-American partisanship is the economic status of the race. Any party that wants to attract and hold African-American political support must be seen as more effective than its rivals in improving the economic health of the black community.

As expected, party identification was generally less sensitive to short-term perceptions of racial interests, evaluations of the economy, and individual economic status, but was more influenced by more stable phenomena such as the status of the regional black economy and one's view of oneself as either a liberal or a conservative. In turn, party identification powerfully shaped one's perception of which party best advances black interests. One exception is Ronald Reagan's influence on partisanship in both years. Reagan supporters were at least 20 percent less likely to support the Democratic party during both years. Reagan was held responsible for the 1981–1982 recession, which devastated African-American communities.[6] Having consistently bypassed and denounced the recognized leadership of the black community, he was viewed as extraordinarily hostile to black aspirations. Reagan's extreme unpopularity in the black community influenced African-American party identification in 1984.[7] An extremely unpopular president can, over the course of his presidency, begin to alter the nature of African-American partisanship.[8] Even a popular Republican president would have difficulty converting African Americans in the absence of an accompanying major improvement in the absolute and relative economic status of African Americans. It was just such a change in perceptions of which party was more likely to improve black economic status that led to the African-American realignment into the Democratic party during the New Deal era.

Support for an Independent Black Political Party

Despite their significant support for the Democratic party since 1964, African Americans have occasionally supported third-party efforts. In particular, in the 1960s African Americans supported a number of independent black political organizations ranging from full-fledged politi-

[6] Indeed, the importance of Reagan approval in the 1984 party identification equation overwhelms evaluations of the economy, which are significant in 1988. As Table 5.2 shows, evaluations of the economy are a powerful feature of the 1984 Reagan approval equation.

[7] See Chapter 6 for a description of the determinants of approval for Reagan. The relationships reported between Reagan approval and partisanship take into account the elements of simultaneity proposed in the initial model.

[8] Longitudinal data would be needed to see if these changes persisted over any substantial period of time. To the degree that we expect current partisanship to be affected by past partisanship, such an effect on African-American partisanship could be quite enduring.

cal parties in Southern states such as Alabama to radical national organizations such as the Student Nonviolent Coordinating Committee
(SNCC) and the Black Panther party. Since the 1972 Gary, Indiana, convention African Americans have periodically attempted to influence
the presidential campaigns through independent candidates (Walters
1988).[9] As Walters describes, these attempts have been at best margin-
ally successful.

Which African Americans are most willing to move outside of
the two-party system to support a black political party? Figure 5.6 displays African-American support for a black political party in 1984 and
1988.[10] Descriptions of the measures used in the analysis can be found
in Appendix 2.

Individual Socioeconomic Status

One would expect those most economically devastated to be most supportive of a black political party. Those who have the least at stake in
the system should be the ones most likely to support strategies that do
not depend on mainstream political institutions. On the other hand,
one would expect more affluent African Americans to be more conservative and more inclined to oppose marginalization from the two-
party political system.

Black Nationalism

Black nationalists have consistently argued that the basis of black oppression is racial and that African-American political, economic, social,
and cultural progress will come through the building and support of
black institutions. Black nationalist beliefs are not the same as a belief
that the fates of individual African Americans are linked to that of the
race as a whole. Many African Americans may believe that their fate is
linked to that of the race but still bitterly disagree about what strategy
to pursue to advance black status (Pinderhughes 1987). Thus, having
the more specific set of beliefs associated with black nationalism should

[9] The Gary convention was convened in an attempt to build a unified black political
strategy. It included African-American nationalists, radicals, and mainstream politicians.
The convention was marked by intense ideological struggles that limited the amount of
unity achieved (Walters 1988).

[10] Only support for an independent political party in 1984 is analyzed, owing to the
availability of the black nationalism measures for this year only.

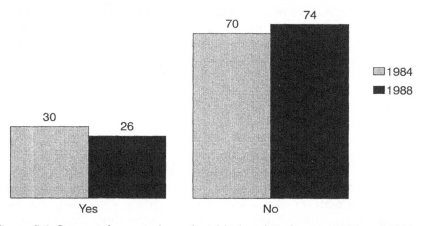

Figure 5.6. Support for an independent black political party, 1984 and 1988 (*Source*: 1984–1988 National Black Election Panel Study)

be a better predictor of support for a black political party. I have used two measures to tap black nationalist sentiments. One evaluates the strength of the belief that one should always support black candidates. The other evaluates the strength of the belief that African Americans should have nothing to do with whites. Those who embrace black nationalist sentiments are more likely to support formation of a black political party.

Support for Jesse Jackson

The Jackson campaigns had the seemingly contradictory effect of bringing new sectors of African Americans into two-party politics and of increasing interest in an independent black political party (Walters 1988). While new voting groups participated in the primaries, much discussion was generated among activists, intellectuals, and academics about whether Jackson specifically and African Americans generally would be better served by the formation of an independent political party (Cavanagh 1985; Walters 1988). Dialogue on the efficacy of a black political party intensified in the period following the Democratic convention, when Jackson supporters felt particularly disenchanted (Morris and Williams 1989). Jackson supporters came from a variety of backgrounds. Many supported Jackson precisely because they believed that he could increase black political independence and decrease dependency on the Democratic party. Indeed, a vocal minority of his supporters expressed the hope that his campaigns would become a vehicle for an independent black political party. Many more hoped that his efforts would lead to the formation of independent grass-roots political organizations that would complement the two-party system. Thus, support for Jackson should also be positively correlated with support for a black party.

Age

Many have speculated that young African Americans have become the African Americans most alienated from mainstream politics (Blauner 1989). Jackson was able to attract some of these young voters. Young African Americans suffer extremely high rates of unemployment, crime, and mortality. These youth, who have no direct experience with the Jim Crow era, may see less utility in working through the system than older African Americans who have seen both the fruits and the failures of the civil rights movement. More generally, younger citizens exhibit more support for third parties, as they generally have weaker attachments to the traditional two-party system (Rosenstone, Behr, and Lazarus 1984). One would expect younger African Americans to be more likely to support a black political party.

Results

All of the hypothesized relationships were strongly confirmed by the analysis. The young, the less affluent, the less educated, those most supportive of Jackson, and those more likely to embrace black nationalist sentiments were more likely than other African Americans to support the formation of a black political party. For example, those who strongly agreed that black candidates should always be supported were 28 percent more likely to support a black political party than those who strongly disagreed. Those who were 17 years old at the time of the interview were 32 percent more likely to support a black political party than those who were 55 years old. Very strong supporters of Jackson were 24 percent more likely to support such a party than strong opponents of Jackson. The least affluent African Americans were 19 percent more likely than the most affluent to support a black party, while the least educated were 17 percent more likely than the most educated. The weakest effect was found in the 9 percent gap between those who strongly agreed that African Americans should have nothing to do with whites and those who strongly disagreed.

Supporters of a black political party constituted a relatively small fraction of the African-American population in both 1984 and 1988. Nevertheless, a substantial number of poor blacks do support an independent black political party. If the present deterioration of African-American economic status at the bottom of the black class structure continues, or if there is an increase in the number of black nationalists, the odds are excellent that there will be increased support for a black political party. As we will see in Chapters 7 and 8, the politics of such a party are likely to be even more unsettling to mainstream American politics than black politics have been up to now.

Conclusion

We have seen that perceptions of political and economic group interests help structure, directly and indirectly, African Americans' short- and long-term evaluations of the major political parties. In addition, short-term political factors such as the evaluations of the Reagan administration also help predict evaluations of the political parties. Party identification in particular is relatively stable—Democratic party identification especially so.

Class divisions were not found to significantly structure African-American partisanship or affect evaluations of which party best advances black interests, although more affluent African Americans were found to show somewhat more support for the Democrats. This result directly contradicts the prediction that the more affluent would favor the Republicans. Class divisions were found to be significant only in the model of support for an independent black political party. Those who were poor, young, and supportive of black nationalist positions were more likely than others to support such a party. The fact that class divisions did not play a major role in determining perceptions of mainstream political institutions but did play a critical role in shaping the debate on black political strategy is significant. This pattern of results will be echoed in the analyses that appear throughout the rest of this book. Though there was relatively weak support for a black political party in 1984 and 1988, economic and political trends suggest that this support could grow in the coming decades.

Appendix 2

Data and Models for Chapter 5

Part A of this appendix provides details of the NBES variables that were introduced for the first time in Chapter 5. Part B details the variables that comprise the components of the models presented in Chapter 5. Part C consists of statistical tables and other supporting materials for the analysis presented in the chapter. Part D consists of a description of how the probabilities are obtained from probit estimates for Table 5.5 and later analyses.

A

The following are the new variables introduced in Chapter 5 from the National Black Election Study 1984–1988.

Party Identification

"Generally speaking, do you usually think of yourself as a Republican, a Democrat, or an independent?" Five-point summary scale, 0 = strong Republican, .5 = independent, 1 = strong Democrat.

"How hard do you think that the Democratic/Republican party works on issues black people really care about?"

0 = not hard at all, 1 = very hard.

Democratic Party works harder on black issues?

This variable is constructed by subtracting the value of an individual's response to the question "How hard do you think that the Republican party works on issues black people really care about?" from the value of that individual's response to the question "How hard do you think that the Democratic party works on issues black people really care about?" Seven-category variable, -1 = Republicans work much harder, 0 = no difference between parties, 1 = Democrats work much harder.

Liberalism/Conservatism

"In general, when it comes to politics, do you usually think of yourself as a liberal, a conservative, or a moderate?" Five-point summary scale, 0 = strong conservative, .5 = middle of the road, 1 = strong liberal.

Reagan Approval

"Do you approve or disapprove of the way Ronald Reagan is handling his job as president?" 0 = disapprove, 1 = approve.

State Black Unemployment Rate

The black unemployment rate for a given state. Recoded from 0 to 1.

Change in State Black/White Unemployment Gap

This variable was constructed by measuring the change from 1983 to 1984 or from 1987 to 1988 in the gap between state black and white unemployment rates. Recoded from -1 to 1.

Support for a Black Political Party

"Do you think blacks should form their own political party?" 0 = no, 1 = yes.

Warmth toward Jackson

"I will ask you to rate [Jackson] on a thermometer that runs from 0 degrees to 100 degrees. Ratings between 50 degrees and 100 degrees mean that you feel favorable and warm toward that person. . . . Ratings between 0 degrees and 50 degrees mean that you don't feel too favorable and are cool toward that person. . . . How would you rate [Jackson] using this thermometer?" Recoded from 0 to 1.

"Do you agree or disagree with the following statement: 'Blacks should always vote for black candidates when they run.'?"

0 = strongly agree, 1 = strongly disagree.

"Do you agree or disagree with the following statement: 'Black people should not have anything to do with whites if they can help it.'?"

0 = strongly disagree, 1 = strongly agree.

B

Individual Socioeconomic Status

Attempts to measure African-American socioeconomic class or status raise thorny questions of theory, operationalization, and available data. I have settled on income as the main measure of socioeconomic status. Education is as much as a resource and cognitive-expertise variable as it is a status variable. Income is more of a pure status variable. Nevertheless, I did test education as a status variable. Level of education and household income were substantively and statistically insignificant predictors of the dependent variables analyzed in Chapter 5 and did not support the class thesis. Occupation variables were not available for 1988. Therefore, income was selected as the status variable in order to preserve comparability across the years of the study.

Individual Perceptions of Racial Group Interests

Both the general and economic components of racial group interests were tested as predictors of African-American evaluations of the two major parties. The economic component proved to be the better predictor. The measures for the determination of absolute and relative black economic status are those introduced in Chapter 4.

Evaluations of the Economy

There are two measures of evaluation of the economy included in this component. One is the the evaluation of the national economy, and the other is the evaluation of household finances. Both measures are described in Appendix 1.

Approval of Reagan's Presidential Performance

This is the Reagan approval measure described in Part A of this appendix.

Party Identification

This is the party identification measure described in Part A of this appendix.

Perceptions of Which Party Best Advances
   Black Issues

This is the measure of the two major parties' relative support for black interests described in this chapter.

Liberalism

This is the single indicator liberal/conservatism measure described in Part A of this appendix.

Local Black Economic Condition

Several measures of unemployment-based black economic conditions at the state level were added to this version of the panel study by the investigator. Statewide unemployment conditions provide a finer indicator of local black economic conditions. The black population is highly urbanized and to a significant degree concentrated. Thus, while local unemployment rates would provide a better indicator, the statewide rates provide an adequate contextual measure of the black economy. In 1984, the statewide black unemployment rate was the best indicator. This variable was recoded to the 0–1 range. In 1988, the change in the gap between black and white unemployment between 1987 and 1988 turns out to be the better indicator.

C

African-American Partisanship

The text that supports Figure 5.5 suggests that there are reciprocal relationships between African-American approval of President Reagan, perceptions of which party works harder on black issues, and African-American party identification. A system of equations approach was used to test the posited simultaneity. Three stage least squares estimators were used to test the model. The results show that there was a reciprocal relationship between African-American party identification and approval of President Reagan, but that perceptions of which party works harder on black issues can be modeled with a single equation. The statistical results from the final model are displayed in Tables 5.2–5.4.

Support for a Black Political Party

Support for a black political party is a simple binary variable where support for a black party = 1, and disapproval = 0. A proper estimator for individual-level data with a binary dependent variable is probit (King 1989). Because the probit estimator is nonlinear, interpretation of the coefficients is not as straightforward as with ordinary least squares. However, the mean effect of each variable can be found by estimating the probit equation while fixing each variable both at its maximum and minimum values and then taking the difference in the generated means. Using support for a black political party as an example, moving from the low to high value of education decreases the probability of supporting formation of a black political party by 17 percent. There are a variety of alternative goodness of fit measures available for dichotomous dependent variable estimators. The percent of correct predictions and the Maddala R^2 are selected for this study. See Maddala (1984) for more details on the R^2 measure. The results from the probit estimation are reported in Table 5.5. Description of how the probabilities were obtained will be presented in the next section.

TABLE 5.2

Relationship between African-American Party Identification and Reagan Approval, 1984

Variable	Dependent Variable: Coefficient (SE)	
	Party ID	Reagan Approval
Reagan approval	−.25	a
	(.07)	
Southern residence	.01	a
	(.01)	
Gender	−.03	a
	(.02)	
Liberalism	.09	a
	(.03)	
State black unemployment	.42	.30
	(.19)	(.38)
Party identification	a	−.66
		(.55)
Belief that Democratic party	a	−.12
works harder on black issues		(.07)
Linked fate	a	−.05
		(.04)
Belief that national economic	a	.29
conditions have improved		(.06)
Improvement in household	a	.09
finances		(.05)
Constant	.75	.59
	(.05)	(.42)
n = 539		
System R^2	.43	

Source: 1984–1988 National Black Election Panel Study. Estimates were obtained using the Systems Procedure of the Shazam econometric program. The estimates are 3SLS estimates.

[a] Not included in equation.

D

These probabilities were obtained by first obtaining the probit estimates for whether the respondent believed that the black rights movement affected her. These estimates were then converted to probabilities. What is reported are the differences in probabilities obtained over the range of each independent variable when the other variables are held constant. See King (1989) for description of these and similar methods.

TABLE 5.3
Relationship between African-American Party Identification and Reagan Approval, 1988

Variable	Dependent Variable: Coefficient (SE)	
	Party ID	Reagan Approval
Reagan Approval	−.20	[a]
	(.07)	
Southern residence	.05	[a]
	(.02)	
Gender	−.06	[a]
	(.03)	
Liberalism	.07	[a]
	(.04)	
Change in state black/white unemployment gap	1.72	1.51
	(.74)	(1.46)
Party identification	[a]	−.29
		(.57)
Belief that democratic party works harder on black issues	[a]	−.22
		(.12)
Linked fate	[a]	−.05
		(.04)
Belief that national economic conditions have improved	[a]	.53
		(.09)
Improvement in household finances	[a]	.15
		(.08)
Constant	.87	.33
	(.03)	(.47)
n = 303		
System R²		.34

Source: 1984–1988 National Black Election Panel Study. Estimates were obtained using the Systems Procedure of the Shazam econometric program. The estimates are 3SLS estimates.

[a] Not included in equation.

TABLE 5.4

Determinants of Perceptions of Whether the Democrats Work Harder on Black Issues, 1984 and 1988.

Independent Variable	Dependent Variable (Belief That Democrates Work Harder): Coefficient (SE)	
	1984	1988[a]
Party identification	.29	.33
	(.07)	(.09)
Liberalism	.22	.12
	(.05)	(.06)
Belief that blacks are economically better off than whites	−.03	−.25
	(.07)	(.10)
Black Economic Status Better?	−.08	−.09
	(.06)	(.11)
Belief that national economic conditions have worsened	−.00	−.09
	(.06)	(.08)
Improvement in household finances	−.04	.05
	(.06)	(.08)
Membership in a black organization	.05	−.07
	(.04)	(.04)
Family income[b]	.07	.18
	(.05)	(.10)
Gender	−.06	−.07
	(.03)	(.04)
Constant	−.00	−.01
	(.08)	(.14)
n	507	224
R^2 (adjusted)	.10	.12

Source: 1984–1988 National Black Election Panel Study. Estimates were obtained using the ordinary least squares procedure from the Shazam econometric program. All variables were recoded from 0 to 1.

[a] This regression uses the Achen (1986) correction for censored data described in Appendix 1.

[b] See Appendix 1 for differences in coding of 1984 and 1988 family income.

TABLE 5.5
Determinants of Support for a Black Political Party, 1984

Independent Variable	Dependent Variable (Support for a Black Political Party): Coefficient (SE)	Change in Probability of Support for a Black Political Party across Range of Variable
Family income	−.69 (.18)	.19
Education (Years)	−1.44 (.40)	.17
Warmth toward Jackson	.97 (.25)	.24
Belief that blacks should always vote for black candidates	.90 (.22)	.28
Belief that blacks should have nothing to do with whites	.30 (.28)	.09
Age	−1.95 (.39)	.51
Constant	.36 (.40)	
n = 706		
Maddala R^2	.14	
Percentage of Correct Predictions	.76	

Source: 1984–1988 National Black Election Panel Study. Estimates are probit estimates derived using the Shazam econometric program. All variables have been recoded from 0 to 1.

6

African-American Political Choice

> In the future we must become intensive political
> activists. We must be guided in this direction
> because we need political strength more desper-
> ately than any other group in American society.
> Most of us are too poor to have adequate eco-
> nomic power, and many of us are too rejected by
> the culture to be part of any tradition of power.
> Necessity will draw us toward the power inher-
> ent in the creative use of politics.
> (Martin Luther King, Jr., *Where Do We Go from
> Here: Chaos or Community?*)

Introduction: African-American Political Choice

African Americans have displayed extraordinary political unity in
their voting decisions from 1964 through the early 1990s. Voting solidarity approached or exceeded 90 percent in the mayoral elections
of Chicago and New York during the 1980s, and in Jesse Jackson's
1988 Democratic party presidential primary campaign. In North
Carolina, African Americans united in opposition to Jesse Helms during the 1990 North Carolina Senate contest. At the same time, modest
variation in vote choice was exhibited, in the first Jackson campaign
(1984), the 1989 Detroit mayoral campaign, and the 1990 Chicago
mayoral campaign. While there has been only one major party realignment of African Americans, black support for the two major political
parties has fluctuated throughout history. Political behavior also includes the decision whether or not to vote. James Blanchard, the
former governor of Michigan, lost a close election in the early 1990s
owing in no small part to a disappointing black voter turnout in
Detroit. African Americans' ability to *act* on their political preferences
is constrained by the dearth of candidates and other officials from the
two major parties willing to advocate and implement those preferences. As African Americans often perceive little difference between
the candidates placed on the ballot by the major parties, abstention

becomes a rational alternative. African-American political choice includes the decision to vote for candidates in national elections, the process of candidate evaluation, and the decision to participate in local politics.

Toward a Framework of African-American Political Choice

African-American political choice is constrained in ways not normally faced by other Americans. Pinderhughes (1987, 113) argues: "[African-American political] loyalty occurs among black voters because they consistently, almost uniformly, commit themselves to the party, faction, or individual candidate that is most supportive of racial reform. Many studies have shown that this pattern repeats itself in the north and the south, in urban and rural areas, before and after the transition to the Democratic party." She goes on to mention that African-American political choice is even more constrained due to the lack of competition between the two parties for the African-American vote. This lack of competition is due in part to the perception that African Americans do not have any options other than the Democratic party and in part to the belief shared by leaders of both parties that competition for the white vote is more important *and* at odds with competition for the black vote. Thus, constraint on African-American political choice is due both to the lack of competition for the black vote and to the salience of race for African-American citizens. As long as race remains salient for African Americans, political debate among African Americans will be confined mainly to discussion of which candidates and factions would best represent African-American interests on economic and racial issues. Those African Americans with the strongest group identification find economic and racial issues the most salient political issues (Conover 1984).

Indeed, many African Americans view their only choices—the same choices they have considered for nearly half a century—as support for the Democratic party, support for radical third-party or other independent political efforts, and abstention. These are viewed as the only choices for advancing African-American group interests. With the new emphasis on electoral politics, the choice for African Americans increasingly has been between supporting the Democratic party and abstention. Consequently, the development of political racial group dynamics and group interests have led to the situation where political participation has to be considered within the sphere of any theory of African American political choice.

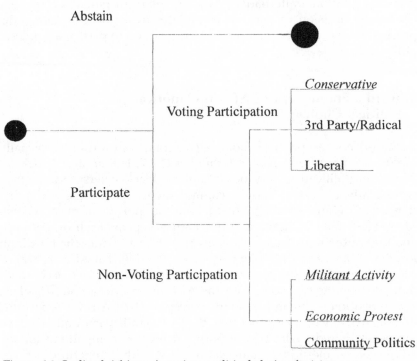

Figure 6.1. Stylized African-American political choice decision tree

Figure 6.1 schematizes the choices facing an African American con-
templating political action. The structural constraints on African Americans' political choice help to prune blacks' decision tree on one branch
while enlarging it on another. The branch of the decision tree that runs
along the participation line forks to include not only voting but also
protest and other community-level forms of participation. As shown
later, community-level activities are a form of political participation
often engaged in by African Americans as an alternative or a supple-
ment to voting (particularly at the national level), given a highly constrained political system with little competition between the parties for
the black vote. Abstention from politics occurs, according to this
model, when the payoff from the *combination* of various selected forms
of participation is more than the cost of participation. Abstention *can* be
a political statement with some positive utility. But the price can be
high in the short to medium term if the result is the election of an official dedicated to cutting programs of benefit to African Americans
and/or implementing programs not in African Americans' interests.

While the participate/not-participate fork of the tree represents a binary choice, the other branches can be viewed as a menu from which citizens can select multiple options. These branches are not mutually exclusive; individuals over time, or at the same time, may well engage in more than one alternative.[1] The constraint in the tree is found in the lack of branches that represent African-American political preferences for leftist and/or nationalist politics.[2] There is also constraint along existing branches that are perceived to have low payoff for African-American group interests.

This constraint is explicitly modeled in the branch of the decision tree that shows vote choice. At the vote choice branch the Republican/right wing branch is highly attenuated (as denoted by the italics). Whether one examines African-American party identification, African-American issue positions, or electoral behavior, the concentration of African Americans on the left of the American political spectrum insures that support for the Democratic Party in recent decades has been overwhelming.[3] The branch of the tree that involves choosing between the parties has been truncated for nearly four decades.

The branch that is labeled third party/radical politics is also usually truncated but is activated periodically, particularly in local black politics. Independent political movements played an important role in Harlem during the 1930s, in Alabama and other Southern states during the 1960s, and in Chicago during the first Washington mayoral campaign in 1983. The Jackson presidential campaigns, particularly the 1984 campaign, which built independent "rainbow coalitions" at the local level, could also be viewed in this context. These independent political movements of African Americans were often sparked by the systematic exclusion of African Americans by both major political parties and increasingly politicized racial consciousness (Barker 1989; Kleppner 1985; McAdam 1982; Naison 1983; Walton 1988). These independent campaigns and alliances can be seen as attempts by African Americans to collectively expand the set of political choices available to them. Expanding the range of choices in American politics, which is highly constrained by the standards of most other Western

---

[1] The idea of viewing participation as a menu of choices is drawn from a paper by Cathy Cohen.

[2] See Pinderhughes (1987), chapter 5, for an excellent discussion of the mapping of dimensions of ideology on African-American beliefs.

[3] See Brady and Sniderman (1985), Dawson (1986), Henderson (1987), and Nie et al. (1979) for the political positioning of African Americans vis-à-vis the party system and the rest of the electorate.

democracies, takes enormous energy, excellent group leadership, and a favorable political environment. It is not difficult to understand why such movements are hard to maintain over long periods of time.

The cognitive mechanisms of racial identity described in Chapter 3 reinforce the structural constraints in the American political system. Further, attributional biases tend to suppress or reinterpret information that is inconsistent with one's schema while (over)emphasizing information consistent with the schema (Taylor 1982). For example, theories of cognitive psychology would predict that information about "positive" policies of the Bush administration would take longer to incorporate into a schema while the information that Bush vetoed a major civil rights bill would dramatically and immediately reinforce African Americans' racial identity, which determines evaluations of the two political parties (Lau 1986). The result of these psychological dynamics at the individual level would be to slow the rate of change in the perception of the political choices available to African Americans.

However, this description of African-American politics is valid only to the degree that large numbers of African Americans perceive a link between their own fate and that of the race. If other interests—for example, economic interests—become more salient, the choices available to African Americans become more numerous, and one should begin to see the type of political heterogeneity described by Dahl (1961). We will discuss whether increasing economic diversity in the African-American community is paralleled by increasing political heterogeneity. Social theorists would expect more affluent African Americans to choose more conservative candidates.

We can test the relative influence of racial group interests and economics on African-American political choice by analyzing support for Jesse Jackson, the presidential vote, and evaluations of Ronald Reagan. Analysis of national African-American voting behavior explores only one aspect of the political choice process outlined in Figure 6.1. In general, the quantitative analysis of survey data is a very limited tool for studying African-American political choice. Relatively rare but important political choice–related events such as economic protests are better studied through historical analysis. In these areas, the analysis of survey data can at best complement other methodologies. As the continued black protest in cities ranging from Birmingham to New York indicates, protest remains an important aspect of black politics in the early 1990s—one that occasionally conflicts with the needs and goals of black electoral politics. While protest is not enough, neither is electoral politics by itself.

Political Choice and Political Support for Jesse Jackson

Black Power, Black Discontent

The presidential campaigns of Jesse Jackson were the strongest national attempts since the late 1960s and early 1970s to expand the political *choices* available to African Americans. The Jackson campaigns
helped to redefine black politics through a combination of the vener-
able black protest tradition and the new wave of electoral politics. En-
joying significant African-American support in 1984, and using the
momentum from his 1984 campaign to advance him further in 1988,
Jackson came as close to uniting the black community at all levels as
anyone had come since the apex of the civil rights movement.

Jackson was confronted with what Walters (1989) calls "shifting opportunities" that made a black presidential candidacy a potentially
powerful tool for uniting and mobilizing African Americans. Several
features of the political environment have been identified as being
particularly critical in providing the basis for the 1984 Jackson campaign (Barker 1989). First, the 1981–1982 Reagan recession had proved
particularly devastating to the African-American community (Barker
1989; Dawson, Brown, and Cohen 1990). The recovery that began in
the mid-1980s left most African Americans behind. The result was
persistent and growing socioeconomic inequality between the races
(Barker 1989).

Second, the 1982 midterm elections fell during the midst of the economic downturn. African-American organizations, as well as the
unions, waged a particularly energetic campaign to mobilize anti-
Reagan sentiment among blacks (Walters 1989). This successful mobilization drive carried over into a series of mayoral campaigns, highlighted by the mass mobilization of the African American community
in Chicago behind Harold Washington's successful 1983 campaign to
become the first black mayor of Chicago. The Chicago campaign demonstrated the power of a mobilized black electorate. African-American
mass electoral movements were shown to be useful tools for gaining, if
not necessarily securing, local black political power.

These mayoral campaigns, besides highlighting the potential power
of a mobilized black electorate, also pointed up the reality of black/
white political polarization *and* the often unsatisfactory performance
of white local and national Democrats in advancing black political
interests. Locally, the battle between blacks and whites for power became so bitter that many lifelong white Democrats *and their leaders* in

TABLE 6.1
African-American Support for Reagan, 1984 and 1988

	1984	1988
Do you approve of President Reagan's performance as president?	18%	24%
How warm do you feel toward Ronald Reagan on a scale of 1 to 100 (1 = cold, 100 = hot)?	29	43
How warm do you feel toward blacks who supported Ronald Reagan on a scale of 1 to 100 (1 = cold, 100 = hot)?	33	a

Source: 1984–1988 National Black Election Panel Study.
[a] Not asked in 1988.

Chicago and Philadelphia switched to the Republican party. Equally disturbing from the standpoint of many black political activists was the lack of enthusiasm of many Democratic politicians such as Walter Mondale and Ted Kennedy for Harold Washington's candidacy (Barker 1989).

As cool as the relationship between African Americans and Democrats was, it was warm compared to the frigidity of that between blacks and the Reagan administration. This was not, as it is occasionally claimed, mainly a dispute between ("overly") liberal black political and civil rights elites and conservative Reagan administration officials. Table 6.1 shows the extent of opposition to Reagan's performance as president and coolness to him personally among African Americans.

As Figures 6.2 and 6.3 suggest, African-American opposition to Reagan was reflected in opposition to Reagan's positions on specific political issues in both 1984 and 1988. African Americans perceive wide variation between the parties on issues of race, economic redistribution, and defense spending. Cognitive theories of group political behavior assume that issues that are highly salient to the group are well understood and that one is able to accurately perceive oneself, other groups, and the political parties and candidates in relation to one's own interests (Brady and Sniderman 1985; Fiske 1986; Lau 1986; Turner 1987; Uhlaner 1989). On these issues, all candidates and groups *except Jesse Jackson* are placed to the right of African Americans. The Republican party and its candidates are placed to the far right—the greatest distance from African Americans. Ronald Reagan was identified with policies and political symbols antithetical to the interests of the great majority of African Americans.

This political environment, as well as the political dynamics of the

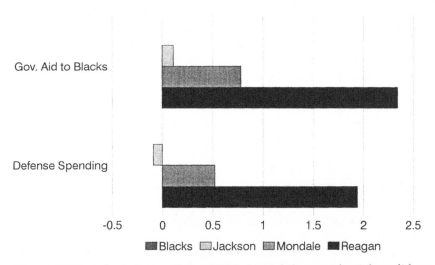

Figure 6.2. Perceived distance between blacks and the presidential candidates on selected issues, 1984. Negative numbers represent positions to the left of the black mean on issues, positive numbers positions to the right of the black mean. (*Source*: 1984–1988 National Black Election Panel Study)

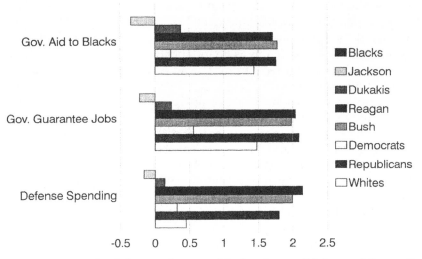

Figure 6.3. Perceived distance between blacks, the candidates, and the parties on selected issues, 1988. Negative numbers represent positions to the left of the black mean on issues, positive numbers positions to the right of the black mean. The white category, unlike the other categories, represents the means of white self-placement on the selected issues. (*Source*: 1984–1988 National Black Election Panel Study)

black community, allowed a consensus to form around the need to challenge the national status quo (Barker 1989). Although consensus developed relatively rapidly among the black elite regarding the need to have a presidential contender, there was some opposition in this group to a Jackson candidacy (Barker 1988, 1989; Reed 1986; Walters 1989). Black elected officials were mixed in their support for Jackson. Political activists ranging from Detroit mayor Coleman Young to the heads of the major civil rights organizations opposed his candidacy (Reed 1986; Walters 1989). In 1984, many black elected officials felt that Jackson had not paid his dues. Moreover, many had a long history of alliances with white Democratic politicians. Specifically, several black elected officials had already pledged their support for Walter Mondale. Jackson fared the worst in states such as Georgia and Alabama, where significant sectors of black leadership opposed him (Henry 1990).

Nevertheless, as Table 6.2 shows, Jackson was able to strengthen his base by winning over many members of the Congressional Black Caucus, many mayors of smaller cities, and, above all, the black clergy. These gains gave him a wide base of support among the black electorate. The data shown in Table 6.2 suggest that Jackson's support in 1984, while broad among all categories of African Americans, was greatest among the better educated. As shown in Table 6.3, in both 1984 and 1988 significant numbers of African Americans felt warm toward Jackson personally, thought his candidacy was a good idea, and stated that they would support Jackson over both of the candidates of the two major parties, even if he ran as an independent. By all indicators Jackson received strong support from African Americans in 1984, and even stronger support in 1988.

A critical aspect of Jackson's campaign that helped him win over many African Americans but may have limited support from American whites was the tone of moral fervor that characterized his speeches and campaign activities. Jackson's oratorical style was rooted in the tradition of the African-American church and African-American culture (Henry 1990; McCormick and Smith 1989). Although aspects of this tradition have been labeled authoritarian and undemocratic by some critics (Reed 1986), Jackson's style resonated deeply with the personal experience of African Americans.

What many of the critics have failed to notice is that Jackson's *politics*, particularly his emphasis on racial collectivism and advancement, are also a shared norm among African Americans. What Reed calls an "intransigent assumption of group black attitudinal uniformity" (32) is not only an assumption, it is a reality (Brady and Sniderman 1985; Dawson 1986; Nie, Verba, and Petrocik 1979; Reed 1986). This fact is

TABLE 6.2
Primary Vote for Jackson, 1984 and 1988

	No. of States	% of Whites Voting for Jackson		% of Blacks Voting for Jackson	
		1984	1988	1984	1988
All states	(13)	5	13	77	92
Region					
Northwest	(5)	4	13	82	93
Midwest	(3)	4	11	79	90
South	(4)	2	6	68	94
West	(1)	9	25	78	93
Respondent Characteristics					
Sex					
Men	(47%)	5	14	76	90
Women	(53%)	4	14	78	94
Ideology					
Liberal	(28%)	9	26	82	93
Moderate	(49%)	3	10	76	92
Conservative	(23%)	3	8	75	93
Religion					
Catholic	(25%)	3	11	72	83
Protestant	(36%)	NA	13	NA	93
Jewish	(6%)	4	8	NA	NA
Age					
18–29	(15%)	6	18	83	93
30–44	(31%)	7	21	83	93
45–59	(24%)	4	13	74	93
60+	(30%)	2	6	66	92
Education					
Less than high school	(11%)	1	10	67	95
High school	(31%)	2	8	77	93
Some college	(26%)	5	14	82	93
College grad	(32%)	9	21	80	91

Source: Adapted from Plissner and Mitofsky 1988, 56–57.

Note: Table is based on thirteen states holding presidential primaries where CBS News and the *New York Times* conducted exit polls in both 1984 and 1988. A comparison of the 1988 Jackson vote within any category in the thirteen states presented in this table and all twenty-four states where exit polls were conducted shows a difference of no more than 2 percentage points. The thirteen states are: Alabama, California, Georgia, Illinois, Indiana, Maryland, Massachusetts, New Jersey, New York, North Carolina, Ohio, Pennsylvania, and Tennessee. In 1984, 17% of Hispanics voted for Jackson; in 1988, 33% did. NA = not available.

TABLE 6.3
African-American Support for Jackson, 1984 and 1988

	1984	1988
Belief that it was good/bad that Jackson ran for president		
Good	87%	91%
Bad	13%	9%
Warmth toward Jackson on a scale of 1 to 100 (1 = cold, 100 = hot)	73	77
If Jackson ran as an independent candidate for president, would you vote for Jackson, Mondale/Dukakis, or Reagan/Bush?		
Jackson	57%	63%
Mondale/Dukakis	37%	34%
Reagan/Bush	6%	3%

Source: 1984–1988 National Black Election Panel Study. Data calculated by the author.

evident when one examines the most salient issues for African Americans—racial and economic issues.[4] Policy disputes among African Americans over questions such as economic redistribution tend to be carried out within the confines of the political left. In addition, intraracial policy debate is still overwhelmed by interracial gaps in public opinion and policy preferences (Kinder, Adams, and Gronke 1989). Normative disputes will continue between those such as Reed (1986) who argue that important class differences among African Americans are obscured by political movements such as Jackson's and those such as Barker (1988) who argue that "developing a unifying strategy" remains a paramount political goal for African Americans. In any event, whether African Americans share common policy preferences, differ in political behavior owing to class status, or perceive a common destiny is an *empirical* question.

Whatever its origin, by 1988 Jackson had achieved near-unanimous African American support among all segments of the population and regions of the country. In New York City, Jackson won 97 percent of the black vote. In Georgia, Jackson improved on his 1984 black vote by nearly 50 percentage points—enough to win the state despite lingering hostility on the part of some black elites (*Public Opinion* 1988). Though support for Jackson among whites was still weak, he was able to win 25

[4] See Table 8.1 for evidence of both the high level of agreement in the black community and the large gap between black and white public opinion on a number of different policy issues.

percent of the white vote in California (Plissner and Mitofsky 1988). Nationally, he won one out of three Hispanic votes in 1988. He won primary Southern states such as Mississippi and Louisiana and also won the important Michigan Caucus. Jackson won 30 percent of the contested primary and caucus votes and went into the Democratic National Convention with 27 percent of the delegates (Plissner and Mitofsky 1988). As in 1984, many Jackson supporters were bitter after the convention because they did not believe that he (and African Americans more generally) received fair treatment. Jackson was remarkably invisible during the Democratic general election campaign. Jackson supporters did not transfer their support to Democratic candidate Michael Dukakis. While Dukakis achieved the normally high levels of support *among those African Americans who voted*, African-American voter turnout in 1988 declined by 5 percent since 1984 as compared to 1 percent for whites (Kinder et al. 1989).

Sources of Support for Jesse Jackson

What are the reasons behind Jackson's massive support among African Americans? Some commentators have argued that black support for Jackson was mainly or solely based on blind loyalty to race or on Jackson's personal charisma. A more accurate explanation is that Jackson's positions on issues were practically identical to those of most African Americans. African Americans' perceptions of racial group interests helped solidify their support for Jackson's candidacy. In addition, African Americans seemed to believe that Jackson had the personality traits necessary for political leadership.

As mentioned previously, the data in Figures 6.2 and 6.3 indicate that African Americans discern major differences between the parties and their candidates on issues perceived as critical to African-American aspirations. Yet close examination also reveals that African Americans, while perceiving Jackson as further left than Dukakis, did not show a clear preference for Jackson's policy positions. Analysis of most survey questions reveals a small absolute difference between the mean black position and the positions where African Americans place the two candidates. The lack of perceived difference between Dukakis and Jackson on the issues may well be an artifact of the American National Election Study. As Shown in Figure 6.3, blacks surveyed in 1984 perceived great distances between Jackson's and Mondale's positions on affirmative action and defense spending, with African Americans' positions being virtually identical to Jackson's on both issues. As on the NES, the distance between the two Democrats and African Americans

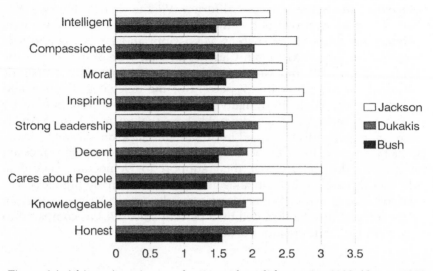

Figure 6.4. African-American evaluations of candidate traits, 1988. (*Source*: 1988 National Black Election Panel Study)

was very small when compared with the distance between African Americans and Ronald Reagan on the same issues.[5] While the evidence from the NBES suggests that African Americans perceived small differences between Jackson and the Democratic candidates, the differences between the Democrats and African Americans were overwhelmed by those between Republicans and African Americans.

On the other hand, in 1988 Jackson had a clear advantage over both major party candidates in terms of leadership traits. Figure 6.4 displays the perceived differences in African Americans' evaluations of the leadership abilities of George Bush, Michael Dukakis, and Jesse Jackson. African Americans strongly believed that Jesse Jackson had superior leadership and character traits. His advantage over both other candidates was clear *on every single measured trait*, and Dukakis's advantage over George Bush was similarly clear. On average, Jackson's lead over Dukakis was about the same as Dukakis's lead over Bush. Thus, while Jackson was clearly preferred over Bush (and other Republicans) owing to both large differences on the issues *and* Jackson's superior perceived leadership ability, Jackson's lead over Dukakis becomes clear once the character and leadership qualities have been factored in.

[5] Unfortunately, the NBES had only two issue placement questions in 1984 and none in 1988.

Who were the Jackson supporters in 1984 and 1988? To answer this question, I measured general affect toward Jesse Jackson in 1984 and 1988 and analyzed specific variables involved in support for Jackson's campaign attempts. As we saw in Table 6.3, African Americans felt very warm toward Jackson, giving him a thermometer score of 73 degrees. This compares to a rating of about 63 degrees for Democratic candidate Mondale and an exceedingly chilly 29 degrees for then-president Reagan.[6] In 1988, Jackson's score was 77 degrees, compared to 67 degrees for Democratic candidate Dukakis and 42 degrees for Republican candidate Bush. The slightly warmer score for Jackson in 1988 than in 1984 reflects the wider support Jackson enjoyed in the black community in this year.

Jackson's high thermometer scores translated into significant support for his candidacy in both 1984 and 1988. Eighty-seven percent of the NBES sample thought it was a good idea for Jackson to run for the presidency despite significant reservations on the part of many black politicians (Barker 1989; McCormick and Smith 1989; Reed 1986; Walters 1989). By 1988 the already robust support for a Jackson presidential candidacy had risen to 91 percent of the survey respondents.

Models of Jackson Support

What were the social variables predicting degree of enthusiasm for Jackson? Particularly in 1984, some sectors of the black population were uneasy about his candidacy. This question will be attacked two ways. First, a model of affect for Jackson will be analyzed. Second, results from an analysis of support for Jackson's candidacy will be presented for both 1984 and 1988. Many of the same factors that predict positive affect toward Jackson could also plausibly be used to predict support for Jackson's candidacy. Therefore, the following description of the variables used to predict warmth toward Jackson will also be used in the other analysis of support for Jackson.

I examined several variables for their possible effect on degree of warmth toward Jackson.[7]

---

[6] The power of norms in the black community is demonstrated by the fact that the thermometer reading for blacks who supported Reagan was almost as low as the thermometer reading for then President Reagan. The mean thermometer reading for black Reagan supporters was a frigid 33 degrees. As suggested in the argument in Chapter 3, blacks perceived as supporting causes or leaders who are considered dangerous for the race are held in contempt.

[7] See Appendix 3 for a detailed description of the individual variables used in each category.

GROUP INTERESTS

To the degree that Jackson was seen as the candidate who would best advance African-American interests, respondents' perceptions of linked fate, relative group status, and racial group interests should predict a high degree of warmth toward Jackson. Those who are most alienated from the two-party system and think that whites have too much power and/or support an independent black political party should be especially likely to support a Jackson candidacy, with its emphasis on massive redistribution of wealth, black pride, and solidarity with the Third World.

ECONOMIC CLASS

Second, the proposition that those with more economic resources would oppose Jackson is tested. Jackson advocated a political agenda that emphasized massive economic redistribution. Such a project would entail new taxes on those with more economic resources and/or cuts in the military. Traditional social theories would predict that such an agenda would not be popular among the more affluent. Conversely, African Americans with fewer resources should be more attracted to such an agenda and thus more supportive of Jackson's candidacy.

ASSESSMENT OF ECONOMIC CONDITIONS

Warmth toward Jackson might well be based on an assessment of the economic health of individual families, the race, and the nation. Presumably, the worse African Americans' assessment of their own relative economic status, the more likely they would be to support Jackson. Furthermore, since the Republican party controlled the presidency for most of the 1980s, they might be seen as responsible for general economic stagnation. Jackson, particularly in 1988, was the only candidate who promised a shift in spending that would protect jobs and aid urban areas to an unprecedented degree. Thus, the more negative one's assessment of the national economy, the more likely one should be to support Jackson's candidacy.

INTEGRATION INTO THE BLACK COMMUNITY

Most theories would predict that integration into the black community and/or exposure to information transmitted through this community should be associated with greater support for Jackson. On the other hand, in 1984 the opposition to Jackson from many black political elites might lead to "mixed" messages *within* black community information networks. Such ambiguity had disappeared by 1988 (Oreskes 1988; Plissner and Mitofsky 1988). I predicted that integration into the black community would translate into support for Jackson.

RESPONSIVENESS OF THE POLITICAL SYSTEM

Support for Jackson could also be a function of African Americans' evaluations of the current responsiveness of the political system. Perceptions of how hard the two parties work on black issues and evaluations of the performance of the current president are elements of this variable. Evaluations of Reagan's performance in particular should be an accurate predictor of support for Jackson. In 1984, Reagan represented all that was racist and bad about America for many African Americans, and Reagan and Jackson symbolized the extreme poles of the American political spectrum. Given the heavy symbolism attached to both candidates' political campaigns, one would expect support for Jackson to be strongly and inversely associated with support for Reagan.

Finally, the Rainbow Coalition was often portrayed as a movement whose basis was found among the poor and in the South. Observers, such as Reed (1986), have questioned the validity of such a portrayal. Consequently, the standard background variables are included to test various hypotheses concerning the demographic nature of support for Jackson.

Warmth toward Jackson

Subjective warmth toward Jackson was determined by the same factors as predicted support for Jackson. The results of the analysis for 1984 and 1988 are presented in Table 6.4. The 1984 results show that the variables that most strongly predicted warmth toward Jackson were associated with African-American racial group interests. The thermometer reading for those who believed that their fate was linked to that of the race as a whole was nearly eight degrees higher than for those who did not believe that such a link existed. Perceptions of racial group interests also indirectly increased support for Jackson. Those who believed that whites had too much influence felt five degrees warmer toward Jackson than those who believed that whites had about the right amount of influence and nearly ten degrees warmer than the few respondents who believed that whites had too *little* influence. Those who believed that African Americans should form an indepen-

TABLE 6.4

Determinants of Warmth toward Jackson, 1984 and 1988

	Dependent Variable (Warmth toward Jackson): Coefficient (SE)	
Independent Variable	1984	1988[a]
Linked fate	.08	.05
	(.02)	(.03)
Family income[b]	.06	.04
	(.02)	(.03)
Support for a black political party	.08	.05
	(.02)	(.03)
Belief that white people have too much influence	.10	.13
	(.04)	(.05)
Approval of Reagan's performance as president	−.07	−.05
	(.02)	(.02)
Southern residence	.05	.03
	(.02)	(.02)
Gender	−.04	−.04
	(.02)	(.03)
Exposure to campaign at church	.04	.03
	(.02)	(.02)
Constant	.54	.81
	(.04)	(.05)
n	802	356
R^2	.10	.07

Source: 1984–1988 National Black Election Panel Study.

[a] The 1984 coefficients were estimated with ordinary least squares. The 1988 estimates were derived using the Achen (1986) correction for selection bias described in Appendix 1.

[b] See Appendix 1 for information on different coding of family income in 1984 and 1988.

dent black political party also felt significantly warmer toward Jackson than those who did not. Clearly, those who believed that their own fate was linked to that of the race, who were concerned about the dominant position of whites, and who believed that African Americans should form their own political party saw strong possibilities in Jackson's candidacy.

The 1984 results show that Jackson's support was stronger among more affluent African Americans. A person whose family income was over $40,000 per year was six degrees warmer toward Jackson, on average, than someone whose family income was less than $10,000 per year. This finding supports Reed's (1986) contention that more affluent African Americans are more likely to support Jackson. Once again, economic status was found to have the opposite effect from that predicted by political theories that associate affluence with conservatism.

Not surprisingly, there was a seven-degree difference in warmth toward Jackson between those who approved and those who disapproved of Reagan's performance as president in 1984. None of the other political variables predicted warmth toward Jackson, nor did the economic evaluation variables. The only variable associated with integration into the black organizations and black information networks that predicted warmth toward Jackson was whether one heard about the campaign at church. Given Jackson's strong roots in the black church, it is not surprising that those whose churches were politically active would be warmer toward Jackson.

Two background variables were especially important in predicting warmth toward Jackson. A consistent finding is that women supported Jackson more often than men.[8] In political participation as well as political choice, a significant gender gap exists between black men and black women (Cavanagh 1985). Residents of the South felt nearly five degrees warmer toward Jackson than residents of other regions of the country. It should be remembered that despite this variability, the average African American in 1984 felt very warm toward Jackson. The interracial gap between blacks and whites far exceeds the intraracial variability among African Americans.[9]

This was even more the case in 1988. Due to the greater support for Jackson in 1988 than 1984, one generally observes a slight attenuation in the effect of several of the causes of positive affect toward Jackson in 1984. Once again, the variables associated with racial group interests best predict warmth toward Jackson. Those who believed that their fate was linked to that of the race were warmer toward Jackson than those who did not perceive such a link. Those who believed that whites had too much influence or that African Americans should form an independent black political party were nearly thirteen degrees warmer toward

[8] My colleague Ron Brown's work on gender and religion in African-American politics leads him to speculate that this may have to do with the importance of the black church. African-American women are the backbone of the black church and are more likely to be exposed to the political messages conveyed in church.

[9] The 1984 and 1988 studies reported, as usual, thermometer readings for all candidates. In both 1984 and 1988 there was a 36-degree gap between black and white thermometer readings for Jackson with blacks giving Jackson scores in the seventies for both years. The difference between blacks' and whites' evaluations of Ronald Reagan is also large during both years—26 degrees in 1984 and 28 degrees in 1988.

Jackson than those who did not share those beliefs. The effect of this variable increased from 1984 to 1988.

Level of household income was not a predictive variable in 1988. There was a slight attenuation in the importance of hearing campaign messages at church as a contributing factor to greater warmth for Jackson. The gender gap in warmth toward Jackson persists in 1988. Jackson's appeals for a coalition based on those who are economically disadvantaged in 1988 did not produce greater warmth from the African American poor for Jackson than in 1984. The other variables had approximately the same effect in 1988 as they had in 1984.

Was It Good for Jackson to Run?

African Americans felt warm toward Jackson in both 1984 and 1988. There was some controversy over his decision to run for president in 1984, at least among black elites, if not among the black masses (Barker 1989; Reed 1986). In general, however, African Americans were strongly supportive of the decision in both 1984 and 1988. In 1984, 87 percent of African Americans thought that it was "good" for Jackson to run. This figure had risen to 91 percent by 1988. Analysis of the basis of support for Jackson's candidacy yields fruitful results despite the skewness of the distributions on these two questions. The results of the analysis are displayed in Table 6.5.

What is striking about the results is the importance of the variables associated with group interests and integration into the black community. The largest impact on support for Jackson's candidacy was made by the belief that one's fate is linked to that of the race. Those who shared this belief were 12 percent more likely to support Jackson's candidacy than those who did not. Economic status played no role in predicting support for Jackson's candidacy in either year.

Most of the other variables had a modest effect. Belonging to a black organization, supporting the formation of an independent black political party, and believing that whites had too much influence increased one's probability of supporting Jackson's candidacy in 1984. Those who identified themselves as liberals were more likely to support the candidacy than self-identified conservatives.

In 1984 several variables had greater effects on support for Jackson's candidacy than in 1988. The importance of perception of linked fate as a predictor of support for Jackson's candidacy declined between 1984 and 1988. Supporting an independent black political party, being a member of a black organization, and believing that whites had too much influence were more important in determining the probability of

TABLE 6.5
Determinants of Support for Jackson's Primary Campaigns, 1984 and 1988

Independent Variable	Dependent Variable (Do You Think It Is Good Jackson Ran?): Coefficient (SE)	
	1984	1988
Linked fate	.12	.08
	(.04)	(.04)
Support for a black political party	.09	.10
	(.02)	(.04)
Membership in a black organization	.07	.09
	(.02)	(.03)
Belief that white people have too much influence	.05	.13
	(.05)	(.06)
Liberalism	.07	.00
	(.04)	(.04)
Constant	.67	.67
	(.06)	(.06)
n	535	301
R^2	.08	.08

Source: 1984–1988 National Black Election Panel Study. Estimates were derived using ordinary least squares. This regression uses the Achen (1986) correction for censored data described in Appendix 1.

supporting Jackson in 1988. Even though the great majority of African Americans supported Jackson's candidacy in 1988, being integrated into the black community and being concerned with the political group interests of African Americans further increased the probability of supporting Jackson.

Summary

As we will see, the model of support for Jackson has a much different structure than models of voting in the presidential campaigns. The factors that made African Americans especially likely to support Jackson over and above the extraordinary levels of general support that he had were his superior perceived leadership traits and his perceived potential for advancing "the state of the race." The beliefs that the major parties did not work hard on black issues, that whites had too much influence in American society, that an independent black political party should be formed, and that one's fate is linked to that of the race all resulted in increased support for Jackson's candidacy.

Ideology played a relatively small role in garnering support for Jackson. At the same time, his appeal to the poor did not bring him especially strong support from that sector of the black community. If status had any effect, it was that in 1984 the more affluent were more likely to support Jackson than the less affluent. However, by 1988 all sectors of the African-American community strongly supported Jackson's candidacy. The general sentiment in the African-American community was that Jackson was the candidate with the best chance of advancing the goals of black America.

The Reagan Factor

Jesse Jackson represented one pole of the electoral arena for African Americans from 1980 to 1988. Ronald Reagan represented the other pole. The near unanimity of support for Jackson was only matched by African-American disapproval of Reagan and his policies.

Group Interests and Support for Reagan

African-American presidential approval was extremely low in both 1984 and 1988. In 1984, 18 percent of blacks approved of Reagan's performance, while in 1988 the figure was 24 percent. It has been argued that in 1984 Reagan encapsulated much of the political and economic woes that confronted black America. The set of economic, social, and group interest variables that has been described earlier was used to predict African-American approval of Reagan in both 1984 and 1988. This discussion is based on the analysis of the interrelation between approval of Reagan's presidential performance and African-American party identification in Chapter 5.[10]

In 1984, those who believed that the Democratic party worked harder than the Republican party on black issues, thought that the national economy had worsened during the past year, and believed that their household finances had also worsened were more likely to disapprove of Reagan's performance. Party identification had a weak effect on presidential approval, showing that even black Republicans had misgivings about his administration.

During the 1988 national election Reagan was not the central symbolic figure for African Americans that he was in 1984. In 1988 he was

[10] The tables on which this discussion is based are found in Appendix 2.

a lame-duck president who was not on the ballot. As we have seen, Reagan's approval was a less important predictor of political choice in 1988 than in 1984. Not surprisingly, the variables unrelated to party had a weaker effect on Reagan's approval rating in 1988. Party identification played a larger role in 1988 than in 1984. However, differences in evaluations of the parties' efforts on behalf of black issues also played a somewhat greater role in shaping attitudes in 1988 than in 1984. The economic evaluation variables played less of a role in 1988. The black community had an extraordinarily unified evaluation of the Reagan presidency. Reagan's approval ratings among African Americans were considerably worse than those of fellow Republican presidents Gerald Ford and George Bush (Dawson, Brown, and Cohen 1990). Presidents can do much to set the tone of race relations, whether through their direct manipulation of symbols (Kennedy), their policies (Johnson, Reagan), or their studied downplaying of racial issues (Nixon's "benign neglect").

The African-American Vote in 1984 and 1988

Jesse Jackson was not on the general election ballot in 1984 and 1988, and Ronald Reagan dominated the political landscape. This served to greatly restrict the choices available to African Americans, both in terms of candidates and in terms of issues of central importance to the black community. Walters (1989) argues that the Jackson campaign highlights the uniqueness of black politics and the ensuing need for detailed separate analysis of it. In particular, he emphasizes how the Jackson campaign clearly demonstrated the importance of what he terms "group improvement" (what is being called here *group interests*) for understanding black politics.

The analysis of the African-American presidential vote presented in this section helps demonstrate some of the similarities and differences between black and white voting patterns and black and white evaluations of presidents. The familiar framework for analyzing African-American political choice, contrasting the importance of racial concerns with those of economic status, is utilized in this analysis. The proposed analysis builds on the analyses of support for the political parties presented in Chapter 5. However, the vote analyses are simpler since the vote decision is considered the last stage of a decision-making process.[11] The proposed antecedents of the vote are discussed.

---

[11] "Simpler," meaning that a single equation can be used to estimate the vote decision.

Group Interests

We have seen that perceptions of racial group interests played a significant role in support for Jackson's primary candidacy. Unfortunately for many African Americans, the general election campaigns of 1984 and 1988 did not evoke symbols and issues central to African-American group interests as Jackson's campaign did. Race was an important feature of the 1988 campaign. George Bush's racist Willie Horton ads pandered to the worst racial stereotypes in the American psyche. Michael Dukakis refused to focus on the issue of race, even to the point of rebuking his vice-presidential candidate, Lloyd Bentsen, when Bentsen challenged Bush on his ads. More to the point, both candidates showed a reluctance to take a stand on issues, ranging from government spending on social programs to civil rights, that were considered important in the black community. As a consequence, one would not expect African-American choice in the general election to be as related to racial group interests as in the Jackson campaigns. The two presidential candidates showed fewer differences on matters of race than in any national election since at least 1976. Nonetheless, the centrality of group interests in African-American politics suggests that such interests should have at least an indirect influence on African-American political choice at the polls. We would expect this to be particularly true in 1984, when Reagan represented the antithesis of African-American group interests for many African Americans. Political choice in the context of this environment could very well be seen, for most African Americans, as a choice between voting for the Democratic candidate and abstaining. Indeed, the Democratic candidate received 90 percent of the African-American vote in both 1984 and 1988. Let us explore the nature of this strong support for Democratic presidential candidates among the African-American community.

Economic Class

According to the traditional theories, increasing economic polarization within a community will lead to the more affluent members' becoming more conservative. Specifically, the more affluent one is, the greater one's likelihood of voting for the Republican candidate. Those who argue that perceptions of group interests drive African Americans' political decision making would expect socioeconomic status to have little or no role in predicting vote choice.

Support for the Political Parties

Numerous students of elections have highlighted the power of party identification as a critical variable in predicting individual political behavior (Campbell et al. 1960; Fiorina 1981; Jackson 1975; Markus and Converse 1979). Another variable is the degree to which one believes that the Democratic (or Republican) party works harder on black issues. Again, one would expect that the probability of voting for the Democratic candidate would increase with the degree to which one believed that the Democratic party worked harder on black issues.

Reagan Approval

We have seen the importance of Ronald Reagan in shaping the racial and economic climate within which black politics operated throughout the 1980s. Particularly in 1984, when Reagan's popularity was at its apex and the recession had just ended, disapproval of Reagan should increase the likelihood of voting for the Democratic candidate.

Liberalism

Reagan started a conservative trend, which was continued by George Bush, that pushed American politics farther to the right of the political spectrum. Indeed, in 1988 Republican candidate Bush attacked liberalism itself as a value outside of the American mainstream. The more liberal the respondent, the more likely they should be to support the Democratic candidate.

Depressed Local Black Economic Conditions

The statewide black unemployment rate served as a proxy for local and regional economic conditions in predicting vote choice. Since Republicans controlled the presidency throughout the 1980s, one assumes that they would be held responsible for local conditions. Therefore, the higher the statewide black unemployment rate, the more likely African Americans should be to vote for the Democratic candidate.

Negative Evaluations of the Economy

Several studies have shown the importance of evaluations of household, group, and national economic conditions in structuring individual vote choice (Fiorina 1981; Kinder et al. 1989). Evaluations of black economic status, which is predicted by the economic component of group interests, are also influential. Since Republicans controlled the presidency throughout the 1980s, one assumes that they would be held responsible for any perceived decline in household, racial, or national economic health.

Results

Table 6.6 displays the change in probability of voting for the Democratic candidate in 1984 and 1988 caused by each variable.[12] In 1984, the key variables in predicting a vote for Mondale were the political, economic evaluation, and group interest–related variables. Status variables played little role in predicting vote choice, and to the degree that they did influence vote choice, they influenced it in the opposite direction from that predicted by traditional theorists.

The importance of group interests in structuring African-American political choice is evident in the 14-percent difference in support for Mondale between those who believed African Americans were financially worse off as a group and those who believed that they were better off than they had been a year before. Perceptions of racial group interests influenced the vote in a number of different ways. In 1984 group interests played a significant role in structuring the vote. The only class variable that played a role in 1984 was level of education, and, once again, this variable had the opposite effect from that predicted. Those who were more educated were somewhat more likely to support Mondale.

The strongest predictors of support for Mondale were party identification and disapproval of Reagan's performance as president. Self-identified Democrats were 34 percent more likely than self-identified Republicans to vote for Mondale. Disapproval of Reagan's performance as president increased the likelihood of voting for Mondale by nearly 20 percent. The strength of Mondale's support in the black community can be gauged by the fact that 78 percent of all African Ameri-

---

[12] The probit estimates from which Table 6.6 were developed can be found in Appendix 3.

TABLE 6.6

Determinants of the African-American Mondale Vote (Probability Version), 1984

Independent Variable	Dependent Variable (Vote for Mondale): % Change in Probability of Voting for Mondale
Democratic identification	.39[a]
Education	.15
Belief that the Democrats work harder on black issues	.08
Approval of Reagan's performance as president	−.18
Belief that black economic conditions have improved	−.14
Belief that national economic conditions have improved	−.12
Age	.10

Source: 1984–1988 National Black Election Panel Study. Estimates are probit estimates derived using the Shazam econometric program.

[a] The methods for deriving the probabilities are detailed in Appendix 2. The probit tables upon which the probabilities are based can be found in Appendix 3.

cans who *approved* of Reagan's performance as president voted *against* Reagan. As expected, those who believed that the Democratic party worked harder on black issues than the Republican party showed stronger support for Mondale than those who thought the Republicans worked harder on these issues. However, in 1984 the direct effect of this variable was small and statistically negligible. Those who thought that national economic conditions were worse were 12 percent more likely to vote for Mondale than those who thought national conditions were better than they had been a year earlier.

Age played a small role in predicting vote choice. Many have predicted that the "new black Republicans" would be found among younger African Americans (Van Dyk 1990), as black youth neither suffered the blatant discrimination of older age cohorts nor were radicalized by the civil rights movement as their parents' generation was. Moreover, this argument goes, this generation is economically the most successful and therefore should be expected to vote its class interests. Although age was a statistically significant variable, African Americans who were 18 years old in 1984 were only 10 percent less likely to vote for Mondale than those who were 80 years old at the time of the election. Overall, those who were older were slightly more likely to vote for Mondale, but even 18-year-olds gave Mondale 86 percent of their vote.

TABLE 6.7
Determinants of the African-American Dukakis Vote (Probability Version), 1988

Independent Variable	Dependent Variable (Vote for Dukakis): % Change in Probability of Voting for Dukakis
Democratic identification	.50[a]
Education	−.09
Belief that the Democrats work harder on black issues	.10
Approval of Reagan's performance as president	−.07
Belief that black economic conditions have improved	−.10
Belief that national economic conditions have improved	.07
Age	−.07

Source: 1984–1988 National Black Election Panel Study. Estimates are probit estimates derived using the Shazam econometric program.
[a] The methods for deriving the probabilities are detailed in Appendix 2. The probit tables upon which the probabilities are based can be found in Appendix 3.

The structure of the African-American vote is somewhat different in 1988 than in 1984. The results for 1988 are displayed in Table 6.7. Perceptions of black economic status had a somewhat greater impact on the presidential vote in 1988 than in 1984. Evaluations of which party worked harder on black issues also had a greater effect in 1988 than in 1984. Those who thought that the Democrats worked harder on these issues than the Republicans were 10 percent more likely to vote for Dukakis. Perceptions of which candidate would best advance the interests of the black community had a modest direct effect on 1988 vote choice in addition to the indirect effects described earlier. Level of education had the opposite effect from the one it had in 1984 but was statistically insignificant.

The absence of Ronald Reagan from the ticket in 1988 removed him as a major factor in the African-American decision-making calculus. The impact of evaluations of Reagan on black vote choice in 1988 declined by more than 50 percent from 1984. Democratic identification was again a powerful factor predicting support for Dukakis. Support for Dukakis was not as strong among Republicans as support for Mondale had been. The mean (black) Republican probability of voting for Dukakis was 47 percent. Still, even among strong Republican identifiers, the probability of voting for the Republican candidate was the equivalent of a coin flip.

Several variables had a much weaker effect in 1988 than in 1984. These include age, level of education, and evaluations of the national economy. All three variables are statistically marginal in 1988 and switch signs. The diminution of the effect of evaluations of the national economy should not be too surprising. While economic conditions in the black community were bad in 1988, memories of the Reagan recession were a bit more distant than they were in 1984. The differences in the 1984 and 1988 models of the black vote do suggest that the political context of American elections—particularly whether racial group interests are salient in a given campaign—structures African-American voting behavior.

Conclusion

African-American political choices and evaluations are shaped by their perceptions of racial group interests and the absolute and relative status of the black community. On the other hand, they are not significantly influenced by individual economic status or level of education. However, the truncation of the American political spectrum and the subsequent limited choices in candidates available to African Americans may mask intragroup differences among African Americans while accentuating interracial differences. As Downs (1957) suggested, two-party political systems tend to produce candidates who tend toward the middle of the political spectrum. That structural tendency, when combined with the readjustment of the entire American spectrum to the right, may make it difficult to discern class differences among African Americans through the examination of the results of national elections and polls of presidential approval.

Indeed, the gulf between black and white political preferences and evaluations of candidates and presidents remains large. In both 1984 and 1988 African Americans overwhelmingly preferred Jesse Jackson. Jackson's politics were significantly outside of the mainstream of the Democratic party as well as the American polity more generally.

But are African Americans as politically liberal on issues of race and economics as their support for Jackson suggests? Or, as some claim, are African Americans considerably more conservative than the conventional wisdom suggests? African Americans' distaste for the enormously popular president Ronald Reagan suggests that the gulf between black and white public opinion continues to widen. Is this gulf a temporary or an enduring phenomenon? Moreover, does this racial gulf mask significant class differences in public opinion and political behavior within the black community?

Appendix 3

Data and Models for Chapter 6

A. African-American Support for Jesse Jackson

The new variables introduced in this section are as follows:

Warmth for Jackson

"I'll read the name of a person and I will ask you to rate that person on a thermometer that runs from 0 degrees to 100 degrees. Ratings between 50 degrees and 100 degrees mean that you feel favorable toward that person or group. Ratings between 0 degrees and 50 degrees mean that you are cool toward that group or person. You may use any number from 0 to 100 to tell me how warm or cold your feelings are for each person. Jesse Jackson. How would you rate him using this thermometer?" Recoded from 0 to 1.

Was It Good Jackson Ran?

This measure is a four-point summary measure built from the following questions: "Some black people feel it was a good idea for Jesse Jackson to run for the Democratic nomination for president. Others disagree and think he should not have run. What do you think? Was it a good idea or a bad idea for Jesse Jackson to have run for president?" "Is that a very good or somewhat good?" "Is that a very bad or somewhat bad?" 0 = very bad, 1 = very good.

B. African-American Vote Choice

The new variables introduced in this section are as follows:

Mondale Vote

"Who did you vote for?" The choices were Reagan, Mondale, and other. The "other" category was dropped from the analysis. The resulting binary variable was coded: 0 = Reagan, 1 = Mondale.

TABLE 6.8
Determinants of the African-American Mondale Vote (Probit Version), 1984

Independent Variable	Dependent Variable (Vote for Mondale): Coefficient (SE)
Democratic identification	2.04
	(.41)
Education	1.26
	(.68)
Belief that the Democrats work harder on black issues	.39
	(.27)
Approval of Reagan's perfor- mance as president	−1.23
	(.22)
Belief that black economic con- ditions have improved	−1.43
	(.42)
Belief that national economic conditions have improved	−1.15
	(.39)
Age	1.22
	(.76)
n	536
Maddala R^2	.25
Percentage of Correct Predictions	.93

Source: 1984–1988 National Black Election Panel Study. Estimates are probit estimates derived using the Shazam econometric program.

Dukakis Vote

"Who did you vote for?" The choices were Bush, Dukakis, and other. The "other" category was dropped from the analysis. The resulting binary variable was coded: 0 = Bush, 1 = Dukakis.

Tables 6.8 and 6.9 contain the probit estimate upon which the vote analyses presented in Tables 6.6 and 6.7 are based. A single equation was used to directly model the vote equations for 1984 and 1988. Appendix 2 describes the modeling of the antecedents to the vote choice equation.

TABLE 6.9
Determinants of the African-American Dukakis Vote (Probit Version), 1988

Independent Variable	Dependent Variable (Vote for Dukakis): Coefficient (SE)
Democratic identification	2.04
	(.56)
Education	−1.49
	(1.01)
Belief that the Democrats work harder on black issues	1.05
	(.51)
Approval of Reagan's performance as president	−.62
	(.35)
Belief that black economic conditions have improved	−1.27
	(.63)
Belief that national economic conditions have improved	.79
	(.62)
Age	−.76
	(.86)
n	259
Maddala R^2	.18
Percentage of Correct Predictions	.92

Source: 1984–1988 National Black Election Panel Study. Estimates are probit estimates derived using the Shazam econometric program.

7

Racial Group Interests, African-American Presidential Approval, and Macroeconomic Policy

WITH CATHY COHEN AND RONALD E. BROWN

> The Negro vote presently is only a partially realized strength. . . . There is no correlation between the numerical importance of the urban Negro vote to the party it supports and the influence we wield in determining the party's program and policies, or its implementation of existing legislation. . . . The new task of the liberation movement, therefore, is not merely to increase the Negro registration and vote; equally imperative is the development of a strong voice that is heard in the smoke-filled rooms where party debating and bargaining proceed. A black face that is mute in party councils is not political representation; the ability to be independent, assertive and respected when the final decisions are made is indispensable for an authentic expression of power.
> (Martin Luther King, Jr., *Where Do We Go from Here: Chaos or Community?*)

Introduction[1]

As we have seen, opposition to Reagan, particularly in 1984, was crucial in shaping African-American political choice. In this chapter we will examine the importance of racial group interests in shaping African-American presidential approval over time. Studying patterns of presidential approval helps us better understand political choice in several ways. In exceptional cases, such as with the Reagan admini-

---

[1] This chapter is drawn from Dawson, Brown, and Cohen (1990) and Dawson, Cohen, and Brown (1990).

stration, a president can signify African Americans' status in society. This has also occurred to various degrees with Presidents Lincoln, Roosevelt, and Kennedy. The symbolic role these presidents play may not be earned—Kennedy was much less enthusiastic about civil rights than Johnson. However, when presidents become this closely identified, for good or ill, with African-American status, African-American perceptions of racial interests should directly predict presidential approval at the individual level.

On the other hand, over time African Americans' approval of the president should be affected not only by the short- and long-term political factors such as scandals and war that generally affect presidential approval, but also by political and economic factors of specific importance to African Americans. Thus, by identifying the factors that are important influences on African-American presidential approval over time, we can better understand which political and economic factors African Americans consider critical.

Historical Trends in African-American Presidential Approval

Ronald Reagan visibly linked the presidency to the future of African-American group interests. Historically, African Americans' perceptions of the relationship between racial group interests and the current administration have helped determine African-American presidential approval. Thus, African Americans use information about group phenomena in their evaluations of the president more than white Americans do. It has been argued that African Americans have used racial group utility as a proxy for individual utility because race has been a critical factor in determining individual African Americans' life chances throughout most of American history (Wilson 1980). The reinforcement of group consciousness over time by indigenous organizations within the black community, particularly the black church, would lead us to predict that group status and relative group comparisons are integral components of models of African-American opinion and choice.[2] Events such as international crises may be evaluated not only in terms of their impact on the country, but also in terms of their effect on African Americans. That is, African Americans may evaluate events not only as Americans but also as a group that has been histori-

---

[2] See Morris (1984) and Allen et al. (1989), for introductions to the political role of the black church.

cally exploited in American society. This "double consciousness" has been recognized as a critical component in African Americans' political behavior since Du Bois described it nearly a century ago (Du Bois 1961).

We would expect the importance of racial group interests to have an impact on two aspects of African-American presidential approval. First, African Americans should be more sensitive to economic phenomena than white Americans. African Americans still lag behind whites on many economic measures. Black unemployment rates are twice those of whites and consistently remain above 10 percent. Black youths and the black elderly are three times more likely than their white counterparts to live in poor households (Farley 1984). African-American wealth also greatly lags that of whites. As we saw in Chapter 2, mean and median wealth of African-American families who earn *more* than $50,000 per year is significantly less than the wealth held by white families who earn *less* than $10,000 per year (Oliver and Shapiro 1989). The combination of these factors leads us to predict that economic factors will play a large role in African-American presidential approval and that this approval will reflect blacks' sensitivity to their relative economic group status.

Second, we would expect African Americans to filter "traditional" factors in presidential approval through evaluations of group utility. For example, blacks would not give all new presidents equal "honeymoons"; rather, their receptions of new presidents would be based on a prediction of the likelihood that the new president will help or harm African Americans.

Further, it is expected that African Americans would apply the filter of group utility to the similar process of evaluating American political parties. Specifically, we would expect African Americans to evaluate the political parties from the standpoint of how effective the major parties have been on black issues. Several scholars have pointed out that since the mid-1960s the Democratic party has been identified by the electorate as representing black interests while the Republican party has been identified as opposing them (Carmines and Stimson 1989; Huckfeldt and Kohfeld 1989). Not surprisingly, African Americans have been overwhelmingly Democratic in their partisan affiliation. The same filters of group utility that create near unanimity among African Americans in their evaluations of the two major political parties also creates near unanimity in African Americans' evaluations of sitting presidents. Because African Americans believe that Democrats will further black interests more than Republicans, we would expect Democratic presidents to garner higher approval ratings. The importance of group utility for African Americans necessitates separate models of black and white public opinion and political behavior. Let us now explore the details of a model of African-American presidential approval.

Explanations of African-American Presidential Approval

Traditionally, the key variables in presidential approval models have been indicators of the performance of the macroeconomy, the effect of wars, and "rally-around-the-flag" variables that measure short-term changes in presidential support in times of crisis, variables that represent other short-term political events such as scandal (e.g., Watergate), and political "honeymoon" periods (see Ostrom and Simon 1985; Hibbs 1987; and Beck 1987 for a short review of the literature). Although these models have provided significant insights into the sources of presidential approval for white Americans, who account for 85 to 90 percent of the data analyzed, they say little or nothing about the sources of the opinions of African Americans.

Traditional Measures of Presidential Approval

Several short-term political factors have been shown to be important in predicting levels of presidential approval. The president is often considered to be responsible for the moral tone of government, the well-being of the nation, and the successful and safe resolution of international crises (Neustadt 1960). Therefore, presidential approval should be damaged by the direct involvement of the president in a scandal that taints his term in office. Similarly, we would expect presidential approval to be damaged when the United States is involved in a war of long duration. On the other hand, presidential approval is thought to increase in times of international crisis, when the nation seems to be under attack and the call is for all Americans to pull together. Some of these variables should affect white and black presidential approval similarly. African Americans are exposed to much of the same political information as white Americans, even though they face different social realities. For example, disapproval of scandal is expected to be similar across the races. However, other events might affect black and white presidential approval differently. The following variables test these propositions.

WAR

Since the Korean War, American involvement in war has been shown to suppress support for the president (Mueller 1973; Hibbs 1987). The number of American soldiers killed in combat should be an important determinant of black approval of the president. Many in the black community perceived, correctly, that blacks suffered higher casualty rates than the rest of the armed services population during the Vietnam War. For example, in 1967 blacks constituted 11 percent of the total population, 14.5 percent of enlisted Army personnel, and 22.4 percent of the Army's killed in action (Franklin 1974). One would expect that the higher the casualty rates, the lower the approval of the president for all Americans. But I would expect African-American approval of the president to be more negatively affected by war casualties than that of whites, for two reasons. First, the perception and reality of *different and adverse* casualty rates for blacks would bring about a quicker negative response to the war by blacks. Second, major black leaders such as Martin Luther King, Jr., Malcolm X, and John Lewis were early and vocal opponents of the war (Franklin 1974; Haines 1988; McAdam 1982; Polenberg 1980). If it is true that African-American leaders during the civil rights and black power movements played an important role in providing information to the African-American people, one would expect war casualties to have a more negative effect on African-American presidential approval than on white presidential approval.

RALLYING AROUND THE FLAG

Short periods of intense crisis have generally been regarded as times when the polity rallies around the executive as a symbol of American unity. Many suspect that black and white Americans interpret these crises very differently. African Americans have historically viewed events in Africa and the Caribbean differently than the government. In general, they have a less interventionist approach to foreign policy questions than white Americans (Walters 1988). Thus, the call to "rally around the flag" is expected to be less effective for African Americans than for white Americans. An example from the 1980s is provided by the invasion of Grenada during the first term of the Reagan administration. Black elites were the only group of American elites to consistently condemn the invasion. Brody and Shapiro (1989) argue that elite response to international crises is the critical element in determining if and how the masses will "rally" around the president. If black elites consistently differ from white elites in their interpretation of international crises, blacks and whites will respond differently to these events. This analysis uses the list of international events proposed by Brody and Shapiro (1989) that excludes U.S.-Soviet summits and events resulting from an ongoing war.

HONEYMOON PHENOMENON

Democratic and Republican presidential honeymoons are modeled separately to test the thesis that for African Americans honeymoons are filtered through expectations of how effective the president will be on black issues. Given the perception by a large majority of African Americans that the Republicans do not work hard on black issues, blacks are not expected to uniformly allow a new president a honeymoon period. Specifically, blacks will allow Democratic presidents honeymoons but not Republicans. On the other hand, whites are predicted to allow presidents of both parties a honeymoon period. A simple dummy variable is used to measure the boost to presidential approval derived from the initial wave of support a president receives after an election.

WATERGATE

As previously suggested, presidents involved in scandal will undoubtedly suffer declining approval ratings. The Watergate scandal had a tremendous impact on Richard Nixon's popularity during his second term. News coverage of Watergate rose steadily, leveling off in the few months before Nixon's resignation. The effect of Watergate on presidential popularity is modeled as a function that rises steadily, levels off, and then declines slightly in the quarter of the resignation.

INFLATION

Finally, inflation has been perceived as a serious economic problem since at least the 1970s by the public (Hibbs 1987; Peretz 1983). Change in the consumer price index can be used to predict presidential approval. An increase in the consumer price index would be expected to lead to lower presidential approval. We would expect both blacks and whites to react negatively to a rise in prices as indicated by an increase in the consumer price index.

Group-Related Predictors of African-American Presidential Approval

GROUP ECONOMIC EFFECTS

Economic phenomena such as unemployment, which is at critical levels in the black community, may play a more important role in presidential approval for blacks than for whites. In the 1984 National Black Election Study (NBES), 62 percent of the respondents cited unemployment as the most important problem facing the nation (Tate et al. 1988). Figure 2.2 displays quarterly nonwhite unemployment rates as compared to quarterly white unemployment rates. Quarterly unemployment rates over 10 percent—rare for the nation as a whole—have been a constant feature of black life since the last quarter of 1974.[3] Even in the midst of a sustained economic recovery, black unemployment rates in the 1980s were substantially above 10 percent. They soared to 20 percent during the recession of the early 1980s and have since leveled off at a still disastrous 13 percent.

For most age groups, black labor force participation trails that of whites by at least 10 percent. For black teenagers the gap is closer to 20 percent. Moreover, while there was a general trend upward during the 1970s and 1980s in American unemployment rates, black unemployment increased more drastically, becoming relatively worse as compared with white unemployment even as both races' unemployment rates climbed. The gap between black and white unemployment exceeded 10 percent during the 1982 recession. It is reasonable to expect that economic problems of this magnitude would have dire political consequences. The conventional wisdom is that high and rising levels of unemployment damage the incumbent party's chances for reelection. Thus, the worse unemployment in the black community becomes, the lower African-American presidential approval will be.

Understanding the importance of the crisis in black unemployment led to its inclusion as a predictor in our model of the difference between black and white unemployment. This measure is used to test the importance of the relative economic status of blacks in African-American presidential approval. Relative economic status been shown to be an important factor in African-American political evaluations. Results

[3] The source for all economic data cited in this article is the Citibase Economic Database.

compiled from the 1984 NBES show that 61 percent of the sample believed that blacks were worse off economically than whites (Tate et al.
1988). Sixty-one percent believed that whites had too much influence
in American society, while 80 percent believed that blacks had too
little influence. Research by scholars such as Brady and Sniderman
(1985) suggests that Americans use information from groups they perceive as holding views which are the polar opposite of their own to
determine their own political view. Turner (1987) also emphasizes
the importance of intergroup social comparisons in the determination
of social behavior. We tested these hypotheses about the importance of
relative group economic status in determining African-American political behavior by using the *difference* between black and white unemployment as a predictor of black presidential approval. As the gap widens, African-American support for the president declines, all other
things being equal.

DEMOCRATIC CONTROL OF THE WHITE HOUSE

The Democratic party has become identified with black interests (Carmines and Stimson 1989; Huckfeldt and Kohfeld 1989). Specifically, the
Democratic party is somewhat more effective in implementing the
macroeconomic (unemployment) and civil rights policies considered
critical by the black community (Dawson, Cohen, and Brown 1990).
Consequently, African Americans' evaluations of how well a president
responds to black group interests are filtered through the political
party of that president. Blacks would be expected to show greater approval of Democratic presidents than of Republican presidents even
after controlling for other economic and political factors. Given that the
white population is more heterogeneous along economic and political
lines, this variable should have a much weaker effect on white presidential approval.

PAST LEVELS OF PRESIDENTIAL APPROVAL

Finally, presidential approval should be related to past performance of
the president. For example, past levels of unemployment, as well as the
current level of unemployment, should have an effect on current presidential popularity. More recent past unemployment levels would be
expected to have more impact than values from the more distant past.
Thus, presidential approval is modeled as a function of current and
past values of the explanatory variables. This phenomenon of current
levels of presidential popularity being influenced by past values of the
explanatory variables can be captured with a geometric distributed lag

model of presidential approval (Kmenta 1986).[4] The coefficient on the level of presidential approval from the previous period, which is bounded by 0 and 1, indicates how much past levels of presidential approval influence current levels. This variable is included in this section because blacks and whites are expected to react differently to past political events.

Estimation of Model

The presidential approval data were compiled from the Gallup presidential approval series provided by the Roper Organization. Quarterly observations on responses to the Gallup question constitute the dependent variable for this time series analysis.[5] The seemingly unrelated regression (SUR) method was used to estimate the two models of presidential approval.[6] The results are presented in Table 7.1.[7]

---

[4] The dynamics of this model can be fairly easily estimated using the Koyck transformation (Kmenta 1986). This transformation captures the dynamic properties of presidential approval by modeling current presidential approval as a function of the most recent past value of presidential approval along with the other explanatory variables.

[5] Gallup provides weighted data so that their sample reflects the national population. The weighted number of blacks in the sample ranged from approximately two hundred to four hundred. A variety of estimators designed to correct for heteroscedasticity were tested on the subperiod of data for which the weighted n's were known. None of these estimators improved or changed the estimation. Quarters with multiple observations were processed by averaging all of the observations for that quarter. Quarters that had missing data were processed by averaging the preceding and following values. The Durbin-H statistic was used to test for serial correlation in models that have a lagged dependent variable (Ostrom 1978). The value of this statistic, reported for both equations in Table 6.8, and examination of the correlogram indicated that serial correlation was not present.

[6] Ordinary least squares estimation would have been the usual method of estimation for this problem. However, when multiple equations may be generated by similar underlying factors, another estimation technique is preferred. Black and white presidential approval is affected by the same cycles of the American macroeconomy and the same electoral calendar, and to a degree share the same national political environment. A statistically more efficient method to estimate the equations is the method of seemingly unrelated regression (SUR). To determine whether the SUR model was appropriate, I tested whether the residuals from the OLS estimation of black and white presidential approval were correlated. They were. Under such a circumstance SUR improves the efficiency of estimates (Kmenta 1986). Version 3.0 of the Regression Analysis of Time Series (RATS) Econometrics Program was used for the estimations.

[7] Numerous specifications were tried in order to test for autocorrelation, find optimal lag structures on the right-hand-side variables, and alternative specifications of the models.

TABLE 7.1

Black and White Models of Presidential Approval, 1961–1985[a]

	Coefficient (SE)	
Dependent Variable	Black Approval	White Approval
Constant	46.48	21.86
	(5.98)	(5.48)
International rally event	−.05	1.62
	(1.04)	(.88)
Watergate	−7.83	−12.65
	(4.03)	(3.56)
Killed in action (1,000s)$_{(t-1)}$	−3.06	−1.94
	(.89)	(.81)
Democratic party honeymoon	17.50	8.23
	(4.89)	(4.07)
Republican party honeymoon	4.20	23.22
	(4.42)	(3.45)
Democratic president	13.83	−1.25
	(1.53)	(.70)
Black/white unemployment gap	−1.79	[b]
	(.57)	
White unemployment rate	[b]	−.68
		(.56)
Percent change in consumer prices	−2.34	−.85
	(.42)	(.33)
Presidential approval$_{(t-1)}$	.38	.70
	(.06)	(.05)
Adjusted R^2	0.94	0.78
Standard error of estimate	6.87	5.88
Durbin-H[c]	−.35	1.26
Number of observations	98	98

Note: The estimates were derived using the seemingly unrelated regression estimator.

[a] The time series data were measured every quarter.

[b] White unemployment was substituted for the difference between white and black unemployment in the estimation of the presidential approval of whites.

[c] Because of the presence of a lagged dependent variable, the Durbin-H statistic is an appropriate test for serial correlation.

Results

There are large differences between the causes of black and white presidential approval. Both the traditional measures of presidential approval and those resulting from the incorporation of the importance of group consciousness for African Americans reveal significant racial differences.

Racial Differences in Traditional Measures of Presidential Approval

The findings in Table 7.1 confirm the belief that African Americans do not "rally around the flag" to the same degree as whites. The African-American rally coefficient (−.05) does not differ statistically or substantively from zero. However, there is evidence for a white rally effect. White presidential approval increases between 1 and 2 percentage points as a result of this effect. The evidence suggests that one should not include rally effects in black models of presidential approval. The evidence from our model when combined with stronger evidence from other models (see Hibbs 1987; Ostrom and Simon 1985) suggests that rally effects should be included in models of white presidential approval. As argued previously, different historical experiences have led to different interpretations of international affairs for blacks and whites. International crises have a greater effect for whites than for blacks on presidential approval. This difference suggests that we need to better understand how elites of different races respond to international crises and influence the public.

Blacks responded to the Watergate crisis more weakly than whites. Black approval of Nixon was already quite low before the Watergate crisis, and Watergate did relatively little to further convince blacks that Nixon was an unsuitable president. African Americans were already convinced that Nixon's behavior in office was scandalous. Conversely, white presidential approval of Nixon was relatively high before the Watergate crisis broke. His approval rating plummeted nearly 13 percentage points among whites.

A difference was also identified between black and white responses to the number of Americans killed in action in Vietnam. The short-term impact is higher for blacks than for whites. The effect of war on black presidential support helps explain the decline in Johnson's popularity among blacks in the latter part of his term in office. The short-term response shows that at the height of the Tet offensive, when nearly five thousand Americans died in a single quarter, black presidential approval declined by 15 percentage points. White presidential approval declined by 10 percentage points during the same quarter. However, as Table 7.2 shows, owing to the more lasting effects for whites of past levels of the presidential approval on current presidential approval, wars eventually depress white presidential approval more than black presidential approval if they continue long enough.[8]

The coefficients on the lagged value of presidential approval imply that only the two previous quarters' events have much impact on current popularity for blacks. However, events nearly two years in the past influence current white presidential approval. While slower to mobilize, aversion to war among whites eventually becomes a potent political force after a long period of extended war. Conversely, one would expect according to the estimates that blacks would (and did) mobilize relatively quickly against a war that involved substantial African-American casualties.

There were large differences between blacks and whites on the honeymoon variables. As expected, blacks gave Democratic presidents a substantial 17.5–percentage point boost in the first quarter of a new presidency. African Americans did not allow Republican presidents a honeymoon. Whites gave significant honeymoons to both Democrats and Republicans. However, the 23–percentage point boost whites give Republicans is nearly three times the boost whites give new Democratic presidents. Racial differences in evaluations of the two major political parties are clearly demonstrated by the length of the honeymoon given new presidents. Such disparities again emphasize the need to model black and white public opinion and political behavior separately.

African-American approval of Democratic presidents is nearly 15 percentage points higher than that of whites when other variables are held constant. This difference is most likely due to the relatively homogeneous support for the Democratic party among blacks, as opposed to the more evenly divided support for the two parties by whites. However, just as important as the difference in magnitude of the parameter estimates is the finding that the signs for the effect of Democrats controlling the White House are different between the races. African Americans strongly support Democratic presidents. On balance, whites have tended to give more support to Republican presidents. As

---

[8] The long-term effects are calculated by determining the mean effect of the mean lag. As Harvey (1981) details, for the Koyck case the long-term effect displayed in Table 7.3 is calculated using the equation $b/(1-x)$, where x is the coefficient on the lagged value of presidential approval.

TABLE 7.2

Short- and Long-Term Effects of Selected Independent Variables on Black and White Presidential Approval (percentage)

Variable	Black Approval		White Approval	
	Short-Term	Long-Term	Short-Term	Long-Term
Long-term political factors				
Effect of one quarter of Democratic presidency	14%	22%	–1%	–4%
Short-term political factors				
Effect of one international rally event in a quarter	<–1%	–1%	2%	5.5%
Effect of one quarter of Watergate scandal	–8%	–13%	–12%	–42%
Effect of 1,000 Americans killed in action during one quarter	–3%	–5%	–2%	–6.5%
Effect of one quarter Democratic honeymoon	11.5%	a	8%	a
Effect of one quarter Republican honeymoon	4%	a	23%	a
Economic Factors				
Effect of 1-percentage-point rise in one quarter in black/white unemployment gap	–2%	–3%	b	b
Effect of 1-percentage-point rise in one quarter in white unemployment rate	b	b	–1%	–2%
Effect of 1-percentage-point rise in one quarter in Consumer Price Index	–2%	–4%	–1%	–3%

[a] Defined as short-term effect.
[b] Not included in this equation.

predicted, the political party of the president has a much greater impact on black than on white presidential approval. Turning to economic variables, the difference between black and white unemployment helps to predict black preidential approval. Interestingly, *while measures of both black unemployment and the difference between the races' unemployment are substantively and statistically significant, the difference between the races' unemployment is the more important single determinant of presidential approval.* This finding is further evidence of the importance of perceived relative group status in influencing African-American political behavior.

For every percentage point that the gap between black and white unemployment widens, presidential approval among African Americans declines by 3 percentage points. White presidential approval barely responded (at weak levels of statistical significance) to the level of white unemployment. Furthermore, white approval rates did not show the same responsiveness to the racial difference in unemployment. As Miller and colleagues (1981) and others have reported, subordinate groups are generally more sensitive to relative group status than dominant groups. Moreover, the more secure economic position of whites in American society may also lead them to discount economic factors in politics more than blacks. White presidential approval declines by less than 1 percentage point for every 1 percentage point rise in the unemployment rate.

African Americans also respond differently than whites to inflation. African Americans respond much more negatively. The black coefficient for the change in the consumer price index was almost three times that for whites. For every 1 percentage point rise in the consumer price index, black presidential approval fell by more than 2 percentage points. This suggests that African Americans are politically sensitive to *both* inflation and unemployment—a result somewhat at odds with previous work that suggested that low-income groups are more averse to unemployment than to inflation (Hibbs 1987; Peretz 1983). In sum, blacks responded more strongly to the economic variables than whites.

The effect of past levels of presidential approval for whites is nearly twice that for blacks (.70 for whites, .38 for blacks). This finding has several implications for differences in group behavior. The relative lack of importance of past levels of approval means that current events are more important for black presidential approval. Second, as Table 7.2 demonstrates, for some variables, such as number of Americans killed in action, the long-range (equilibrium) impact for whites is greater than that for blacks even though the contemporaneous impact is greater for blacks.

Finally, the coefficients for the previous level of presidential approval can be interpreted to mean that whites have longer political memories vis-à-vis presidential approval than blacks. Events three quarters in the past have a negligible effect on current African-American presidential approval. For whites, it takes ten quarters for past events to have the same negligible effect that three quarters have for blacks. Events two years in the past have for whites the same effect that events two quarters in the past have for blacks. This phenomenon can be explained in part by the greater number of political and social phenomena African Americans must attend to. In addition to the events that all Americans must attend to, racial issues demand close attention. Furthermore, the economic marginality of a substantial sector of the black population results in a deficiency of resources that can be devoted to tracking political trends. The combination of the precariousness of many African-American lives and the need to track a wider range of phenomena could well explain African Americans' somewhat greater propensity to emphasize more recent events. The salient question for African Americans when evaluating recent political events is, "What have you done for us lately?" This evaluation process is separate from the historical legacy that shapes African Americans' orientation toward the political system—a legacy that is acquired early on and is continually reinforced through African-American political and social institutions.

The differences between black and white presidential approval indicate major differences along racial lines in the factors influencing presidential approval. Not only do the two races often disagree in their assessments of the president, but the reasons behind these assessments differ as well. The strength of black association with the Democratic party has led to a high level of black approval of Democratic presidents. The more evenly distributed party affiliation among whites makes the party affiliation of the president a weaker indicator of white presidential approval. Blacks are less likely to "rally around the flag" and allow a new Republican president an extended honeymoon period than whites. The perception of differential rates of those killed in action leads to a more negative impact of war on presidential popularity among blacks than among whites in the short term. Blacks respond more negatively than whites to adverse economic conditions. In general, all of these results are consistent with my arguments concerning the importance of group evaluations in African-American public opinion and the need to consider separate structural models when examining group public opinion.

African-American Economic Interests and Macroeconomic Policy

We have already observed the larger impact that unemployment has on black presidential approval than on white presidential approval, as well as the larger impact that the gap between black and white unemployment has on black presidential approval than on white presidential approval. The political importance of black economic status, particularly relative black economic status, was discussed at length in Chapter 3. It was argued there that the comparison between in- and out-groups on salient issues is an integral aspect of the formation of social identity.

In Chapter 2 evidence was marshaled that government had indeed played a role in improving African-American economic status. The state helped to expand the black middle class by providing more employment in the state sector and enforcing fair employment and affirmative action regulations that served to open up both white-collar and blue-collar jobs, the latter particularly in the South. Not only the government in general but also which party is in control of the government is a critical factor in African-American economic advancement.

African Americans are particularly vulnerable to shifts in American macroeconomic performance. According to Jaynes and Williams (1989, 294), "Blacks have a strong interest—stronger than the white majority—in national policies that hold unemployment low and keep the economy expanding. At the same time, their sensitivity to the nation's macroeconomic performance is a symptom of their marginality and inferiority in economic status. The sustained rapid growth of the nation's economy during World War II and for a quarter century thereafter was extremely important to blacks' gains in economic status. . . . National and international economic trends since 1973 have been much less benign." If this is true, then perceptions of African-American economic group interests may be a powerful predictor of party identification, candidate choice, and presidential approval. Thus, the economic analysis of racial inequality as a result of macroeconomic performance provides potentially fruitful grounds for analyzing the political stances of African Americans.

There is a tradition of work that traces different macroeconomic phenomena to partisan control of the presidency. For example, Hibbs and Dennis (1988) find that income inequality declines under Democratic administrations. This phenomenon is due mainly to the reduction of unemployment under Democratic administrations and the increase of transfer payments as Democratic control of Congress increases. The black community would be a prime beneficiary of Democratic control of the executive and Congress, while many middle-income whites would see money redistributed away from themselves. Consequently, political differences in party identification, support for particular presidential administrations, and support of various tax policies could all stem at least in part from very different economic interests.[9]

---

[9] For a fuller discussion of these points in the context of popular support for varying tax policies, see Sears and Citrin (1985). Their analysis of the Proposition 13 referendum campaign provides valuable insight into how whites and blacks evaluated this campaign.

African-American Unemployment and Political Control of the Presidency

Unemployment within the black community is tied to which party is in control of the presidency. This is politically significant since unemployment has often been regarded as the most critical problem in the black community (Dawson, Cohen, and Brown 1989). In order to examine this relationship, I studied quarterly nonwhite unemployment rates from 1954 to 1985.[10] I also analyzed the data to see if there was a relationship between the gap between black and white unemployment and partisan control of the presidency.[11] Table 7.3 presents the results of analyses of the effect of partisan control on nonwhite and white unemployment rates.

The results help explain why, for many blacks, measures of relative group economic status predict political choice and presidential approval. Black unemployment declines by about 2.5 percentage points when a Democrat occupies the White House for two terms. On average, a Republican administration in power for two terms is associated with a rise in black unemployment of nearly 2.5 percentage points. The effect of a Democrat in the White House for two terms on white unemployment is a 1.34–percentage point decrease—about half of the decrease found in black unemployment. Our estimation of the transfer function model indicated that there is a three-quarter delay before a new administration's policies begin to take effect. This model reflects a more realistic view of how policies take hold than models that assume that policies attain their full force from the moment they are implemented (Hibbs 1987).

The greater magnitude of the interparty shifts in black employment confirm findings from other studies. Given the high priority awarded to employment policies by black elites and the black public, it is reasonable to posit that the perception of interparty differences in performance on unemployment would lead to a strengthening of black ties to the Democratic party. More generally, these differences should reinforce the propensity to take into account the economic status of the group and its relationship to the government in making *political choices*.[12]

---

[10] Nonwhite, as opposed to black, statistics are available during this period. The largest component of nonwhite unemployment continues to be black unemployment.

[11] The following results for both sets of analysis were obtained using the ARMAX transfer function estimator provided by the RATS program.

[12] Hibbs and Dennis (1988) provides evidence about the differences in economic policy outputs depending on which party controlled the presidency and/or the White House.

TABLE 7.3

Effect of Democratic Presidents on Unemployment, 1954–1985

Variable	Lag	Coefficient (SE)	
		Nonwhite Unemployment	White Unemployment
Constant	0	11.10	5.25
		(0.22)	(0.11)
Impact of Demo-cratic president (ω_0)	3	−0.26	−0.16
		(0.15)	(0.08)
Impact of past values (δ_1)	1	0.79	0.75
		(.18)	(.19)
Equilibrium party difference in impact on un-employment $2 \times [\omega_0/(1 - \delta_1)]$		2.48	1.34
Noise terms			
AR1[a]	1	1.37	1.54
		(0.08)[a]	(0.07)[a]
AR2[a]	2	−0.41	−0.60
		(0.08)[a]	(0.07)[a]

[a] AR1 and AR2 terms are the autoregressive coefficients (rho) in the noise terms. The unemployment autoregressive specifications follow a second-order autoregressive process commonly found in unemployment time series. The equations were estimated using the transfer function routine of the Regression Analysis of Time Series package for IBM-compatible PCs.

The Difference between White and Black Rates of Unemployment

The large interparty differences with regard to black unemployment could also be explained by the assertion that the Republican party historically has been more concerned with inflation and that, consequently, unemployment rises for everyone under Republican administrations. To examine this theory, I analyzed the gap between black and white unemployment rates for the period from 1954 to 1985. The results, presented in Table 7.4, are enlightening. Whether the Democrats are in power has a substantively and statistically significant effect on the size of the gap between black and white unemployment. Under a Republican administration, all other things being equal, the gap widens by an average of more than 1.2 percentage points over two terms (the path that black unemployment follows over time is almost identi-

TABLE 7.4
Effect of Democratic Presidents on the Gap between Black and White Unemployment, 1954–1985

Variable	Lag	Coefficient (SE)
Constant	0	5.88
		(0.99)
Impact of Democratic president (ω_0)	4	−0.16
		(0.09)
Impact of past values (δ_1)	1	0.74
		(0.21)
Equilibrium party difference in impact on unemployment $2 \times [\omega_0/(1 - \delta_1)]$		1.24
Noise terms		
AR1[a]	1	0.96
		(0.03)[a]

[a] First-order autoregression (AR1) is found in the time series on the gap between black and white unemployment. The equation was estimated using the transfer function routine of the Regression Analysis of Time Series package for IBM-compatible PCs.

cal to the path followed by white unemployment in Figure 2.2). Not only is the absolute level of black unemployment worse under Republicans, but the relative level vis-à-vis whites is worse as well.

Much more work needs to be done on the distributional effect of the party in power on racial groups. While these results do not speak to other aspects of black economic life (such as the impact of inflation, tax policy, or government transfer payments), they do suggest that to the extent that black Americans perceive unemployment and other economic difficulties as the main problem facing the nation, Republicans will have difficulty winning black converts. The data also provide further support for the suspicion that black bloc voting is based on a fair assessment of the relative merits of the candidates and their programs for group economic advancement. It should be noted that during the 1980s neither party put much of a dent in the absolute levels of black unemployment. As long as this continues to be the case, employment policies will remain high on the political agenda of black America. Indeed, as Linda Williams (1987) has argued, the continued economic distress of the black community has been a major disappointment of African Americans involved in the political arena.

Politics and government have not proved to be sufficient to correct the economic problems of the black community. As Wilson (1980) points out, affirmative action programs cannot address the problems of structural readjustments in the political economy or employment problems in a slack labor market. While Wilson argues, probably correctly, that these programs largely benefited the better-educated, better-trained, and better-off minorities, in light of the Reagan administration's actions he may wish to revise his belief that these programs were solidly in place and could not be undercut significantly in a hostile environment. Sowell (1975) and Walter Williams (1982) to the contrary, an economically activist state seems to have been a necessary (although not sufficient) condition for black progress.

Conclusion

Time series analysis also demonstrates that African Americans' political evaluations are shaped by perceptions of racial group interests and by the different outputs that blacks receive from the political and economic system. African Americans suffer more from unemployment and bear more of that burden under Republican administrations than under Democratic regimes. However, African-American unemployment rates remain high under both parties' control. As a result, African Americans weight economic conditions more heavily than whites do in their evaluations of presidents. Our analyses of presidential approval and unemployment provide further confirmation of the need for separate analyses of black and white political phenomena.

8

Group Interests, Class Divisions, and African-American Policy Preferences

> There were two kinds of slave, the house Negro
> and the field Negro. The house Negroes, they
> lived in the house with master, they dressed
> pretty good, they ate good. . . . On that same
> plantation there was the field Negro. The field
> Negroes were the masses. The Negro in the field
> caught hell. . . . He hated his master.
>   (Malcolm X, *Malcolm X Speaks*)

> It is clear that the black community was never
> monolithic. Intraracial class differences shaped
> perspectives almost as much as life in a Jim
> Crow city did. . . . Nevertheless, the wide range
> of [African-American] persons and personalities
> who called Norfolk home shared a point of
> agreement: throughout the years, they were
> determined to act in their own interests.
>   (Earl Lewis, *In Their Own Interests: Race, Class,
> and Power in Twentieth-Century Norfolk, Virginia*)

Introduction: Class Divisions and Policy Preferences

Class divisions have so far been relatively absent in our analysis of African-American political choice. It has already been suggested that the lack of internal heterogeneity in African-American partisanship and political choice could be due to the significant truncation of the American political spectrum on the left when compared with the choices available in other Western, industrialized countries. The well-documented isolation of African Americans on the left of the spectrum could mask important political cleavages within the black community that would be apparent in other political communities (Brady and Sniderman 1985; Gilliam 1986; Hamilton 1982; Nie, Verba, and Petrocik 1979; Pinderhughes 1987). Moreover, Pinderhughes (1987) and others have suggested that African-American political beliefs do not map neatly onto a single left-right spectrum but are better understood through the incorporation of an economic policy dimension and a racial group status dimension.

Scholars such as Pinderhughes have argued that the intersection of racial and economic domination has produced complex patterns of political beliefs that have had several major consequences for black politics. First, black politics and public opinion are "constrained but not controlled" by white politics. Second, the interaction of status and economic dimensions has helped create a multidimensional issue space, in which the economic policy dimension maps relatively well onto a traditional left-right scale while other dimensions are specific to African Americans, such as the black nationalist-integrationist dimension, which has no real counterpart among white Americans. Historically, there have been severe political divisions among African Americans about the desirable degree of integration into American society, just as there have been political divisions about means even when there has been agreement over ends.

However, African Americans' low social status throughout most of American history has led to *both* African-American occupation of the left of the political spectrum *and* the truncation of mainstream political debate on the left. Table 8.1 illustrates blacks' leftist leanings on issues of economic redistribution, racial policies, and government spending. The combination of blacks' low socioeconomic status and historical relationship to the federal government has led African Americans to be relatively pro-government.

The deep and profound political divisions between blacks and whites highlighted in Table 8.1 have also served to mask political variation among African Americans. Hamilton (1982) and others have documented a very slow shift toward conservatism in some arenas of African-American public opinion. However, eight years after the "conservative revolution" heralded by the election of Ronald Reagan, extraordinary political divisions persisted between blacks and whites. As Table 8.1 shows, 20– and 30–percentage point gaps between blacks and whites on some issues are not uncommon, and often the two races end up on opposite sides of critical policy questions. These enormous gaps serve to overwhelm what would normally be considered significant variation in African-American public opinion, thus helping to explain the seeming homogeneity of African-American political behavior. Normally the reference for evaluating black political behavior is white political behavior. In addition, most public opinion polls do not contain many questions that are crucial to African-American discourse. Thus the nature of the questions included in these polls tends to conceal variation in African-American public opinion.

TABLE 8.1
Differences between Black and White Public Opinion, 1988 (percentages)

	Whites	Blacks
Issues		
Supports increased spending on government services	33	63
Supports decreased defense spending	31	47
Supports government health insurance	39	49
Believes government should provide jobs and a good standard of living	21	57
Believes men and women should have equal roles	68	68
Supports increased federal spending on:		
Social security	53	82
Food stamps	16	49
Fighting AIDS	71	83
Protecting the environment	64	58
Financial aid to college students	39	72
Assistance to the unemployed	24	65
Child care	53	78
Public schools	61	83
Care for the elderly	73	90
The homeless	61	90
The war on drugs	74	82
Supports decreased federal spending on:		
Aid to Nicaraguan Contras	50	51
Star Wars	40	53
Space and scientific research	31	25
Approves of U.S.–Soviet nuclear treaty	90	71
Opposes use of U.S. military to protect oil shipments	32	50
Supports greater cooperation with Russia	43	42
Opposes limits on foreign imports	34	22
Political identifications		
Considers self a liberal	27	41
Considers self a Democrat	40	83
Likes something about the Democratic party	51	63
Dislikes something about the Democratic party	48	20
Likes something about the Republican party	52	22
Dislikes something about the Republican party	47	50
Candidate and public figure evaluations		
Likes something about Bush enough to vote for him	59	19
Dislikes something about Bush enough to vote against him	52	47

TABLE 8.1 *(continued)*

	Whites	Blacks
Likes something about Dukakis enough to vote for him	44	61
Dislikes something about Dukakis enough to vote against him	63	22
Disapproves of Reagan's handling of his job as president	34	75
Thinks Jackson would make the best Democratic candidate	13	59

Source: 1988 American National Election Study.

The different dimensions of African-American public opinion have significant implications for the strategies of African-American politicians. The more successful black politicians (such as Jesse Jackson and Harold Washington) emphasize the collective racial dimension of black public opinion, the less destructive we would expect the internal divisions among African Americans to be. These politicians often sacrifice some white support to gain overwhelming black support. Even more mainstream black politicians, such as Tom Bradley and Douglas Wilder, use the belief among some African Americans that black politicians are always more supportive than white politicians of African-American racial interests to gain substantial black support regardless of their actual stands on economic issues. These politicians try to broaden their appeal outside of the black community by adopting issue positions considerably to the right of those espoused by most African Americans. Does the lack of viable political options available to African Americans mask real class-based differences in African-American public opinion?

Models of African-American Public Opinion and Policy Preferences

We have seen that the two key sets of issues for African Americans are racial issues and issues of economic redistribution. The 1984–1988 National Black Election Panel Study (NBES) allowed for the construction of two measures of different aspects of African-American racial group interests and one measure of economic redistribution. One of the racial measures focuses on government policies aimed at African Americans and other "minorities." The other variable is designed to measure the degree of autonomy from white society desired by African Americans.

The black utility heuristic suggests that group interests should play a role in shaping policy preferences across all three domains, as all three historically have been centrally tied to African-American group interests. However, class-based political theories would suggest that class variables should play the greatest role in shaping attitudes toward economic redistribution. Let us build models of each issue domain.

Measurement Model

Models of African-American attitudes on economic redistribution, racial policies, and black autonomy are built. Further, both the overall concept and the individual indicators of the abstract concept and policy preferences are measured with error. The method of confirmatory factor analysis allows one to build measurement models of the political concepts of interest, the latent variables, which are then corrected for measurement error. It is desirable, where possible, to include several indicators of the higher-level concepts in the measurement model.[1] The 1984 NBES contains more of the issue and policy preference questions needed for the analysis of black public opinion than the 1988 version and thus was used in the following analyses.[2] What follows is a description of the latent concepts and the indicators used to measure each one. Appendix 4 contains the actual question wording for each of the variables discussed in this chapter.

Economic Redistribution

As several authors (Hamilton 1982; Kilson 1983) have suggested, redistributive policies (which call for transfer of economic resources from the more affluent to the less affluent) are likely to detect incipient class

[1] See Bollen (1989) for an excellent discussion of the theoretical, philosophical, and practical aspects of both confirmatory factor analysis and the more general subject of structural equation models. It is not possible to directly measure individual African Americans' beliefs on economic redistribution, government racial policy, and black political autonomy. What is possible is to measure several public opinion indicators that are the result of these overarching concepts. For example, one's attitudes toward a government guarantee of a job or income, level of spending on food stamps, and so on should be significantly shaped by one's overall beliefs about economic redistribution. Because of the availability of several measures of black public opinion in 1984, it is possible to build multiple indicator models of the main concepts.

[2] The NES and similar surveys do not include the variables needed to test the group interests thesis. They also generally do not have sufficient blacks within the survey to enable one to take advantage of the ordinal variable estimators used in this analysis.

divisions in African-American public opinion if such divisions exist. The results from these authors' studies suggest that African Americans remain liberal *when compared to whites* on questions of economic policy. Hamilton has argued that the historical experiences of African Americans in the private sector and with the federal government would incline African Americans toward government intervention in the economy. This measure of attitudes toward economic redistribution will be used to determine whether there are class divisions *among* African Americans in this domain. Attitudes toward economic redistribution were determined using the following four indicators.[3]

1. How strongly does the respondent approve or disapprove of a government guarantee of jobs or income?

2. Does the respondent believe that government spending on unemployment compensation should be increased, be decreased, or remain about the same?

3. Does the respondent believe that government spending on Medicare should be increased, be decreased, or remain about the same?

4. Does the respondent believe that government spending on food stamps should be increased, be decreased, or remain about the same?[4]

These four indicators all measure the degree to which one supports government support for the economically disadvantaged. They cover concerns ranging from the popularly supported Medicare program to the belief that the government should be the employer/income guarantor of last resort. A more precise model of attitudes toward economic redistribution based on these indicators is developed below.

Government Racial Policies

A fiercely contested issue in the American polity, especially since the late years of the Carter administration, has been government policies designed to eliminate racial inequality or aid minority citizens. These policies have been a particular focus of the efforts of the civil rights

---

[3] Other indicators were tested as components of the three latent variables. They were shown through confirmatory factor analysis not to be part of the model for these concepts. What is reported here are the items that were found to fit the models. Details on the final measurement model follow.

[4] These four indicators, if combined in an additive scale, have a reliability of .66. The reliability measure is Cronbach's alpha. For details on the calculation of this measure of how well the indicators cohere to form a scale, see Carmines and Zeller (1979). Bollen (1989) points out that this measure actually underestimates the reliability of the type of scale used in this section.

movement, women's organizations, and minority group advocacy organizations. The policies have been bitterly opposed by most conservative organizations and some white ethnic organizations, and have on occasion been one of the tension points between the African-American and Jewish communities (Reed 1986). We saw in Table 8.1 that the average white and black citizen in the NBES sample placed themselves on opposite sides of this issue.

Government policies on race clearly should evoke racial group interests. If one sees one's fate as linked to that of all African Americans, one will be more likely to support government intervention on behalf of minorities. On the other hand, as Kilson (1983) points out, this is an issue domain that could evoke conflicting feelings in the black middle class. To the degree that one believes that one's own status is owed to or protected by government economic programs, one will support such programs. Even if one believes that his or her own skills and abilities are sufficient to ensure affluent status, a sense of racial solidarity might lead one to support these programs. On the other hand, someone who had adopted a more individually oriented approach to economic success, or believed that these programs stigmatize successful African Americans (Loury 1985) might oppose these programs.

The following statements of belief were used to measure one's attitudes toward government efforts to aid African Americans.

1. The federal government should make every effort to improve the social and economic position of blacks and other minority groups.

2. Because of past discrimination, minorities should be given special consideration in hiring decisions.

3. Improving schools in black neighborhoods is more important than busing children to achieve integration.

4. The government should not make a special effort to help blacks and other minorities because they should help themselves.[5]

Each of these indicators measures acceptance or rejection of government intervention on behalf of minorities in general and African Americans specifically.

Black Autonomy

From David Walker's appeal for slave rebellions, through large-scale efforts of African Americans to return to Africa, to the revolutionary black nationalism of Malcolm X, many black intellectuals and political

---

[5] These four indicators, when combined, have a modest reliability of .51.

activists have advocated the cultural and/or political separation of blacks from whites. Black nationalists have viewed African Americans' relationship with white America as necessarily adversarial. This attitude is reflected in modern times by the drive for black nationalism, black autonomy, and an independent black political voice (Allen, Dawson, and Brown 1989; Dawson, Brown, and Allen 1990; Gurin, Hatchett, and Jackson 1989).

The core concepts behind black nationalism have historically been the development of independent political strategies (Carmichael and Hamilton 1967; X 1966), black and African culture, economic independence, and an African-American land base. The NBES does not have sufficient indicators to fully model black nationalism. The somewhat broader concept of black autonomy is constructed using a subset of the core concepts of black nationalism. These measures are similar but not identical to measures developed by Allen, Dawson, and their colleagues (Allen, Dawson, and Brown 1989; Dawson, Brown, and Allen 1990). They cover the political, cultural, and social dimensions of black autonomy. The following statements of belief were used to construct the measurement model for black autonomy.

1. Blacks should give their children African names.
2. Blacks should always vote for black candidates.
3. Blacks should have nothing to do with whites.
4. Blacks should form an independent political party.[6]

These four indicators measure the degree of desired political, social, and cultural autonomy from whites. Malcolm X, the most influential black nationalist of the second half of the twentieth century, incorporated all three aspects of black nationalism into his program. The Nation of Islam has emphasized economic and spiritual nationalism. The US Organization of the 1960s begun by Ron Karenga (the creator of the now popular African-American holiday celebration of Kwanza) emphasized cultural nationalism. Marcus Garvey's one million–strong United Negro Improvement Association of the 1920s advocated black cultural and social autonomy.

We would expect that those who are economically more successful would be less likely to support radical black autonomy and black nationalism. Indeed, Malcolm X's "Speech to the Grassroots" makes the point, as have many speeches by nationalist leaders, that black nationalism is supported much less strongly by more affluent African Americans (X 1965). Perceptions of linked fate should have a positive effect on support for black autonomy and should act as a constraint on class divisions.

---

[6] These four indicators form a scale with a reliability of .62.

Causes of African-American Public Opinion and Policy Preferences

Table 8.2 displays the results of the measures of the three main latent variables for 1984. The results show that, generally, African Americans strongly support government economic redistribution. African-American support for economic redistribution is much stronger than white support.[7] African Americans also strongly support government aid to minorities, although a majority also espouse self-help concepts. Finally, a large majority are skeptical about uncritical support for black candidates, the formation of a black political party, and social isolation from whites. Thus, support for black autonomy is considerably less than support for government racial policy and economic redistribution. We will subsequently analyze the differences in support for these concepts among different socioeconomic strata of African Americans.[8]

To determine whether there is systematic class-based variation among African Americans on these issues, we will begin with a review of the bivariate cross-tabulations between the three variables under consideration before moving to the multivariate analysis. Figure 8.1 clearly shows that several of the indicators vary significantly by class. However, multivariate analysis is necessary to discern the presence and strength of class effects after controlling for the effects of other factors, including the group interests variables. The three dependent variables measuring African-American attitudes toward economic redistribution, government racial policy, and black autonomy were constructed from the factor scores derived from the confirmatory factor analysis described in Appendix 4.[9] A description of the independent variables used in the multivariate analysis follows.

Determinants of African-American Public Opinion on Racial and Economic Issues

Political scientists and social psychologists have repeatedly demonstrated that political and social issues become salient to the degree that they evoke group interests (Uhlaner 1989; Turner 1987). We saw in

---

[7] See Table 8.1 for a more detailed comparison of white and black differences on policies of economic redistribution.

[8] See Appendix 4 for a description of the measurement model that was constructed for each of the three policy constructs.

[9] Factor scores provide weights that describe each indicator's statistical contribution to the latent variable. Statistical packages that estimate either exploratory or confirmatory factor analytic models routinely provide the calculation of the factor scores as an option.

TABLE 8.2
African-American Public Opinion on Key Policy Domains, 1984

Redistributive Policies

Government guarantee job or income?
agree	45%[a]
disagree	31%[a]

Government should increase or decrease spending on:
Food Stamps
increase	49%
decrease	10%

Jobs
increase	82%
decrease	05%

Medicare
increase	79%
decrease	02%

Racial Policies

Special consideration for minorities in hiring because of past discrimination?
agree	61%
disagree	39%

Government should work to improve position of blacks?
agree	88%
disagree	12%

Government shoud work to improve black schools not concentrate on busing?
agree	82%
disagree	18%

No government aid to blacks but blacks should help themselves?
agree	74%
disagree	26%

Black Autonomy

Blacks should study African language?
agree	37%
disagree	63%

Blacks should whenever possible vote for black candidates?
agree	18%
disagree	82%

TABLE 8.2 *(continued)*

Redistributive Policies

Blacks should whenever possible have nothing to do
with whites?

agree	04%
disagree	96%

Blacks should form an independent black political
party?

agree	29%
disagree	71%

Source: 1984–1988 National Black Election Panel Study.

[a] Totals do not sum to 100% because of omission of intermediate categories.

Chapter 3 that both economic and racial policies have historically been tied to African-American group interests. Consequently, we would expect that perceptions of linked fate will shape all three of the issue domains.

Household and racial group economic health were tested to determine what effect they had on African-American public opinion about economic redistribution. Evaluations of racial group economic health would be expected to have the same effect as perceptions of linked fate. Perceptions of poor black economic health should lead to stronger support of redistributive policies. However, poor household economic health is posited to have the opposite effect. It is easier to be altruistic when one's own financial condition is healthy. In addition to the measures of group interests developed in earlier chapters, partisanship, ideology, and self-interest were all tested to determine their influence on African-American public opinion. Party identification, a variety of objective and subjective indicators of social and economic status, self-placement on a political spectrum, and membership in a black organization were tested for their impact on attitudes toward economic redistribution.

In addition to the likelihood of receiving political messages in church discussed earlier, one new religious variable was added. Several political scholars have commented on the impact of religious belief systems on African-American public opinion (Allen, Dawson, and Brown 1989; Dawson, Brown, and Allen 1990; Jackson 1987). An analogue to the religiosity measure used in the Allen and Dawson analyses was devel-

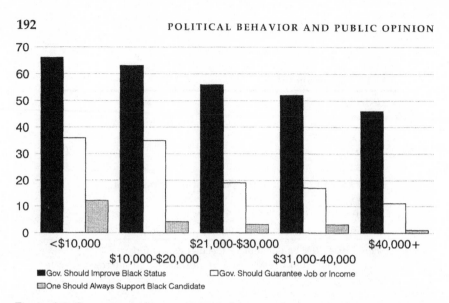

Figure 8.1. Percentage of respondents who strongly agree with selected items from racial and economic issue domains by income category (*Source*: 1984–1988 National Black Election Panel Study)

oped to test for the independent effect of black religiosity on African-American public opinion.[10] All of these variables and their construction are detailed in Appendix 4.

Results

Economic Redistribution

The effects of economic status on attitudes toward economic redistribution are evident in Table 8.3. Level of family income had the greatest effect on these attitudes. The more affluent one is, the less supportive one is of economic redistribution. Level of education had the same ef-

---

[10] A measurement model was also developed to build this construct. The three indicators used to build the religiosity variable were the frequency of church attendance, how important religion is in one's life, and to what degree religion guides one's life. Since the 1984 NBES had only three indicators appropriate for the religiosity measure, the confirmatory factor model was exactly identified. Thus, the global measures of fit are inappropriate for model evaluation (Bollen 1989). However, the reliability of these three measures using Cronbach's alpha is .77. Further, the individual component fits are excellent, suggesting that these three indicators satisfactorily measure a higher-order religiosity construct.

TABLE 8.3
Determinants of Opposition to Economic Redistribution, 1984

Independent Variable	Dependent Variable (Economic Redistribution): Coefficient (SE)
Linked fate	−.04
	(.02)
Family income	.09
	(.02)
Education	.04
	(.04)
Exposure to the campaign at church	−.01
	(.01)
Liberalism	−.05
	(.02)
Improvement in household finances	−.03
	(.02)
Belief that blacks are economically better off than whites	.04
	(.02)
Membership in a black organization	.02
	(.01)
Democratic identification	−.06
	(.03)
Constant	.45
	(.04)
n	322
R^2	.16

Source: 1984–1988 National Black Election Panel Study. The coefficients are ordinary least squares estimates derived using the SPSSX program.

fect, although it was weaker. Not surprisingly, most of the effects are weak. Perceptions of linked fate act as a constraint on class divisions. Regardless of economic status, the stronger the perceived link, the more likely one is to support policies of economic redistribution. Moreover, if one had perceived a decline in black economic status, one was also more likely to support policies of economic redistribution. On the other hand, if one's household finances had declined, one was less likely to support economic redistribution—indicating that individual financial health was seen as a prerequisite to helping others. Liberal ideology, Democratic party identification, and having heard about political campaigns in church all had small to moderate positive effects on support for economic redistribution. Membership in a black organization had a small and statistically marginal effect on attitudes toward economic redistribution. Perceptions of racial group interests and political liberalism both served as constraints on a strong tendency among more affluent and educated African Americans to oppose policies of economic redistribution.

Government Racial Policies

Class-based divisions also played a role in shaping African-American attitudes toward government racial policies. Nevertheless, as expected, the results in Table 8.4 show that perceptions of linked fate played the greatest role in predicting support for government racial policies. Perceptions of deteriorating black economic status and liberal political persuasion also predicted support for government racial policies. The higher one's income, the more likely one was to *oppose* affirmative action and similar policies. While all effects *except* those of linked fate and degree of liberalism were substantively marginal, if the finding on income is confirmed by other studies, it might show the retreat by the black middle class from affirmative action programs that they may feel stigmatize their accomplishments. On the whole, the expectation that the perception of linkage between individual and group interests would dominate in policy areas where race is clearly salient is supported by this analysis.

Black Autonomy

Class divisions played a significant role in shaping views on the desirable degree of autonomy from whites. As Table 8.5 shows, the higher one's income and education, the *less* likely one was to support black autonomy. Support for black autonomy is quite different from support for government pro-minority policies. Rather than emphasizing reform from within the system, it focuses on developing policies and strategies within the black community and rejects cooperation with whites as a strategy for black advancement. The more affluent and educated one is, the more likely one is to reject this approach. Class divisions historically have been prominent in debates over whether to support a black nationalist agenda. The Marcus Garvey–W.E.B. Du Bois debate in the early twentieth century was to a significant degree framed as a debate between the black middle class (Du Bois's "talented tenth") and less affluent African Americans. Certainly the debate between Malcolm X and Martin Luther King in the 1960s was often interpreted as a con-

TABLE 8.4
Determinants of Opposition to Racial Policies, 1984

Independent Variable	Dependent Variable (Support for Racial Policy): Coefficient (SE)
Linked fate	−.08
	(.02)
Family income	.04
	(.02)
Education	.00
	(.05)
Exposure to campaign at church	−.02
	(.01)
Belief that blacks are economically better off than whites	.03
	(.03)
Liberalism	−.07
	(.03)
Constant	.57
	(.04)
n	468
R^2	.07

Source: 1984–1988 National Black Election Panel Study. The coefficients are ordinary least squares estimates derived using the SPSSX program.

frontation between Malcolm X's angry urban poor and the more middle-class–based civil rights movement. During the 1984 and 1988 elections both Jesse Jackson and Minister Louis Farrakhan of the Nation of Islam made strong appeals to the most economically distressed within the black community. However, Farrakhan, a black nationalist, garnered more support from the urban poor.

Perceptions of linked fate also played the expected role in African-American attitudes toward black autonomy. The stronger the perception of a link between group and individual interests, the stronger one's support for black autonomy. However, the effect of linked fate was weaker than the effects of education and income. Linked fate played a smaller role as a constraint here than it did in the domain of economic redistribution. Class is the main determinant of African Americans' support of various strategies for black advancement.[11] Religiosity had a weak positive effect on support for black autonomy.

[11] See Dawson (1986) for a similar finding on orientation toward the capitalist system. Grass-roots African Americans were much more likely to reject the capitalist system as inherently unfair than elite black Americans.

TABLE 8.5
Determinants of Opposition to Black Autonomy, 1984

Independent Variable	Dependent Variable (Support of Black Autonomy): Coefficient (SE)
Linked fate	−.04
	(.02)
Family income	.09
	(.02)
Education	.14
	(.04)
Religiosity	.07
	(.05)
Constant	.63
	(.03)
n	657
R²	.08

Source: 1984–1988 National Black Election Panel Study. The coefficients are ordinary least squares estimates derived using the SPSSX program.

The Constraint of Racial Identity on African-American Class Divisions

The results reported above strongly suggest that there are significant class divisions in African-American public opinion and policy preferences. Policies that require increased government spending on welfare and other programs of economic redistribution are less strongly supported by more affluent African Americans. The truncation of the American political spectrum masks significant class-based differences in African-American public opinion. If more political options were available to blacks in American society, we would see greater heterogeneity in African-American political behavior.

Nevertheless, even when we are discussing policies of economic redistribution, it is important to remember that racial identity and the perception of group interests serve as powerful constraints on incipient class divisions. Those with strong perceptions of linked fate were more inclined toward liberal or nationalist positions on the survey questions, regardless of socioeconomic factors, than those who did not perceive such a linkage.

Perceptions of linked fate were *not* associated with individuals' absolute economic status but rather with their perceptions of disparities

between black and white status. As perceptions of interracial disparities declined and as individual African Americans' perceptions of
linked fate declined, class distinctions became more pronounced. Class
divisions could *either* decline or increase, given long-term trends in African Americans' perceptions of the racial divide, the maintenance of
residential and social segregation, and the presence of politicians and
political movements that continue to emphasize the collective aspects
of black life and black politics.

Nevertheless, even increasing class divisions in African-American
policy preferences do not necessarily imply that political conflict
among African Americans will increase. Class-based political movements would have to be able to develop within African-American communities in order for class conflict to become a focus of black politics.
While indigenous class conflict has been a periodic feature of black
politics, attempts by groups outside of the black community to reorient
black politics more along the lines of class have generally been unsuccessful (Kelley 1990; Naison 1983).

Second, both informal and formal united fronts will play a less significant role in black politics than they have in the past because the
growing economic polarization in the black community will make it
more difficult to unite groups that have increasingly severe political
disagreements. The civil rights movement, the Marcus Garvey movement, and the campaigns of both Harold Washington and Jesse Jackson
were united fronts that combined a number of different organizations,
interests, and black social classes in pursuit of common goals that were
thought to advance the racial interests of the entire group. While
these formations (particularly the Garvey movement) harbored class
conflict, their primary function was to unite disparate elements within the African-American community in pursuit of a common goal. The
Negro Convention movement of the antebellum era and the African
Liberation Day movement of the early and mid-1970s also down-
played intraracial divisions while emphasizing interracial divisions.
There was internal struggle within all of these formations, but their
overriding goal, which they usually achieved, was increased black
unity.

As discussed previously, class divisions are masked by the large interracial gaps shown in Table 8.1. These racial gaps found in American
public opinion tend to overwhelm the intraracial gaps explored in this
chapter. As long as racial divisions remain prominent, racial issues
will take precedence over class divisions. This gap exists even on the
redistributive domain where the intraracial gap is the largest. It is true
that, overall, African Americans remain liberal on economic questions

(Hamilton 1982). It is harder to discern at what point affluent African Americans decide that they are more similar politically to whites than to less affluent and more radical African Americans.

The question will remain unanswered as long as racial harassment is perceived as a common feature of black middle-class life. Interracial gaps in American public opinion will have to decrease before African-American class conflict becomes prominent. These gaps have the potential to decrease through a number of modalities. For example, the American public could move to the left of the political spectrum, or the racial climate could improve sufficiently that more affluent African Americans feel that they can begin to act on their class preferences.

Finally, the question of representation in the political arena of the aspirations and preferences of the less affluent must be confronted. At least within the electoral arena, a black nationalist position that *combines* economic radicalism with a clearly nationalist political stance is not to be found. In his last years Martin Luther King clearly represented a class-based radical egalitarianism while Malcolm X represented a radical black nationalist approach. During the last year of both men's lives a significant convergence between their two original positions occurred. They both began to focus on the economic issues of concern to the most disadvantaged African Americans and the need to understand African Americans' position in the United States within the context of the anticolonial struggles of the 1950s and 1960s. During the last year of his life Malcolm X espoused the need for a broad African-American nonsectarian movement, while during the last year of his life Dr. King spoke about the need for more radical analysis of the circumstances of African Americans.

The most prominent representatives of these two trends in the late 1980s were Minister Louis Farrakhan of the Nation of Islam and the Reverend Jesse Jackson. Jackson has consistently distanced himself from black nationalism while maintaining an agenda of economic radicalism. Minister Farrakhan was the most consistent public advocate of black nationalism in the late 1980s. During the 1980s, leaders in the mold of Malcolm X and organizations such as the Student Nonviolent Coordinating Committee (SNCC) and the Black Panthers, which combined these two forms of radicalism, were not prominent within the black community and were absent from the electoral arena. The analysis given here suggests that a political program that combined nationalism with economic radicalism would still have significant support within the black community. Those such as Linda Lichter (1985) who claim that black leadership is out of touch with a significant segment of the black community are probably correct about the *fact* but not in their description of the political gap between the community and leadership. In many areas, the community is more radical than the leaders.[12]

Summary

We have seen that class divisions among African Americans exist in important issue domains. The greatest class-based diversity is found around the issues of economic redistribution and black autonomy. A large majority of African Americans support extensive economic redistribution, but a significant drop-off in support occurs at the upper end of the income distribution. Perceptions of linked fate act as a liberal counterbalance to the greater conservatism of the more affluent. A large majority of African Americans are opposed to the more radical versions of black nationalism, with those at the bottom of the income distribution much more supportive of nationalist positions than the rest of the sample. On this measure, perceptions of linked fate were positively correlated with the propensity to adopt nationalist positions.

The focus of this chapter has been on the degree to which economic status influences African-American public opinion and policy preferences. Wilson (1987) and Marable (1983) have both argued that the impoverishment of the most economically distressed black communities has created a substantial gulf between the poorest African-American communities and the rest of black society.

---

[12] Lichter's own data showed that the black masses were more likely than black elites to reject capitalism (Dawson 1986; Lichter 1985).

Appendix 4

Data and Models for Chapter 8

Part A of this appendix contains the question wording for variables used in the measurement model. Part B presents the confirmatory factor analysis upon which the measurement models of the policy domains are based. Part C contains the details of the analysis presented in Chapter 8.

A

Redistributive Policy

GOVERNMENT GUARANTEE OF JOB OR INCOME

"Some people feel that the government in Washington should see to it that every person has a job and a good standard of living. . . . Where would you place yourself on this scale, or haven't you thought much about this?" Seven-point scale, 0 = Government should let each person get ahead on his/her own, 1 = Government should guarantee job and good standard of living.

GOVERNMENT SPENDING

"If you had a say in making up the federal budget this year, what programs would you like to see increased, decreased, or kept the same: food stamps? government jobs for the unemployed? Medicare?" Three-point scale, 0 = decreased, 1 = increased.

Racial Policy

The following variables were presented as statements with which the respondent was asked to agree or disagree.

SPECIAL CONSIDERATION

"Because of past discrimination, minorities should be given special consideration when decisions are made about hiring applicants for jobs." Four-point scale, 0 = strongly disagree, 1 = strongly agree.

GOVERNMENT AID

"The government in Washington should make every possible effort to improve the social and economic position of blacks and other minority groups." Four-point scale, 0 = strongly disagree, 1 = strongly agree.

BUSING

"Improving schools in black neighborhoods is more important than busing children to achieve racial integration." Four-point scale, 0 = strongly disagree, 1 = strongly agree.

SELF-HELP

"The government should not make any special effort to help blacks and other minorities because they should help themselves." Four-point scale, 0 = strongly disagree, 1 = strongly agree.

Black Autonomy

The first three variables listed below were presented as statements with which the respondent was asked to agree or disagree, while the fourth variable was posed as a question.

AFRICAN LANGUAGE

"Black children should study an African language." Four-point scale, 0 = strongly disagree, 1 = strongly agree.

BLACK CANDIDATES

"Blacks should always vote for black candidates when they run." Four-point scale, 0 = strongly disagree, 1 = strongly agree.

RELATIONS WITH WHITES

"Blacks should not have anything to do with whites if they can help it." Four-point scale, 0 = strongly disagree, 1 = strongly agree.

BLACK POLITICAL PARTY

"Do you think blacks should form their own political party?" Two-point scale, 0 = no, 1 = yes.

B

Confirmatory factor analysis was used to build the measurement model for each latent variable.[13] Table 8.6 presents the results from the measurement model for each dependent variable in Chapter 8.

---

[13] The PRELIS and LISREL VII programs combine to allow one to estimate confirmatory factor analysis based on correlation matrices designed for ordinal-level variables. Asymptotic variances and covariances were used to calculate the measurement models using the weighted least squares estimator. See Joreskog and Sorbom (1988) for the im-

TABLE 8.6

Measurement Coefficients for African-American Policy Domains

Construct	Item	Unstandardized λ (SE)	θ_8^a (SE)
Economic redistribution			
Government guarantee of job	X_1	.29 (.05)	.92 (.07)
Spending on food stamps	X_2	.67 (.07)	.64 (.11)
Spending on jobs	X_3	.64 (.07)	.73 (.11)
Spending on Medicare	X_4	.72 (.08)	.55 (.13)
Racial policies			
Affirmative action	X_1	.51 (.07)	.74 (.08)
Government aid to blacks	X_2	.66 (.08)	.56 (.12)
Improvement of black schools	X_3	.33 (.05)	.89 (.06)
Self-help for blacks	X_4	.34 (.05)	.88 (.06)
Black autonomy			
African languages	X_1	.40 (.04)	.84 (.06)
Support black candidate	X_2	.88 (.09)	.22 (.16)
Nothing to do with whites	X_3	.53 (.05)	.72 (.08)
Black political party	X_4	.38 (.05)	.86 (.06)

The overall fit of the economic redistribution factor is very good. The χ^2, χ^2/df, and goodness of fit indexes are all very reasonable. All of the indicators are statistically significant. The goodness of fit of both the global and individual components is also acceptable for the black autonomy variable. The χ^2 is borderline for the racial policies variable. However, given the relatively large size of the sample, the sensitivity of the χ^2 measure to sample size, and the reasonable value for the χ^2/df index, the fit for this variable is also reasonable. The confirmatory factor analysis provides a satisfactory representation of the three aspects of African-American public opinion under consideration.

provements in LISREL that allow the use of ordinal-level data while relaxing the assumption of multinormality.

TABLE 8.6 *(continued)*

Construct	Item	Unstandardized λ *(SE)*	$\theta_\delta{}^a$ *(SE)*
Measures of Model Goodness of Fit			
Economic redistribution			
n = 559			
X^2 = .30			
df = 2			
p = .86			
Racial policies			
n = 795			
X = 5.91			
df = 2			
p = .05			
Black autonomy			
n = 734			
X^2 = 3.23			
df = 2			
p = .20			

Source: 1984–1988 National Black Election Panel Study.
[a] This and following coefficients θ_δ.

C

The variables used in Tables 8.3 through 8.5 are described in detail in Appendixes 1 and 2. All variables have been recoded from 0 to 1. All estimations are OLS and were completed using the SPSSX program.

9

Epilogue: Racial Group Interests, Class, and the Future of African-American Politics

> When a people are mired in oppression, they re-
> alize deliverance when they have accumulated
> the power to enforce change. When they have
> amassed such strength, the writing of a program
> becomes almost an administrative detail. . . . The
> powerful never lose opportunities—they remain
> available to them. The powerless, on the other
> hand, never experience opportunity—it is al-
> ways arriving at a later time. . . . Our nettlesome
> task is to discover how to organize our strength
> into compelling power so that government can-
> not elude our demands. We must develop from
> strength, a situation in which the government
> finds it wise and prudent to collaborate with us.
> It would be the height of naivete to wait pas-
> sively until the administration had somehow
> been infused with such blessing of goodwill that
> it implored us for our programs. The first course
> is grounded in mature realism; the other is a
> childish fantasy.
> (Martin Luther King, Jr., *Where Do We Go from
> Here: Chaos or Community?*)

Overview of the Results

What happens to African-American politics when a growing number of African Americans move from behind the mule? Alternatively, what happens to African-American politics when the mule disappears, when there is no reasonable expectation of earning a decent living, for another growing segment of African Americans? The answer is twofold.

First, within the realm of mainstream American partisan politics, African-American political behavior remains powerfully influenced by African Americans' perceptions of group interests. What is perceived as good for the group still plays a dominant role in shaping African-American partisanship, political choice, and public opinion. Perceptions of group interests are not associated with economic status. Within the confines of mainstream American politics, individual economic status plays a small role in shaping African-American political choice.

However, individuals' economic status plays a large role in shaping African-American public opinion in several issue domains. This is the second part of the answer to the question about what happens to black politics as economic polarization among African Americans increases. Attitudes toward economic redistribution are greatly affected by individual economic status. More affluent African Americans are much less likely to support economic redistribution than those with fewer resources. Although the majority of African Americans remain on the left of the American political spectrum on these issues, the most affluent African Americans hold views more consistent with those of the conservative white mainstream.

Significant class divisions are also found on questions concerning the desirable degree of African-American political, social, and cultural autonomy from white America. Less affluent African Americans are more likely to support the formation of an independent black political party, organizational efforts that exclude whites, and social disengagement from white America. Militant black nationalism with an economic component is gaining widespread exposure in urban black communities through the music of rap artists such as Public Enemy, X-Clan, and Sister Souljah. If poverty continues to spread among African Americans, support for black nationalism and support for economic redistribution could grow rapidly. What implications do these results have for the politics of race and class?

Class

If poverty spreads among African Americans, more African Americans may come to see the need for an independent black political party as the two major parties are seen as increasingly irrelevant to solving the economic crisis gripping many black communities. Yet disenchantment with the party system among the black poor could remain unmobilized, because the poor participate in the political system at lower levels than more affluent African Americans. On the other hand, mobilization campaigns aimed at the black poor *built around the politics of the black poor* could be fruitful.

Growing support for black nationalism and economic redistribution could be accompanied by increasingly evident class divisions among

African Americans if the spread of poverty is accompanied by the continued rise in intraracial inequality discussed in Chapter 2. Although class divisions in African-American politics have existed for over a century, they are often masked by other factors and by the methods often utilized to study black politics.

Race

First and foremost, class divisions in African-American politics have been masked by the extraordinary economic, social, and political differences that remain between blacks and whites. Gaps in unemployment rates, wages, mortality rates, and poverty between the races remain large. Socially, residential segregation of African Americans appears to be a permanent feature of the American landscape. By the 1980s both racial violence and the political use of racism were surging across the nation, as seen in the Howard Beach and Bensonhurst incidents in New York when black teenagers were killed by white mobs, the exploitation of the Willie Horton case during the 1988 presidential campaign, and Jesse Helms's inflammatory attack on affirmative action in the 1990 North Carolina Senate race.

The high degree of racial polarization in the economic and social spheres is reflected in the political gulf between the races. In public opinion, voting behavior, partisan loyalties, and evaluations of political candidates, the races adopt opposite positions more often than not. Ronald Reagan, the most popular president among white Americans since Franklin D. Roosevelt, was for African Americans the most despised president since early in the century. Jesse Jackson, the most popular black leader since Martin Luther King, Jr., is generally viewed with great suspicion and some distaste by white Americans, regardless of ideological background.

A further implication of the vast political gulf between the races is the lack of political choices available to African Americans, particularly in the electoral arena. Numerically, blacks make up a small fraction of the electorate. Consequently, both major parties often find it strategically advantageous to ignore the black vote while pursuing the white vote. The need to appeal to white voters forces even the most radical of African-American candidates for public office to moderate their public stands on issues such as economic redistribution and black nationalism. The left wing of African-American politics is far to the left of the Democratic party of Bill Clinton on issues of economic redistribution, foreign policy, and racial policy. For example, as detailed by Smith (1990) and his colleagues, the pro–Third World orientation of Jackson's presidential campaigns has solid roots in the African-American community. This is a foreign policy orientation at odds with that of mainstream America.

Thus, the historical tendency among African Americans to build all-encompassing black united fronts has been balanced by the caution of many modern black politicians concerned about losing white support. Black politicians have increasingly adopted positions to the right of mainstream black America. On the other hand, white politicians of both major parties since 1972 have consistently sought to distance themselves from the liberal end of the American polity. The lack of political options for African Americans at both the state and national levels has caused interracial political differences to be accentuated while masking intraracial differences among African Americans. In the late 1980s African Americans felt their only real option was the liberal wing of the Democratic party.

Still, survey analyses of African-American politics are likely to overestimate the degree of political unity within the African-American community. First, measures of many of the issues that historically have divided the black community, such as which leadership trend to support (Malcolm vs. Martin, Jackson vs. Farrakhan, etc.), and the proper role of whites in black rights organizations, are not included in most surveys. Second, the segments of the black community most at odds with mainstream American politics—namely, the black poor—are the most poorly represented in most surveys. This problem will become accentuated if the most affluent African Americans increasingly reside in predominantly white communities. These affluent African Americans will also be hard to identify and represent. Furthermore, as Collins (1990), Higginbotham (1992), and many others have forcefully argued, gender and class interact with race in a profound manner. A black woman working in a textile mill, a black male judge, and a young inner-city gang member all experience race differently—just as a white woman who is a corporate lawyer experiences gender differently than a Chicana who works in a cannery. The question of how racial identity shapes individual black politics given the interaction of increasingly complex social identities demands multiple research approaches, including the use of small focus groups, storytelling, case studies of black organizations in a given community, participant observation, analysis of popular culture, and historical analysis.

The results of our analysis suggest the need for the development of separate models of African-American political behavior and public opinion. The historical legacy of black politics has led to the development of different heuristics, institutional frameworks, leadership styles, and behavioral patterns. If there is a convergence between the social and economic circumstances of some strata of African Americans and white Americans, this convergence may also extend to patterns of political behavior and public opinion. Under what conditions might such a convergence occur?

Race, Class, and the Future of African-American Politics

The economic health of black America and the country's racial climate both need to be considered when speculating about the future of black politics. Continued economic decline could have a dramatic radicalizing effect on black politics. On the other hand, growing economic prosperity in the black community is likely to gradually reduce the demand for redistributive policies while severely curtailing nationalist tendencies.

Of course, these forecasts are predicated on a stable racial climate. A hostile racial climate is likely to encourage all classes of African Americans to continue to perceive a strong link between group and individual utility. On the other hand, an improving racial climate opens up the possibility for cross-racial, multiethnic coalitions. Let us explore four possible future scenarios.

Four Futures

Pluralist Dream

The only way that African-American politics may yet develop as Dahl (1961) and the pluralists envisioned is if *both* the racial and economic environments steadily improve. African-American economic progress would mitigate radical tendencies among African Americans. Like the white American working class, African Americans would trade a radical vision of American society for the promise of economic security. Pluralists argue that the diminishing of racial (or ethnic) solidarity is a prerequisite if a group is to become fully integrated; thus increasing racial harmony is necessary. For multiple individual identities and societal cleavages to have their ameliorating effect, it is necessary that no single identity—whether race, class, or religion—remain politically dominant. Under this scenario, African Americans would politically, if not culturally, assimilate (let's be blunt) as they pursued their individual interests. African-American politics would no longer be homogene-

ous but would converge with mainstream American politics. The likelihood of such a scenario developing seems minimal, given the long-
term erosion of the American economy and the concurrent maintenance of often virulent racial hostility.

Unite and Fight

What if the economic environment stagnated or deteriorated while
the racial climate improved? This scenario could very well lead to the
multiracial class alliances envisioned by the American left periodically
over the last hundred years. An improved racial climate, combined
with increased class conflict within the African-American community,
would tend to weaken the perceived linkage between racial group and
individual utility. Yet, given the poor economic status of large segments of the African-American community, class identity would likely
take the place of racial identity as the primary factor influencing black
politics. In this scenario affluent African Americans' politics would
continue to converge with those of their their white middle-class counterparts. Aversion to policies of economic redistribution would increase among these affluent African Americans. We would see a "unite
and fight" phenomenon driven by class; for example, cases in which
black and white middle-class parents united to fight to keep their
schools from being "harmed" by working-class and poor children
would become more frequent.

Two Black Movements

What if the economic environment improved but the racial environment deteriorated? This is probably the least predictable of the scenarios. On one hand, the continued prosperity of the black middle class
could very well lead this group to be somewhat averse to policies of
economic redistribution. On the other hand, continued racial hostility
aimed at all African Americans would do little to reduce the usefulness
of the black utility heuristic. What would be quite likely is serious conflict over strategies and tactics within the black community. Middle-
class African Americans would tend to emphasize strategies and tactics
that emphasized protection of the civil and human rights of the race,
but would be hostile to the more militant suggestions coming from
the black poor. This last point would depend, of course, on *how badly*
race relations had deteriorated. In Detroit in 1925, a black doctor,

O. H. Sweet, defended his home with armed force from a lynch mob. The black middle class has accepted armed self-defense as necessary for survival during periods of extreme racial tension such as at the end of World War I (Franklin 1974; Lipsitz 1988). However, the more normal condition, during periods of all but the most severe racial oppression, has been marked by class-based disputes between strata of African Americans about the preferred strategy for survival.

The Politics of Isolation

What would be the consequences of a continued deterioration in *both* the economic climate and the racial climate? The result would be the increasing political and perhaps spatial isolation of African Americans. The inner cities and near suburbs would become impoverished communities that would be politically powerless and physically isolated from the rest of American society. Residential segregation would continue to prevent all but a few African Americans from escaping the black ghetto. The hard-earned gains of the black middle class, enabled by civil rights and black power movements, would be precarious as politicians like Jesse Helms and David Duke were able to capitalize on white frustration and racism in order to erode them. Radical politics might not flourish only among less affluent African Americans but might spread to the black middle class. African Americans' participation in third-party and other independent political movements is most likely in this scenario. Specifically, these conditions would be the most favorable for the creation of an independent black political party. The end result of this scenario could depend on how the growing Hispanic and Asian populations fared under this regime. Without allies, African Americans as a whole would face an exceedingly difficult future.

This scenario seems increasingly more likely. The Los Angeles rebellion in May 1992 severely distressed the black community nationwide and revealed the tensions between blacks and whites and within the black community. Numerous testimonials from middle-class blacks followed the first Rodney King verdict, which acquitted four white Los Angeles police officers caught on videotape savagely beating a black motorist, stating that the verdict reinforced blacks' feeling that they had no chance at justice within America, despite their accomplishments. Further, black leaders emphasized the importance of the events in Los Angeles and the urban turmoil generally found within the nation for a longer period than did their white counterparts in national leadership. Black leaders accused the major presidential candidates of ignoring urban issues. However, significant divisions were evident in the black community over what tactics to pursue to rectify the problems of African Americans. As the gulf between blacks and whites on economic, social, and political dimensions remained wide, the potential for both widening divisions within the black community and increased isolation from the rest of the nation continued strong.

Policy Implications

The future of African-American politics will be powerfully shaped by the American state. Political institutions such as the Supreme Court and political leaders such as Ronald Reagan have had enormous influence on the racial climate within the country. State and local governments have determined whether African-American property rights are to be respected. The state still determines the degree to which African Americans in the labor market are protected from discrimination, the quality of schooling available to the great majority of African Americans, and whether economic advancement can be translated into better neighborhoods and schools for African Americans, as it can for virtually all other Americans.

Government and party politics have been shown to be at least partly responsible not only for the level of economic woe found among African Americans, but also for how economic hardship is distributed between the races. Perhaps even more important, the political leadership of the United States often sets the moral tone for race relations for the country as a whole. Ronald Reagan's refusal to recognize or respond to any established element of the black community, George Bush's Willie Horton ads and veto of a major civil rights bill, the attempted distancing of the Democratic party from African-American interests, John Silber's comments about Boston's black community, and the naked racial hatred engendered by the Jesse Helms campaign all symbolize the American political leadership's ability to manipulate the politics of race to its advantage. Though many have argued, probably correctly, that the American state is relatively weak, for African Americans the state at all levels has helped define the boundaries of the possible in all spheres of life.

It is the task of African-American politics to weather the changes in economic and racial climate such that all African Americans' interests are advanced. This will be a difficult task, not only because of the environment in which black politics must operate, but also because of the political divisions within the black community. In the recent past, intense class divisions within St. Louis's black community did not prevent both materially poor, working-class Ivory Perry and the black upper classes' scions, the Branton brothers, from being persecuted for resisting racism as youths and growing into men who, each in his own way based on his class background and training, were fighters for black rights. Political divisions based on class status are not new within the black community. What may be new is that the emerging black middle class may see the relentless fight for the rights and survival of the black poor as "futile." Many of Ivory Perry's former comrades viewed his continued struggles on behalf of the black poor as, at best, "naive" and "quixotic" (Lipsitz 1988). They and many of his opponents could not understand why he did not cash in on his years of struggle as so many of them had. The future of African-American politics may well depend on how the racial and economic environment of twenty-first-century America dictates which African Americans perceive that their fates remain linked.

Bibliography

Achen, Christopher H. 1982. *Interpreting and using regression.* Quantitative Applications in the Social Sciences, no. 29. Beverly Hills: Sage Publications.

———. 1986. *The statistical analysis of quasi-experiments.* Berkeley: University of California Press.

———. 1989. Prospective voting and the theory of party identification. Paper presented at the Annual Meeting of the American Political Science Association, Atlanta, Georgia, 30 August–3 September.

Alkalimat, Abdul, and Doug Gills. 1984. Black power vs. racism: Harold Washington becomes mayor. In *The new black vote: Politics and power in four American cities,* ed. Rod Bush, 53–179. San Francisco: Synthesis Publications.

Allen, Richard L., Michael C. Dawson, and Ronald E. Brown. 1989. A schema-based approach to modeling an African-American racial belief system. *American Political Science Review* 83: 421–41.

Allen, Richard L., and Cheng Kuo. 1990. Communication and beliefs about structural inequality. Paper presented at the Annual Meeting of the International Communications Association, Dublin, Ireland, 24–29 June.

Anderson, Bernard. 1982. Economic patterns in black America. In *The state of black America: 1982,* ed. James Williams, 1–32. New York: The Urban League.

Baker, Houston A., Jr. 1984. *Blues, ideology, and Afro-American literature: A vernacular theory.* Chicago: University of Chicago Press.

Banfield, Edward. 1970. *The unheavenly city.* 2d ed. Boston: Little, Brown.

Barker, Lucius J. 1988. *Our time has come: A delegate's diary of Jesse Jackson's 1984 presidential campaign.* Urbana: University of Illinois Press.

———. 1989. Jesse Jackson's candidacy in political-social perspective: A contextual analysis. In *Jesse Jackson's 1984 presidential campaign: Challenge and change in American politics,* ed. Lucius J. Barker and Ronald W. Walters, 3–34. Urbana: University of Illinois Press.

Baron, Harold M. 1971. *The demand for black labor.* Cambridge, Mass.: Radical America.

Beck, Nathaniel. 1987. Alternative dynamic specifications of popularity functions. Paper presented at the Fourth Annual Meeting of the Political Methodology Society, Duke University, 6–9 August.

Black Enterprise Magazine. 1983. Comparative unemployment rates: Spring 1982–Spring 1983. *Black Enterprise Magazine,* July, 31.

———. 1984. Unemployment rates among black teenagers (16–19 years): During the last four recessions. *Black Enterprise Magazine,* January, 32.

Blauner, Bob. 1989. *Black lives, white lives: Three decades of race relations in America.* Berkeley: University of California Press.

Bluestone, Barry, and Bennett Harrison. 1982. *The deindustrialization of America.* New York: Basic Books.

Bobo, Lawrence. 1983. Whites' opposition to busing: Symbolic racism or realistic group conflict? *Journal of Personality and Social Psychology* 45: 1196–1210.

Bobo, Lawrence, and Franklin D. Gilliam, Jr. 1990. Race, sociopolitical participation and black empowerment. *American Political Science Review* 84: 377–94.

Bobo, Lawrence, and James R. Kluegel. 1991. Modern American prejudice: Stereotypes, social distance, and perception of discrimination toward blacks, Hispanics, and Asians. Paper presented at the Annual Meeting of the American Sociological Association, Cincinnati, Ohio. 23–27 August.

Bollen, Kenneth A. 1989. *Structural equations with latent variables*. New York: John Wiley and Sons.

Boston, Thomas D. 1988. *Race, class, and conservatism*. London: Unwin Hyman.

Bound, John, and Richard Freeman. 1990. What went wrong? The erosion of the relative earnings and employment of young black men in the 1980s. Unpublished manuscript.

Brady, Henry E., and Paul M. Sniderman. 1985. Attitude attribution: A group basis for political reasoning. *American Political Science Review* 79: 1061–78.

Brody, Richard A., and Catherine R. Shapiro. 1989. A reconsideration of the rally phenomenon in public opinion. In *Political behavior annual*, ed. Samuel Long, 2: 77–102. Boulder, Colo.: Westview Press.

Brown, Elsa Barkley. 1989. To catch the vision of freedom: Reconstructing Southern black women's political history, 1865–1885. Unpublished manuscript.

Brown, Roger. 1986. *Social psychology*. 2d ed. New York: Free Press.

Brown, Ronald E., Richard L. Allen, and Michael C. Dawson. 1990. Gender based differences in racial belief systems. Unpublished manuscript.

Burnham, Walter Dean. 1983. *The current crisis in American politics*. New York: Oxford University Press.

Butler, Richard, and James J. Heckman. 1977. The government's impact on the labor market status of black Americans: A critical review. In *Equal rights and industrial relations*, by the Industrial Relations Research Association, 235–281. Madison, Wis.: Industrial Relations Research Association.

Campbell, Angus, Phillip E. Converse, Warren E. Miller, and Donald E. Stokes. 1960. *The American voter*. New York: John Wiley and Sons.

Carmichael, Stokely, and Charles V. Hamilton. 1967. *Black power: The politics of liberation in America*. New York: Vintage Books.

Carmines, Edward G., and James A. Stimson. 1989. *Issue evolution: Race and the transformation of American politics*. Princeton: Princeton University Press.

Carmines, Edward G., and Richard A. Zeller. 1979. *Reliability and validity assessment*. Beverly Hills: Sage Publications.

Cavanagh, Thomas E. 1985. The black vote in the 1984 presidential election. Paper presented at the Annual Meeting of the American Political Science Association, New Orleans, 29 August–1 September.

Cole, Robert E., and Donald R. Deskins, Jr. 1988. Racial factors in site location and employment patterns of Japanese auto firms in America. *California Management Review* 31: 9–22.

Coleman, Milton. 1986. Blacks' dim view of Reagan has grown even dimmer. *Washington Post*, 3 February, national weekly edition.

Collins, Patricia Hill. 1990. *Black feminist thought: Knowledge, consciousness, and the politics of empowerment*. Boston: Unwin Hyman.

Conover, Pamela Johnston. 1984. The influence of group identification on political perception and evaluation. *Journal of Politics* 46: 760–85.

————. 1988. The role of social groups in political thinking. *British Journal of Political Science* 18: 51–76.

Culp, Jerome, and Bruce H. Dunson. 1986. Brothers of a different color: A preliminary look at employer treatment of white and black youth. In *The black youth employment crisis*, ed. Richard B. Freeman and Harry J. Holzer, 233–59. Chicago: University of Chicago Press.

Dahl, Robert A. 1956. *Preface to democratic theory*. Chicago: University of Chicago Press.

————. 1961. *Who governs?* New Haven: Yale University Press.

Darden, Joe T., Richard C. Hill, June Thomas, and Richard Thomas. 1987. *Detroit: Race and uneven development*. Philadelphia: Temple University Press.

Darrity, William A., and Samuel Myers, Jr. 1980. Changes in black-white income inequality, 1968–1978: A decade of progress? *Review of Black Political Economy* 10: 354–79.

Datcher-Loury, Linda, and Glenn C. Loury. 1986. Effects of attitudes and aspirations on labor supply. In *The black youth employment crisis*, ed. Richard B. Freeman and Harry J. Holzer, 377–99. Chicago: University of Chicago Press.

Dawson, Michael C. 1986. *Race, class and the formation of Afro-American political attitudes: 1972–1983*. Ph.D. diss., Harvard University.

Dawson, Michael C., Ronald E. Brown, and Richard L. Allen. 1990. Racial belief systems, religious guidance, and African American political participation. *National Review of Political Science* 2: 22–44.

Dawson, Michael C., Ronald E. Brown, and Cathy Cohen. 1990. African American presidential approval and racial differences in models of political behavior. Unpublished manuscript.

Dawson, Michael C., Cathy Cohen, and Ronald E. Brown. 1990. Political parties and African American unemployment. Unpublished manuscript.

Dawson, Michael C., and Ernest J. Wilson III. 1991. Paradigms and paradoxes: Political science and African American politics. In *Political science: Looking to the future*, ed. William Crotty, 1: 189–234.

Debets, P., and E. Browner. 1986. *MSP: A program for Mokken Scale Analysis for polychotomous items*. Amsterdam: Technisch Centrum Universiteit van Amsterdam.

Dennis, Christopher D. 1983. The impact of political and economic variables on the distribution of net income in the United States (1947–70). Ph.D. diss., University of Georgia.

Detroit Area Study. 1989. Separate and unequal: The racial divide: Strategies for reducing political and economic inequalities in the Detroit area. A report to the Detroit tri-county area by the University of Michigan Detroit Area Study, December, Ann Arbor, Michigan.

Dionne, E. J., Jr., and Richard Morin. 1990. Analysts debate: Did more blacks vote Republican this year? Doubts arise about exit poll that found sharp increase in support. *Washington Post*, 10 December, final edition.

Donohue, John, and James J. Heckman. 1989. Continuous versus episodic change: The impact of affirmative action and civil rights policy on the economic status of blacks. Unpublished manuscript.

Downs, Anthony. 1957. *An economic theory of democracy*. New York: Harper and Row.

Drake, St. Clair, and Horace R. Cayton. 1970. *Black metropolis: A study of Negro life in a Northern city*. New York: Harcourt, Brace and World.

Du Bois, W.E.B. 1935. *Black reconstruction*. New York: Harcourt, Brace, and Company.

―――. 1961 (orig. 1953). *The souls of black folk*. Greenwich, Conn.: Fawcett Publications.

Ellwood, David T. 1986. The spatial mismatch hypothesis: Are there teenage jobs missing in the ghetto? In *The black youth employment crisis*, ed. Richard B. Freeman and Harry J. Holzer, 233–59. Chicago: University of Chicago Press.

Elster, Jon. 1989. *Solomonic judgements: Studies in the limitations of rationality*. Cambridge: Cambridge University Press.

Farley, Reynolds. 1984. *Blacks and whites: Narrowing the gap?* Cambridge, Mass.: Harvard University Press.

Farley, Reynolds, and Walter R. Allen. 1987. *The color line and the quality of life in America*. New York: Russell Sage Foundation.

Feldman, Stanley. 1983. Economic individualism and American public opinion. *American Politics Quarterly* 11: 3–29.

Fiorina, Morris. 1981. *Retrospective voting in American national elections*. New Haven: Yale University Press.

Fiske, Susan T. 1986. Schema-based versus piecemeal politics: A patchwork quilt, but not a blanket, of evidence. In *Political cognition: The 19th annual Carnegie symposium on cognition*, ed. Richard R. Lau and David O. Sears, 41–54. Hillsdale, N.J.: Lawrence Erlbaum Associates.

Foner, Eric. 1988. *Reconstruction: America's unfinished revolution, 1863–1877*. New York: Harper and Row.

Franklin, John Hope. 1974. *From slavery to freedom: A history of Negro Americans*. 4th ed. New York: Knopf.

Freeman, Richard B. 1976. *Black elite: The new market for highly educated black Americans*. New York: McGraw-Hill.

Freeman, Richard B., and Harry J. Holzer. 1986. The black youth employment crisis: Summary of findings. In *The black youth employment crisis*, ed. Richard B. Freeman and Harry J. Holzer, 233–59. Chicago: University of Chicago Press.

Frye, Hardy T. 1980. *Black parties and political power: A case study*. Boston: G. K. Hall.

Gates, Henry L., Jr. 1984. Criticism in the jungle. In *Black literature and literary theory*, ed. Henry L. Gates, Jr., 1–24. New York: Methuen.

Geddes, Barbara, and John Zaller. 1989. Source of popular support for authoritarian regimes. *American Journal of Political Science* 33: 319–47.

Gerber, Elisabeth R., and John E. Jackson. 1990. Endogenous preferences and the study of institutions. Paper presented at the Annual Meeting of the American Political Science Association, San Francisco, 30 August–2 September.

Giddings, Paula. 1984. *When and where I enter: The impact of black women on race and sex in America.* New York: William Morrow and Company.

Gilliam, Franklin D., Jr. 1986. Black America: Divided by class? *Public Opinion* 9: 53–57.

Goodwyn, Lawrence. 1978. *The Populist movement: A short history of the agrarian revolt in America.* Oxford: Oxford University Press.

Granovetter, Mark S. 1973. The strength of weak ties. *American Journal of Sociology* 78: 347–67.

Greenstone, J. David, and Paul E. Peterson. 1973. *Race and authority in urban politics: Community participation and the war on poverty.* New York: Russell Sage Foundation.

Gurin, Patricia, Shirley Hatchett, and James S. Jackson. 1989. *Hope and independence: Blacks' response to electoral and party politics.* New York: Russell Sage Foundation.

Gwaltney, John L. 1980. *Drylongso: A self-portrait of black America.* New York: Vintage Books.

Haines, Herbert H. 1988. *Black radicals and the civil rights mainstream, 1954–1970.* Knoxville: University of Tennessee Press.

Hamilton, Charles V. 1982. Measuring black conservatism. In *The state of black America*, ed. James Williams, 113–40. New York: The National Urban League.

Hamilton, Charles V., and Donna C. Hamilton. 1986. Social policies, civil rights, and poverty. In *Fighting poverty: What works and what doesn't*, ed. Sheldon H. Danziger and Daniel H. Weinberg, 297–311. Cambridge, Mass.: Harvard University Press.

Hardin, Russell. 1991. Self interest, group identity. Paper prepared for the Committee on Contributions of Behavioral and Social Science to the Prevention of Nuclear War, National Research Council.

Harris, William H. 1982. *The harder we run: Black workers since the civil war.* Oxford: Oxford University Press.

Harvey, Andrew C. 1981. *The econometric analysis of time series.* Oxford: Philip Allan.

Hechter, Michael. 1986. Rational choice theory and the study of race and ethnic relations. In *Theories of race and ethnic relations*, ed. John Rex and David Mason, 264–79. New York: Cambridge University Press.

Heckman, James J. 1976. Simultaneous equation models with and without structural shift in the equations. In *Studies in non-linear estimation*, ed. Stephen M. Goldfeld and Richard E. Quandt, 235–72. Cambridge, Mass.: Ballinger Publishing.

Heckman, James J., and Brook S. Payner. 1989. Determining the impact of federal antidiscrimination policy on the economic status of blacks: A study of South Carolina. *American Economic Review* 79: 138–77.

Henderson, Lenneal J., Jr. 1987. Black politics and American presidential election. In *The new black politics: The search for political power*, 2d ed., ed. Michael B. Preston, Lenneal J. Henderson, Jr., and Paul L. Puryear, 3–29. White Plains, N.Y.: Longman.

Henry, Charles P. 1990. *Culture and African American politics*. Bloomington: Indiana University Press.

Hershey, R. D. 1989. The hand that shaped America's poverty line as the realistic index. *New York Times*, 4 August, national edition.

Hibbs, Douglas A., Jr. 1987. *The American political economy: Macroeconomics and electoral politics in the United States*. Cambridge, Mass.: Harvard University Press.

Hibbs, Douglas A., Jr., and Christopher Dennis. 1988. Income distribution in the United States. *American Political Science Review* 82: 467–90.

Higginbotham, Evelyn Brooks. 1992. African-American women's history and the metalanguage of race. *Signs* 17: 251–74.

Higgs, Robert. 1977. *Competition and coercion: Blacks in the American economy, 1865–1914*. Cambridge: Cambridge University Press.

Hochschild, Jennifer L. 1981. *What's fair? American beliefs about distributive justice*. Cambridge, Mass.: Harvard University Press.

———. 1989. Equal opportunity and the estranged poor. *The Annals* 501: 143–55.

———. 1993. Middle class blacks and the complexities of success. In *Prejudice, politics, and the American dilemma*, ed. Paul Sniderman, Philip Tetlock, and Edward G. Carminer. Stanford: Stanford University Press.

Holzer, Harry J. 1989. The spatial mismatch hypothesis: What has the evidence shown? Unpublished manuscript.

Huckfeldt, Robert R., and Carol Weitzel Kohfeld. 1989. *Race and the decline of class in American politics*. Urbana: University of Illinois Press.

Hughes, Langston. 1974. Democracy. In *Selected Poems of Langston Hughes*, 285. New York: Vintage Books.

Iyengar, Shanto. 1990. Shortcuts to political knowledge: The role of selective attention and accessibility. In *Information and democratic processes*, ed. John A. Ferejohn and James H. Kuklinski, 160–85. Urbana: University of Illinois Press.

Iyengar, Shanto, and Donald R. Kinder. 1987. *News that matters: Television and American opinion*. Chicago: University of Chicago Press.

Jackman, Mary R., and Robert W. Jackman. 1983. *Class awareness in the United States*. Berkeley: University of California Press.

Jackson, Byran O. 1987. The effects of racial group consciousness on political mobilization in American cities. *Western Political Quarterly* 40: 631–46.

———. 1989. Linking racial group consciousness to the political participation of black Americans: An organizational perspective. Unpublished manuscript.

Jackson, John E. 1975. Issues, party choices, and presidential votes. *American Journal of Political Science* 19: 61–85.

Jaynes, Gerald D. 1986. *Branches without roots: Genesis of the black working class in the American South, 1862–1882*. New York: Oxford University Press.

Jaynes, Gerald D., and Robin M. Williams, Jr., eds. 1989. *A common destiny: Blacks and American society*. Washington, D.C.: National Academy Press.

Johnson, James H., Jr., and Melvin L. Oliver. 1990. Economic restructuring and black male joblessness in U.S. metropolitan areas. Unpublished manuscript.

Jones, Mack H. 1987. The political thought of the new black conservatives: An analysis, explanation and interpretation. In *Readings in American political issues*, ed. Franklin D. Jones and Michael O. Adams, 23–49. Dubuque, Iowa: Kendall/Hunt.

Joreskog, Karl G., and Dag Sorbom. 1988. *LISREL 7: A guide to the program and applications.* Chicago: SPSS.

Kahneman, Daniel, and Amos Tversky. 1982. The simulation heuristic. In *Judgement under uncertainty: Heuristics and biases*, ed. Daniel Kahneman, Paul Slovic, and Amos Tversky, 190–200. New York: Cambridge University Press.

Kelley, Robin. 1990. *Hammer and hoe: Alabama Communists during the Depression.* Chapel Hill: University of North Carolina Press.

Kilson, Martin. 1981. Black social classes and intergenerational poverty. *The Public Interest* 54: 58–78.

———. 1983. The black bourgeoisie revisited. *Dissent*, Winter, 85–96.

Kinder, Donald R., Gordon S. Adams, and Paul W. Gronke. 1989. Economics and politics in the 1984 presidential election. *American Journal of Political Science* 33: 491–515.

Kinder, Donald R., and D. Roderick Kiewiet. 1981. Sociotropic politics. *British Journal of Political Science* 11: 129–61.

Kinder, Donald R., Tali Mendelberg, Michael C. Dawson, Lynn M. Sanders, Steven J. Rosenstone, Jocelyn Sargent, and Cathy Cohen. 1989. Race and the 1988 American presidential election. Paper presented at the Annual Meeting of the American Political Science Association, Atlanta, Georgia, 30 August–3 September.

King, Gary. 1989. *Unifying political methodology: The likelihood theory of statistical inference.* New York: Cambridge University Press.

King, Martin Luther, Jr. 1967. *Where do we go from here: Chaos or community?* Boston: Beacon Hill Press.

Kirschenman, Joleen, and Kathryn M. Neckerman. 1991. "We'd love to hire them, but . . .": The meaning of race for employers. In *The urban underclass*, ed. Christopher Jencks and Paul E. Peterson, 203–32. Washington, D.C.: The Brookings Institution.

Kleppner, Paul. 1985. *Chicago divided: The making of a black mayor.* DeKalb: Northern Illinois University Press.

Kmenta, Jan. 1986. *Elements of econometrics.* 2d ed. New York: Macmillan.

Koepp, Stephen. 1985. Teenage orphans of the job boom. *Time*, 13 May, 47.

Landes, William M. 1968. The economics of fair employment laws. *Journal of Political Economy* 76: 507–52.

Landry, Bart. 1987. *The new black middle class.* Berkeley: University of California Press.

Lau, Richard R. 1986. Political schemata, candidate evaluations, and voting behavior. In *Political cognition: The 19th annual Carnegie symposium on cognition*, ed. Richard R. Lau and David O. Sears, 95–126. Hillsdale, N.J.: Lawrence Erlbaum Associates.

Leonard, Jonathan S. 1984a. Splitting blacks? Affirmative action and earnings inequality within and across races. National Bureau of Economic Research,

Working Paper Series, no. 1327. Cambridge, Mass.: National Bureau of Economic Research.

———. 1984b. What promises are worth: The impact of affirmative action goals. National Bureau of Economic Research, Working Paper Series, no. 1346. Cambridge, Mass.: National Bureau of Economic Research.

———. 1986. Comment. In *The black youth employment crisis*, ed. Richard B. Freeman and Harry J. Holzer, 185–90. Chicago: University of Chicago Press.

Levy, F. 1980. The intergenerational transfer of poverty. The Urban Institute, Working paper no. 121-02. Washington, D.C.: The Urban Institute.

Lewis, Earl. 1991. *In their own interests: Race, class, and power in twentieth-century Norfolk, Virginia*. Berkeley: University of California Press.

Lichter, Linda S. 1985. Who speaks for black America? *Public Opinion*, August–September, 41–44, 58.

Lipsitz, George. 1988. *A life in the struggle: Ivory Perry and the culture of opposition*. Philadelphia: Temple University Press.

Loury, Glenn C. 1983. Economics, politics, and blacks. *Review of Black Political Economy* 12: 43–54.

———. 1985. Beyond civil rights. *New Republic*, 7 October, 22–25.

Maddala, G. S. 1984. *Limited-dependent and qualitative variables in econometrics*. New York: Cambridge University Press.

Marable, Manning. 1983. *How capitalism underdeveloped black America: Problems in race, political economy, and society*. Boston: South End Press.

———. 1985. *Black American politics: From the Washington marches to Jesse Jackson*. London: Verso Press.

Markus, Gregory B. 1988. The impact of personal and national economic conditions on the presidential vote: A pooled cross-sectional analysis. *American Journal of Political Science* 32: 137–54.

Markus, Gregory, and Phillip Converse. 1979. A dynamic simultaneous equation model of the electoral choice. *American Political Science Review* 73: 1055–70.

Massey, Douglas S. 1990. American apartheid: Segregation and the making of the underclass. *American Journal of Sociology* 95: 1153–88.

Massey, Douglas S., and Nancy A. Denton. 1988. Residential segregation of blacks, Hispanics, and Asians by socioeconomic status and generation. *Social Science Quarterly* 69: 797–817.

McAdam, Doug. 1982. *Political process and the development of black insurgency, 1930–1970*. Chicago: University of Chicago Press.

McClosky, Herbert, and John Zaller. 1984. *The American ethos: Public attitudes toward capitalism and democracy*. Cambridge, Mass.: Harvard University Press.

McCormick, Joseph P., II, and Robert C. Smith. 1989. Through the prism of Afro-American culture: An interpretation of the Jackson campaign style. In *Jesse Jackson's 1984 presidential campaign: Challenge and change in American politics*, ed. Lucius J. Barker and Ronald W. Walters, 96–107. Urbana: University of Illinois Press.

McKelvey, Richard D., and Peter C. Ordeshook. 1986. Information, electoral equilibria, and the democratic ideal. *Journal of Politics* 48: 909–37.

McLanahan, Susan. 1983. Family structure and the reproduction of poverty. Discussion paper 720A-83, Institute for Research on Poverty, University of Wisconsin, Madison.

Mead, Lawrence M. 1986. *Beyond entitlement: The social obligations of citizenship.* New York: Free Press.

Miller, Arthur H., Patricia Gurin, Gerald Gurin, and Oksana Malanchuk. 1981. Group consciousness and political participation. *American Journal of Political Science* 25: 494–511.

Morris, Aldon M. 1984. *The origins of the civil rights movement: Black communities organizing for change.* New York: Free Press.

Morris, Lorenzo, and Linda F. Williams. 1989. The coalition at the end of the rainbow: The 1984 Jackson campaign. In *Jesse Jackson's 1984 presidential campaign: Challenge and change in American politics,* ed. Lucius J. Barker and Ronald W. Walters, 227–48. Urbana: University of Illinois Press.

Moss, Phillip, and Chris Tilly. 1991. *Why black men are doing worse in the labor market: A review of supply-side and demand-side explanations.* New York: Social Science Research Council.

Mueller, John E. 1973. *War, presidents and public opinion.* New York: John Wiley and Sons.

Murray, Charles. 1984. *Losing ground: American social policy, 1950–1980.* New York: Basic Books.

Naison, Mark. 1983. *Communists in Harlem during the Depression.* New York: Grove Press.

Nelson, W. Dale. 1990. Race-motivated crimes on rise. *Ann Arbor News,* 29 October.

Neustadt, Richard. 1960. *Presidential power.* New York: Wiley.

Nie, Norman H., Sidney Verba, and John R. Petrocik. 1979. *The changing American voter.* 2d ed. Cambridge, Mass.: Harvard University Press.

Oliver, Melvin L., and Thomas M. Shapiro. 1989. Race and wealth. *Review of Black Political Economy* 17: 5–25.

Oreskes, Michael. 1988. Jackson's success earns the trust of many who once feared him. *New York Times,* 13 March, national edition.

Ostrom, Charles W., Jr. 1978. *Time series analysis: Regression techniques.* Beverly Hills: Sage Publications.

Ostrom, Charles W., Jr., and Dennis M. Simon. 1985. Promise and performance: A dynamic model of presidential popularity. *American Political Science Review* 2: 334–58.

Page, Benjamin I. 1978. *Choices and echoes in presidential elections: Rational man and electoral democracy.* Chicago: University of Chicago Press.

Painter, Nell Irvin. 1977. *Exodusters: Black migration to Kansas after Reconstruction.* New York: Knopf.

———. 1987. *Standing at Armageddon: The United States, 1877–1919.* New York: Norton.

Peretz, Paul. 1983. *The political economy of inflation in the United States.* Chicago: University of Chicago Press.

Peterson, Paul E. 1979. Organizational imperatives and ideological change: The case of black power. *Urban Affairs Quarterly* 14: 466–84.

Pinderhughes, Dianne. 1987. *Race and ethnicity in Chicago politics*. Urbana: University of Illinois Press.

———. 1990. The articulation of black interests by black civil rights, professional, and religious organizations. In *The social and political implications of the 1984 Jesse Jackson presidential campaign*, ed. Lorenzo Morris, 125–34. New York: Praeger.

Pinkney, Alphonso. 1984. *The myth of black progress*. New York: Cambridge University Press.

Piven, Francis Fox. 1974. The urban crisis: Who got what and why. In *The politics of turmoil: Essays on poverty, race and the urban crisis*, ed. Richard A. Cloward and Francis Fox Piven, 165–201. New York: Pantheon Books.

Plissner, Martin, and Warren Mitofsky. 1988. The changing Jackson voter. *Public Opinion*, July–August, 56–57.

Polenberg, Richard. 1980. *One nation divisible: Class, race, and ethnicity in the United States since 1938*. New York: Viking Press.

Poulantzas, Nicos. 1974. *Political power and social classes*. London: New Left Books.

Preston, Michael B. 1987a. The election of Harold Washington: An examination of the SES model in the 1983 Chicago mayoral election. In *The new black politics: The search for political power*, 2d ed., ed. Michael B. Preston, Lenneal J. Henderson, Jr., and Paul L. Puryear, 139–71. White Plains, N.Y.: Longman.

———. 1987b. Introduction. In *The new black politics: The search for political power*, 2d ed., ed. Michael B. Preston, Lenneal J. Henderson, Jr., and Paul L. Puryear, vii–ix. White Plains, N.Y.: Longman.

Przeworski, Adam. 1975. Institutionalization of voting patterns, or is mobilization the source of decay? *American Political Science Review* 69: 49–67.

———. 1985. Marxism and rational choice. *Politics and Society* 14: 379–409.

Public Opinion. 1988. What we've learned from the voters this year. May–June, 21–25.

Quan, Robert Seto. 1982. *Lotus among the magnolias: The Mississippi Chinese*. Jackson: University of Mississippi Press.

Ransom, Roger L., and Richard Sutch. 1977. *One kind of freedom: The economic consequences of emancipation*. Cambridge: Cambridge University Press.

Reed, Adolph L., Jr. 1986. *The Jesse Jackson phenomenon*. New Haven: Yale University Press.

Reich, Michael. 1981. *Racial inequality: A political-economic analysis*. Princeton: Princeton University Press.

Robinson, Deborah Marie. 1987. *The effect of multiple group identity among black women on race consciousness*. Ph.D. diss., University of Michigan, Ann Arbor.

Rokeach, Milton. 1976. *Beliefs, attitudes, and values: A theory of organization and change*. San Francisco: Jossey-Bass.

———. 1979. Changes and stability in American value systems, 1969–1971. In *Understanding human values*, ed. Milton Rokeach, 129–47. New York: Free Press.

Rosenstone, Steven J. 1982. Economic adversity and voter turnout. *American Political Science Review* 72: 22–45.

Rosenstone, Steven J., Roy L. Behr, and Edward H. Lazarus. 1984. *Third parties in America: Citizen response to major party failure*. Princeton: Princeton University Press.

Sawhill, Isabel V. 1988. Poverty in the U.S.: Why is it so persistent? *Journal of Economic Literature* 26: 1073–1119.

Schlozman, Kay L., and Sidney Verba. 1979. *Injury to insult: Unemployment, class, and political response*. Cambridge, Mass.: Harvard University Press.

Sears, David O., and Jack Citrin. 1985. *Tax revolt: Something for nothing in California*. Cambridge, Mass.: Harvard University Press.

Shaw, Nate. 1974. *All God's dangers: The life of Nate Shaw*. New York: Avon Books.

Shefter, Martin. 1977. New York City's fiscal crisis: The politics of inflation and retrenchment. *The Public Interest* 48: 98–127.

Shingles, Richard. 1981. Black consciousness and political participation: The missing link. *American Political Science Review* 75: 76–91.

Simon, Herbert A. 1985. Human nature in politics: The dialogue of psychology with political science. *American Political Science Review* 79: 293–304.

Singletary, Otis A. 1957. *Negro militia and Reconstruction*. New York: McGraw-Hill.

Sitkoff, Harvard. 1978. *A new deal for blacks: The emergence of civil rights as a national issue*. Vol. 1: *The Depression decade*. New York: Oxford University Press.

Smith, James P., and Finnis R. Welch. 1989. Black economic progress after Myrdal. *Journal of Economic Literature* 27: 519–64.

Smith, Robert C. 1990. From insurgency toward inclusion: The Jackson campaigns of 1984 and 1988. In *The social and political implications of the 1984 Jesse Jackson presidential campaign*, ed. Lorenzo Morris, 215–30. New York: Praeger.

Sowell, Thomas. 1975. *Race and economics*. New York: Longman.

Stone, Clarence N. 1989. *Regime politics: Governing Atlanta, 1946–1988*. Lawrence: University of Kansas Press.

Tajfel, Henri. 1981. *Human groups and social categories: Studies in social psychology*. New York: Cambridge University Press.

Tate, Katherine, Ronald E. Brown, Shirley J. Hatchett, and James S. Jackson. 1988. *The 1984 National Black Election Study Sourcebook*. Ann Arbor: Institute for Social Research, University of Michigan.

Taylor, Shelley E. 1982. The availability bias in social perception and interaction. In *Judgement under uncertainty: Heuristics and biases*, ed. Daniel Kahneman, Paul Slovic, and Amos Tversky, 190–200. New York: Cambridge University Press.

Thomas, Karen, M. 1989. Parents in a class conflict. *Chicago Tribune*, 28 March.

———. 1990. One school, different worlds: Class conflict at heart of South Loop busing dispute. *Chicago Tribune*, 13 August.

Tufte, Edward R. 1978. *Political control of the economy*. Princeton: Princeton University Press.

Turner, John C. 1987. *Rediscovering the social group: A self-categorization theory*. Oxford: Basil Blackwell.

Turner, Margery A., Michael Fix, and Raymond J. Struyk. 1991. *Opportunities denied, opportunities diminished: Discrimination in hiring.* Washington, D.C.: The Urban Institute.

Uhlaner, Carole J. 1989. Rational turnout: The neglected role of groups. *American Journal of Political Science* 33: 390–422.

Updegrave, Walter L. 1989. Race and money. *Money*, December, 152–72.

U.S. Bureau of the Census. 1968. *Statistical abstract of the United States: 1968.* Washington, D.C.: U.S. Bureau of the Census.

————. 1969. *Statistical abstract of the United States: 1969.* Washington, D.C.: U.S. Bureau of the Census.

————. 1970. *Statistical abstract of the United States: 1970.* Washington, D.C.: U.S. Bureau of the Census.

————. 1971. *Statistical abstract of the United States: 1971.* Washington, D.C.: U.S. Bureau of the Census.

————. 1974. *Statistical abstract of the United States: 1974.* Washington, D.C.: U.S. Bureau of the Census.

————. 1975. *Statistical abstract of the United States: 1975.* Washington, D.C.: U.S. Bureau of the Census.

————. 1978. *Statistical abstract of the United States: 1978.* Washington, D.C.: U.S. Bureau of the Census.

————. 1990. *Statistical abstract of the United States: 1990.* Washington, D.C.: U.S. Bureau of the Census.

U.S. Department of Commerce. 1985. *Money income of households, families, and persons in the United States: 1983.* Current Population Reports, Series P-60, no. 146. Washington, D.C.: U.S. Department of Commerce.

U.S. Department of Labor, Bureau of Labor Statistics. 1989. *Handbook of labor statistics.* Bulletin 2340, August.

Van Dyk, Ted. 1990. Will Powell run with Bush in '92? *New York Times*, 6 September, national edition.

Verba, Sidney, and Gary R. Orren. 1985. *Equality in America: The view from the top.* Cambridge, Mass.: Harvard University Press.

Walters, Ronald W. 1988. *Black presidential politics in America: A strategic approach.* Albany: State University of New York Press.

————. 1989. The emergent mobilization of the black community in the Jackson campaign for president. In *Jesse Jackson's 1984 presidential campaign: Challenge and change in American politics*, ed. Lucius J. Barker and Ronald W. Walters, 35–54. Urbana: University of Illinois Press.

Walton, Hanes, Jr. 1972. *Black political parties.* New York: Free Press.

————. 1988. The National Democratic party of Alabama and party failure in America. In *When parties fail: Emerging alternative organizations*, ed. Kay Lawson and Peter H. Merkl, 365–88. Princeton: Princeton University Press.

Weiss, Nancy J. 1983. *Farewell to the party of Lincoln: Black politics in the age of FDR.* Princeton: Princeton University Press.

West, Cornel. 1982. *Prophesy deliverance! An Afro-American revolutionary Christianity.* Philadelphia: Westminster Press.

White, Kenneth J., Shirley A. Haun, Nancy G. Horsman, and S. Donna Wong.

1988. *Shazam econometrics computer program: User's reference manual, version 6.1.* New York: McGraw-Hill.

Wilkerson, Isabel. 1990. Middle-class blacks try to grip a ladder while lending a hand. *New York Times,* 25 November, national edition.

Williams, Linda F. 1987. Black political progress in the 1980s: The electoral arena. In *The new black politics: The search for political power,* 2d ed., ed. Michael B. Preston, Lenneal J. Henderson, Jr., and Paul L. Puryear, 87–135. White Plains, N.Y.: Longman.

Williams, Walter E. 1982. *The state against blacks.* New York: McGraw-Hill.

Williamson, Joel. 1965. *After slavery: The Negro in South Carolina during Reconstruction, 1861–1877.* Chapel Hill: University of North Carolina Press.

————. 1984. *The crucible of race: Black-white relations in the American South.* Oxford: Oxford University Press.

Wilson, William J. 1980. *The declining significance of race.* 2d ed. Chicago: University of Chicago Press.

————. 1987. *The truly disadvantaged: The inner city, the underclass, and public policy.* Chicago: University of Chicago Press.

Woodward, C. Vann. 1966. *The strange career of Jim Crow.* 2d rev. ed. New York: Oxford University Press.

Wright, Erik Olin, David Hachen, Cynthia Costello, and Joey Sprague. 1982. The American class structure. *American Sociological Review* 47: 709–26.

Wright, Richard. 1966. *Black boy.* New York: Harper and Row.

X, Malcolm. 1966. *Malcolm X Speaks.* New York: Grove Press.

Zafar, Rafia. 1989. White call, black response: Adoption, subversion, and transformation from the colonial era to the age of abolition. Ph.D. diss., Harvard University.

Index

Made in United States
North Haven, CT
14 August 2023

40278581R00150